REPATRIATION
UNDER CONFLICT
IN CENTRAL AMERICA

REPATRIATION
UNDER CONFLICT
IN CENTRAL AMERICA

Edited by

Mary Ann Larkin
Frederick C. Cuny
Barry N. Stein

Hemispheric Migration Project
Center for Immigration Policy and Refugee Assistance
Georgetown University

and

The Intertect Institute

Center for Immigration Policy and
Refugee Assistance
Georgetown University
P.O. Box 2298 - Hoya Station
Washington, D.C. 20057-1011

Intertect Institute
3511 North Hall Street
Dallas, TX 75219

ISBN: 0-924046-17-1

Cover Photo ©1988, Donna DeCesare, Impact Visuals: Refugee leaders hold meeting with NGO and UNHCR representatives during the journey from Mesa Grande, Honduras to Santa Marta, El Salvador in 1988.

This photo is from a photo essay in progress on Salvadoran migration and its effects in Central and North America that photographer Donna DeCesare began in 1988.

CONTENTS

PREFACE

by Mary Ann Larkin

Central America has witnessed a decade of violence and upheaval that has forced over two million people from their homes. Social and political crises erupted into violence in three countries of the region: El Salvador in 1980, where a reformist military coup was reversed by hardline elements; Guatemala in 1981, with the massacre of numerous indigenous communities in the highlands; and Nicaragua in the late 1970s with the revolution and, again in 1984, with the U.S.-backed Contra resistance.

The outmigration was ostensibly caused by the violence, driven by the profound social and economic inequalities that each day seemed to worsen. The landed and wealthy minorities reaped the gains of what was great economic growth in the 1960s. However, the Central American development gains were stymied by the world oil recession in the early 1970s. When popular organizations emerged that began to make increasingly vocal demands for land and jobs, at a time when resources were scarce, the organizations were put down by ever more powerful militaries. Guerrilla movements that previously had been small and scattered began to grow and challenge the military, providing those in power with the justification they needed for increased repression.

By the 1980s, it was war.

Massive numbers of people were fleeing widespread counter-insurgency attacks. Thousands fled the generalized and random violence that occurs in the course of war, especially in rural areas. Labor, religious, and other community leaders whose work was believed to challenge the government fled individual persecution. Added to this, the economic collapse that resulted from the war pushed even greater numbers of people to other cities and other countries to seek jobs that could support them and their families.

Where did they go? Over 80 percent of the people who left their countries moved northward to Mexico and the United States.[1] Most of these people were not recognized as refugees. However, the population treated in this volume were mostly poor, rural families who traveled to

immediate safety across the border. Salvadorans in this category fled to
Honduras where several camps were established for them.
Guatemalans most often fled to settlements in the department of
Chiapas in Mexico; in 1984, about one-half of the recognized refugees
were relocated away from the border to Campeche and Quintana Roo
in the Yucatán Peninsula. Nicaraguan Miskito and Sumu indigenous
communities fled to Honduras and to Costa Rica, as did Mestizo
refugees later.

Whether an individual or community fled to a different region
within their own country or crossed the border to another country was
never an arbitrary choice. Rather, the destination of uprooted peoples
depended on a number of variables. One variable was geography. I was
once told that Salvadorans in Morazán found it easier to cross to
Honduras than to try to go back toward the capital in the face of the
approaching military. Guatemalans, we are told, often fled first within
their country where hundreds of thousands were displaced by the
violence. Days, weeks, or months later, many of these persons crossed
into Mexico. For others, destination was determined by following
traditional labor migration routes where the trails were familiar and
friendly contacts could be found. Nicaraguan Miskito communities fled
to the safety of their sister communities in Honduras, where they
migrated seasonally.

Crossing the border did not mean automatic recognition of
refugee status. In Mexico's often contradictory policy toward refugees,
Guatemalans that crossed into the Soconusco area of southern Chiapas
were ultimately not regarded as refugees, while those that crossed the
border further north were given refugee assistance by official and
international agencies.

That relatively few of all the Central Americans who fled their
countries were recognized as refugees led to a debate that raged for
years over who would be officially considered a refugee and who would
be dismissed as an undocumented labor migrant. Central Americans
who bypassed the camps in the country of first asylum, having the
means, skills, contacts, or ambition to find work to support their
families, effectively forfeited their chance to be treated as refugees.

Of the refugees who stayed in the region, one-third or
approximately 150,000 at any one time received assistance and were
recognized as refugees by the United Nations High Commissioner for
Refugees (UNHCR). The studies in this volume focus primarily on
repatriations from this group of officially recognized refugees, largely
because the population is identified and the data exist. There are little

existing data on undocumented refugees in exile or on their spontaneous return.

Research on the feasibility of Salvadoran and Guatemalan repatriation was taboo in the international community at least until 1985, even though, as we now know, spontaneous returns of refugees were already taking place. There was a general fear that to discuss prospects for their repatriation was somehow to validate it as an immediate option, and that this, in turn, could lead to *non*voluntary repatriation, particularly from those countries that were not happy about hosting the refugees. Repatriation, of course, was always mentioned theoretically as the best solution to any refugee crisis. Nonetheless, there was a general consensus in the international community that conditions were not safe enough to recommend repatriation as long as the conflicts and human rights abuses continued at home.

Even at the time of the Cartagena Declaration in 1984, a document which is known for having broadened the definition of the refugee in Central America to include those fleeing generalized violence, repatriation is mentioned only in the context of assuring against the *non*voluntary return of refugees, or *nonrefoulement*.

Several things helped to break that taboo in international discourse. The authors here cite the visit of UN High Commissioner Jean Pierre Hocke in 1985 as a turning point in the refugees' consideration of the inevitability of repatriation. The refugees and agencies working with them began to consider their future options: refugees could settle in the host country (if it would have them), accept relocation to a third country (a very difficult, if not impossible, option), or they could repatriate. Also, the agreements reached under the Central American Peace process created an expectation of peace that would permit repatriation. The Esquipulas II Agreement in 1987 was the first high level mention of the need to attend to refugees and repatriates. Much later, the Tela Agreement in August 1989 discussed the dismantling and repatriation of the Nicaraguan Contra forces and refugees.

By the time of the International Conference on Central American Refugees (CIREFCA) in mid-1989, the taboo was broken. At the request of the governments of the region and Mexico, the United Nations High Commissioner for Refugees and the United Nations Development Program co-sponsored that meeting and its follow-up. CIREFCA was not just a meeting, but the start of a process to attend to the refugee crisis in the region. It promised to design a strategy to assist refugees, displaced persons, and repatriates within the framework

of national and regional development. And, furthermore, the
CIREFCA process would help to facilitate funding for refugee projects.
After a slow and troubled beginning, a second meeting of CIREFCA
was held in 1990 in which it was reported that progress was being made,
that funds were being raised, and that development projects were
including these populations. By 1991, however, just over one-half of the
priority projects were funded and only 18 were operational.[2]

These international events by no means triggered refugee
repatriation, as you will read in the case studies to follow. The
diplomatic and international initiatives are noted here as a backdrop to
the repatriation issue. The decision of refugees to repatriate is based
on a series of factors, primary among them the pursuit of protection (if
not security) and the chance to regain control over their lives, control
often lost to camp administrators and refugee leaders.

It seems totally unfathomable that refugees would decide to
return while the conditions still exist that first led them to flee. Yet,
they do return, in Central America and in similar instances around the
world.

The studies in this volume form part of a worldwide study of
spontaneous repatriation which is directed by Fred Cuny and Barry
Stein, as described in the next chapter. The Hemispheric Migration
Project collaborated with them in focussing on the three Central
American cases individually and in a regional context.

The HMP had previously sponsored the groundwork in Central
America with Marvin Ortega's research on the repatriation of
Nicaraguan Miskito indigenous communities from Honduras, Ricardo
Stein's research on the decision to repatriate by Salvadoran refugees in
Mesa Grande, and Beatriz Manz report on the difficulties faced by the
first Guatemalan repatriates from Mexico.[3]

When we embarked upon this project in 1989, conditions were
quite different from what they are today. Salvadoran refugees in Mesa
Grande were sporadically repatriating in large groups, and we had the
first inkling that refugees in the Colomoncagua and San Antonio camps
in Honduras were also considering repatriation. With Nicaragua, there
was little expectation at that time that conditions would so change there
as to permit the large-scale return from Honduras of any but the
Miskito and other indigenous groups. Finally, Guatemalan refugees in
Mexico appeared to be intrigued by the example of the Salvadoran
refugees who were going home, but they themselves were ever more
resolved *not* to repatriate until certain conditions were met at home.
Since that time, much has changed, as the cases show.

Initial drafts of these chapters were shared with participants in a series of meetings on repatriation held in December, 1990.[4] Representatives of research institutions, governmental and nongovernmental agencies, and international organizations based in the region and the United States participated in a two-day conference at Georgetown University. The authors then conducted briefings at the State Department, Congress, InterAction in New York, and the United Nations in Geneva, co-hosted by the International Organization for Migration and the United Nations High Commissioner for Refugees. At these meetings the policy ramifications of the research were discussed with those individuals on the repatriation front lines which allowed the authors to refine the chapters presented here.

For the Hemispheric Migration Project, we hope that the research reported here contributes to the understanding of repatriation and to the policy debate about when and how to assist refugees on their journey home. The cases illustrate the positive nature of international humanitarian assistance, as well as the sometimes destructive nature of that assistance when administered under prolonged emergency conditions and without consultation with the beneficiary populations. Repatriation assistance, as with refugee assistance in exile, requires consultation with the refugees and consideration of the long-term reintegration and development issues. Ultimately, the refugees decide when conditions are right for their return. The role of the international community in assistance and protection is still being forged in cases of repatriation under conflict.

REFERENCES

[1]Sergio Aguayo and Patricia Weiss Fagen, **Central Americans in Mexico and the United States: Unilateral, Bilateral, and Regional Pespectives** (Washington, D.C.: Center for Immigration Policy and Refugee Assistance, Georgetown University, 1988), 1.

[2] United Nations High Commissioner for Refugees and United Nations Development Program, CIREFCA Joint Support Unit, **Status Report on Implementation of the Concerted Plan of Action of the International Conference on Central American Refugees** (San José, Costa Rica, March 1991), 3.

[3] Marvin Ortega, **Nicaraguan Repatriation to Mosquitia** (Washington, D.C.: Hemispheric Migration Project, Center for Immigration Policy and Refugee Assistance, Georgetown University, 1991); Ricardo Stein, "The Spontaneous and Planned Return of Repatriates and Displaced Persons", in **1989 Central American Refugees** (Washington, D.C. and San José, Costa Rica: Center for Immigration Policy and Refugee Assistance, Georgetown and Consejo Superior Universitario Centroamericano, 1989); Beatriz Manz, **Repatriation and Reintegration: An Arduous Process in Guatemala** (Washington, D.C.: Hemispheric Migration Project, Center for Immigration Policy and Refugee Assistance, Georgetown University, 1988).

[4]Mary Ann Larkin, **Conference Report: Repatriation Under Conflict: The Central American Case** (Washington, D.C.: Hemispheric Migration Project, Center for Immigration Policy and Refugee Assistance, Georgetown University, 1991).

ACKNOWLEDGEMENTS

The editors of this volume wish to acknowledge the Ford Foundation and the Hemispheric Migration Project of Georgetown University's Center for Immigration Policy and Refugee Assistance for their financial support of the research and its dissemination. As well, we appreciate the support of the United Nations High Commissioner for Refugees, which generously offered Patricia Weiss Fagen the time to conduct the research. The UNHCR also facilitated the researchers' access to refugee camps and data on refugees and repatriation.

We would be remiss if we did not acknowledge the analytical contributions of Ricardo Stein to this research during the early meetings of the researchers. His understanding of the motivations and timing of spontaneous repatriation in the region contributed substantively to the case studies.

In the early meetings on the project, we are grateful for the participation of Patricia R. Pessar of the Hemispheric Migration Project in the design of the case studies. We are also most grateful to Charles B. Keely of CIPRA who made instructive comments on the drafts. In addition, the participants of the series of meetings on Central American Repatriation in December 1990 contributed greatly to this book by sharing their experience with us and exchanging views on the research.

In the preparation of this manuscript, we wish also to thank the following individuals for their dedicated work: Charles Becker for editing and translation, Diane Kuntz and Hazel Sirett for editing, the Center for Migration Studies for the index, Roxana Díaz for production, and Kristin Stoneking and Thomas Wentworth for assistance in production.

ABBREVIATIONS

ACRN	Nicaraguan Resistance Civic Association
AID	U.S. Agency for International Development
ASAI	Salvadoran Association for Comprehensive Support
CEAR	Commission for the Assistance of Repatriated and Displaced Persons
CEB	Christian Base Community
CEDEN	Evangelical Committee for Development and National Emergency
CIAV	International Commission for Assistance and Verification
CIPRA	Center for Immigration Policy and Refugee Assistance
CIREFCA	International Conference on Central American Refugees
CNR	National Coordinator for Repopulation
COFREGUA	The Conference of Guatemalan Religious Persons
COMAR	Mexican Commission for the Assistance of Refugees
CONADES	Salvadoran National Commission for Assistance to the Displaced Population
CONARE	Honduran National Commission for Refugees
CRIPDES	Christian Committee for the Displaced of El Salvador
CRS	Catholic Relief Services
DIGEPARE	National Directorate for Refugees
ERP	Peoples Revolutionary Army
FASTRAS	Federation for Salvadoran Labor Empowerment and Solidarity
FDR	Democratic Revolutionary Front
FECCAS	Christian Peasant Federation
FEDECOPADES	Federation of Farming Cooperatives of El Salvador
FMLN	Farabundo Martí National Liberation Front
FSLN	Sandinista National Liberation Front
FUNDPROCOOP	Foundation to Promote Cooperatives
GAM	Group of Mutual Support
HMP	Hemispheric Migration Project
ICRC	International Committee of the Red Cross
INRE	Nicaraguan Repatriation Institute
INSSBI	Nicaraguan Institute of Social Security and Welfare
INTA	Guatemalan Institute for Agrarian Transformation
MIDINRA	Ministry for Agricultural Development and Land Reform
MSF	Médecins sans Frontières (Doctors Without Borders)
OAS	Organization of American States
ONUCA	United Nations Central America Unit
ORDEN	Nationalist Democratic Organization
PAC	Peace and Autonomy Commission
PAR	Refugee Assistance Project
PEC	Special Plan of Economic Cooperation for Central America

PRODERE	Development Project for Refugees, Displaced, and Returnees
SARG	Secretariat for the Assistance of Guatemalan Refugees
UNDP	United Nations Development Program
UNHCR	United Nations High Commissioner for Refugees
UTC	Union of Rural Workers

CHAPTER I

INTRODUCTION

by Barry N. Stein and Frederick C. Cuny

Voluntary repatriation is generally viewed as the most desirable durable solution for refugees; however, it has received relatively little study. The papers in this volume were prepared as part of a five-year International Study of Spontaneous Voluntary Repatriation which has been supported by the Ford Foundation. A very fortuitous aspect of the study has been the cooperation with Georgetown University's Hemispheric Migration Project, which co-sponsored these case studies on returns to El Salvador, Guatemala, and Nicaragua. These studies, and the related meetings and conferences held in January and December 1990, have been critical to the analytical framework of the International Study in that they have elucidated the major patterns and concepts, and have formulated recommendations regarding refugee-induced repatriation. Other full or partial case studies in the International Study include returns to Sri Lanka, Afghanistan, Cambodia, Burundi, and Ethiopia.

This introduction will, first, provide a background regarding voluntary repatriation and spontaneous repatriation in order to explain why these case studies were undertaken; and, second, indicate the main research findings that have come from these and the other case studies.

SPONTANEOUS VOLUNTARY REPATRIATION

When the International Study of Spontaneous Voluntary Repatriation began in 1986, there were approximately ten million refugees worldwide; as of 1991, the estimated total exceeds seventeen million refugees. The principal reason for the increase in the number of refugees is the lack of durable solutions to refugee problems. A durable solution requires the integration, whether through citizenship or permanent status, of a refugee into a society. Resettlement in a third country, settlement in the country of asylum, or voluntary repatriation are the three classic durable solutions. However, for many refugees, long-term temporary asylum is the only option available. Once the refugees are admitted, many remain in the place of asylum seemingly forever. Refugee problems demand durable solutions, not only because of the cost and burden on host countries and the international community, as well as the waste of the refugees' lives, but also because in their second, third and fourth generation refugees can become a violent and destabilizing social element.

In any given year, less than one percent of the world's refugees escape the limbo of refugee status either by resettling in third countries or by obtaining citizenship in their country of asylum. *If the number of refugees is to be reduced significantly, it will be by means of voluntary repatriation.* Oddly, although repatriation is considered the ideal option, it is also the most difficult to implement for assistance agencies such as the United Nations High Commissioner for Refugees (UNHCR), nongovernmental organizations (NGOs), other United Nations (UN) agencies, and bilateral actors. Repatriation assistance is where these agencies have their greatest limitations of mandate and resources. Nonetheless, despite the international agencies' limitations, voluntary repatriation has become the most common durable solution. Since 1985, over one million refugees have repatriated, although over 90 percent did so in an irregular fashion.

Contemporary international beliefs and principles regarding repatriation hold that return to the refugee's homeland will be purely voluntary, that it will be assisted and monitored under the terms of a tripartite agreement between the United Nations High Commissioner for Refugees (UNHCR), the governments of the refugee's country of origin and of asylum, and that the refugee's complete safety and socioeconomic integration will be assured.

Unfortunately, it is a rare case that entails such orderly and organized return. Thus, international activities based on the above assumptions may be irrelevant to the needs of most refugees.

Today, most voluntary repatriations occur during conflict, without a decisive political event such as national independence, without any change in the regime or the conditions that originally caused flight. Countless individual refugees and sizeable groups of well-organized refugees return home in the face of continued risk, frequently without an amnesty or a repatriation agreement or program, without the permission of the authorities in either the country of asylum or of origin, without international knowledge or assistance, and without an end to the conflict that caused the exodus. The fact that large numbers of refugees choose to return without the "protection" of the UN is an indicator of the efficacy of the protection process, and the fact that many refugees are willing to forgo assistance indicates how aid is regarded during this point in a refugee's exile. The fact that refugees are returning to their homelands under these circumstances requires new thinking about voluntary repatriation and the ways of promoting it.

The three case studies in this volume were selected as examples of the above conditions. Their detailed narratives of the chronology of events and the roles of the refugees, the governments, and the assistance agencies, are critical in the development of a new perspective on repatriation, distinct from the conventional wisdom regarding international assistance to return movements. This new perspective calls for assistance agencies to respond in their work to the refugees' decisions rather than attempt to design and direct returns before refugee participation is sought.

The refugees are the main actors in the contemporary practice of voluntary repatriation. They are the main decision-makers and determine the modalities of movement and the conditions of reception. Refugee-induced repatriation is a self-regulating process on the refugees' own terms. The refugees apply their own criteria to their situation in exile and to conditions in their homeland and will return home if it is safe and better by their standards.

> *This protection is defined as the perceived "space" or opening*
> *in society that provides the refugees not only some measure of*
> *physical protection, but also material and moral support.*
> *Space can be seen so narrowly as to give a single refugee the*
> *freedom to choose to return to the community of origin, or it*
> *can be understood so broadly as to permit a collective return*
> *of a community.**

Many of the returnees are in desperate circumstances — in part because their return receives woefully inadequate international support, but they do not flee again.

RESEARCH FINDINGS

Our findings can be categorized into three main areas; as the range of repatriation, including that which occurs without the assistance or protection of the international community; phases of repatriation; and the decision-making of refugees confronted with unsatisfactory options.

The Range of Repatriation

Generally, if international agencies and governments do not initiate, manage, and organize a voluntary repatriation, the international agencies refer to it as an unorganized or spontaneous repatriation. However, the failure or inability to provide repatriation assistance does not mean there is a lack of organization. Refugee-run agencies, guerrilla forces, and host governments may provide substantial organization. Unfortunately, due to the lack of international participation, return and reintegration resources are likely to be inadequate.

To a certain degree, it is better to avoid labelling types of repatriation and to concentrate instead on examining the range of repatriation experiences. It is useful to describe a repatriation experience with respect to where it falls along one or more continuums or spectrums. For example, one continuum might begin with unorganized, unassisted repatriation at one end and continue to organized, internationally assisted repatriation at the other end. In between are repatriations which are organized or assisted to varying degrees by the refugees themselves or various local or international actors. A second continuum which can be used to characterize repatriation indicates the degree to which it is voluntary, encouraged, induced, or forced. A third continuum charts whether a repatriation is undertaken by an individual, small group, or more sizeable collective. Finally, a fourth continuum might reflect changes in the degree of political conflict which spurred the original flight. Today, most repatriation occurs under adverse conditions or conflict. These circumstances raise serious questions of coercion and protection of refugees.

Some of the points along a political conflict spectrum would represent: (1) return after fundamental political change such as independence (Zimbabwe, Namibia) or victory (Eritrea, Ethiopia); (2) return after a political settlement or major political change (Nicaragua); (3) return after a political settlement that does not end the political conflict and which leaves the contending parties with substantial political and military power (Afghanistan, Sri Lanka, Angola); (4) return to areas not controlled by the government of the country of origin (perhaps controlled by rival political, local, or foreign forces, such as in Tigray, Iraq, Afghanistan, El Salvador, Cambodia); (5) return to a country controlled by the government that originally caused the flight (Guatemala); (6) return caused by deteriorating political security conditions in the host country (the post-1985 return from southern Sudan to Uganda, the 1989-1991 return from Somalia to Ethiopia); and, (7) forced return of impressed refugees to a conflict zone (Cambodia).

Repatriation Phases and Decisions

In examining refugee-stimulated repatriation under conflict it is necessary to take a split screen view of two interacting factors simultaneously; the phases of repatriation and the purpose of refugee decision-making. These two factors constantly interact in the course of the repatriation process.

In our conceptual framework, we have identified four main phases of repatriation: (1) the "ricochet" effect or immediate repatriation of newly arrived refugees; (2) relocation-stimulated repatriation; (3) the evaluation of community and alienation; and, (4) major repatriations. The timing of these phases is not rigid, and the process may be drawn out or swift. The various phases may flow in smooth succession, or they may be jumbled by events. The key factors driving the events are the assistance decisions and attitudes of the host country, changing conditions within the homeland, the location of the refugees in their refuge, and the evolution of refugee communities at sites where refugees are concentrated. Also influencing this process is the fact that most borders are relatively porous allowing refugees to visit and communicate with their homeland.

Ricochet Repatriation — If the exodus was sudden, such as the result of military action or a stampede away from danger, a substantial number of people who might not have felt personally threatened or whose sympathies were not in line with the majority of the refugees will immediately seek ways to return. These initial repatriations will be spontaneous and unassisted and can be termed "ricochet repatriations."

Relocation-stimulated Repatriation — The next phase is the host government's round-up of refugees scattered along the border and their movement to refugee camps to facilitate the process of aiding and controlling the refugees. At this point, refugees must decide whether to accept host government control and reside in the camps or try to elude the authorities and find a place to live away from other refugees. For those who stay in the camps, repatriation will inevitably become a less immediate option. But for those refugees who settle outside the camps, repatriation is more likely to be a viable alternative, especially if they are unable to find work in the country of asylum.

   Community and Alienation — One of the more interesting common denominators found in the case studies is the formation by uprooted peoples of politically organized, cohesive communities. Rounded up by the host government and relocated to refugee camps, refugees are placed in unaccustomed communal situations which may change their way of life and crowd them in with strangers. Under these circumstances refugees show an impressive ability to organize and congeal into a new community with its own mores and values. Frequently, refugee organizations are formed that ally with insurgent groups. Refugees come to believe that their situation is a key part of the political equation in the struggle of their group for social, cultural, or economic change.

   Some refugees will be indifferent or alienated from the emerging refugee community, its values, and common cause. These aloof refugees, seeking control over their own lives, are likely to move away from the camp or settlement or to repatriate. As a UNHCR official once commented, "We must not forget that, like governments, refugee leaderships are not immune to the attractiveness of repression in order to achieve a political goal or maintain stability within the community."

   As time passes, the available space for repatriation is likely to increase. At home, the locus of the conflict may change; the levels of violence may decrease; political or economic changes may occur. The border may become more porous as a result of internal changes in the homeland. Cross-border trade may normalize, providing an opportunity for families in the camps and spontaneously-settled refugees to send scouts back to check on conditions and to find out if it is viable for small numbers of people to go back. Returns by internally displaced persons to particular regions will be carefully noted by refugees and may trigger some repatriation.

   Gradually more and more people will begin to leave. They are generally people who are on the periphery of the mainstream refugee community, or those who feel they no longer belong. The refugee organizations may oppose the return of these less committed refugees, feeling that repatriation somehow undercuts the political or moral position of the refugee comunity. Repatriations during this period may expand the political space at home, although not always significantly.

Secondary Relocation-stimulated Repatriation — At some point, in almost every refugee situation, the host government will decide, or at least propose, to relocate refugees from camps near the border to camps or formal settlements in the interior. This relocation may be dictated by political concerns, as was the case of Guatemalans in Mexico, or by operational concerns, as was the case in Sudan. Whatever the reason, imminent relocation forces the refugees to decide whether to accept the transfer and the disruption it is likely to cause to both the refugees' lives and to the established sense of community, or to leave the camps and attempt either to integrate into the surrounding communities or to repatriate.

A key consideration is the perceived breakup of the sense of community that has evolved in the camps. If more refugees show an interest in repatriation than the existing political conditions and organization of assistance allows, then organizational attitudes start to change, and agencies working with the refugees actively begin to seek ways to expand the space for repatriation.

Major Repatriations — UNHCR participation is the final stage in the repatriation process. In response to governmental pressures (usually from the host government and then from the country of origin), UNHCR will begin to provide assistance, in some cases reluctantly. Whether or not this is carried out as part of a formal tripartite agreement may depend on the way the repatriation is perceived by the international community.

Decision-Making

There are two points to note about refugee decision-making. First, not all refugees are alike; there will be varied responses to forced location often rooted in different levels of mobility, urbanization, education, and economic status among the refugees. Second, refugee responses vary over a long period of time. The refugee community will behave differently at the beginning, when there is generally a conservative risk-aversive response; in later years, greater initiative and risk-taking will occur.

Our perspective of refugee decision-making views the refugees as individuals who make "rational" choices among unsatisfactory options, and who strive for an outcome that achieves relative security and some degree of control over their lives.

Although refugees are commonly thought of as powerless, and they certainly are in relative terms, it is well to recall that the decision to flee, to stay, or to return home, is an action and a choice. (The choice is often influenced by geography; those near the border cross it and become refugees; others, far from the border, flee to the cities and become internally displaced persons. Their status differs, but the cause of flight is often identical.)

The decision to flee obviously reflects the refugees' belief that their power over others and over their own lives is inadequate to provide protection from insult, injury, imprisonment, or death. Refugees make their moves to flee, to repatriate, and to accept settlement or resettlement on the basis of decisions that are made through a comparison of alternatives.

In comparing alternative choices, refugees attempt to conserve and strengthen their control over their own lives and to reduce the possibility that further stress will occur. Not surprisingly, refugees seek security. In clinging to the familiar, refugees attempt to move the shortest distance not only in terms of space in order to remain in contact with a familiar habitat, but also in terms of the psychological and sociocultural context of their lives.

Initially, refugees can be expected to follow a conservative strategy. They cope with the stress of flight to an unfamiliar habitat by clinging to the familiar and changing no more than necessary.

In the relocation phase of repatriation, refugees consider the move to refugee camps or further inland to settlements as a threat to their identity. It would move them from a known to an unknown world, further away from kin and familiar territory. Returning home to a previously established social identity with rights and obligations can be seen as allowing the refugee to retain more power, stability, and control over their own lives.

The passage of time is likely to alter the refugees' approach to decision-making, although not the goal of the decisions — security and control.

The later stage of decision-making is marked by increased initiative and risk taking. The turning point is when the refugees have regained much of their former standard of living and degree of self-sufficiency. The refugees' willingness to take risks may focus on repatriation if the community's condition in the host country is hopeless, isolated, or precarious.

Conservative risk-aversive refugees will act as individuals and will avoid contact with government and international agencies; i.e., they will be suspicious of anything official. Thus, they will repatriate spontaneously. Over time, as initiative and risk-taking re-emerge in the refugee community, the refugees will be willing to confront their hosts, their homeland, and the international community with requests for officially sanctioned, but refugee stimulated repatriation.

CONCLUSION

As these case studies indicate, the ability of refugees to take matters into their own hands and organize repatriations is a hopeful sign. But often they are forced into this position by hopelessness, danger, and lack of assistance. The mass repatriations to conflict zones in El Salvador grew out of the hostile, hopeless situation in the closed refugee camps in Honduras.

The international community has failed to provide durable solutions for millions of refugees. Although repatriation should not be viewed as a panacea, there remains a need, despite significant protection concerns, to promote voluntary repatriation actively, even at times under conflict. In an imperfect world in which most refugees are offered only long-term temporary asylum, there is a need to assist refugees in going home. Confronted with unsatisfactory options, the refugee must still search for the best available alternative.

Rather than adopt a passive international approach, there are circumstances in which repatriation should be carefully and actively promoted even before the formal end of hostilities. It is evident from the number of repatriations to date that the end of conflict is not a precondition for repatriation; thus, other political options need to be explored. Protection, security, and more control over one's fate are the key variables of repatriation under conflict. We must find ways to work with, respond to, and respect the refugees' decisions.

REFERENCE

*Mary Ann Larkin, **Conference Report: Repatriation Under Conflict: The Central American Case**, (Washington, D.C.: Hemispheric Migration Project, Center for Immigration Policy and Refugee Assistance, Georgetown University, 1991):15.

HONDURAS

Tegucigalpa
*

EL SALVADOR

NICARAGUA

PACIFIC OCEAN

CARIBBEAN SEA

COSTA RICA

MOSQUITIA
Prumnitara
Sixatigni
Koko
Mocorón
Tapalwas
Tapamlaya
Las Vegas · · Teupacenti
Danlí
Waspan
Bonanza
Trojes
EL PARAISO
RAAN
Puerto Cabezas
(Northern Atlantic
Autonomous Region)*
Choluteca
N. SEGOVIA
Yali
JINOTEGA
ESTELÍ
MATAGALPA
CHINANDEGA
LEON
Masaya
Chontales
Managua *
Granada
Bluefields
(Southern Atlantic
Autonomous Region)*
Rio San Juan
Tilaran
Limon
San Jose *

Scale

0   25   50   75   100

Kilometers

* Atlantic Coast Headquarters

CHAPTER II

NICARAGUAN REPATRIATION FROM HONDURAS AND COSTA RICA

by Marvin Ortega and Pedro Acevedo

INTRODUCTION

The Central American peace agreements and the policy changes undertaken by the government of Nicaragua to encourage repatriation are the products of national and international efforts to assist Nicaraguan refugees in Honduras and Costa Rica in returning to their country.

The following activities are among the most important undertaken by the Nicaraguan government, with the support of international agencies, to encourage repatriation. These are: The Autonomy Law (1987) for ethnic groups; the Amnesty Law for the Miskitos (1988); the discussions with the Resistance (1988); the groundwork for holding elections on February 25, 1990; and the 1989 National Dialogue between the opposition parties and the Sandinista Front.

The 1989 National Dialogue led to a number of agreements: (a) a broad and unconditional amnesty that took effect with the final implementation of the plan for Contra demobilization; (b) suspension of the military draft between September 1989 and February 1990; (c) release from jail of political party activists and political prisoners; and (d) the Constitutional Reform for the hand-over of power after the February 1990 elections.

On March 23, 1990, the Nicaraguan government and the Resistance signed a treaty in Toncontín, Honduras for the demobilization and disarmament of the Resistance before April 20, 1990. Under this agreement, the Resistance was to retreat into zones that the Organization of American States (OAS) and the United Nations (UN) had marked off for this purpose. Thus, on April 6, 1990, the OAS and UN opened five security zones (each of which covered an area of 3,000 square km) where the disarmament and demobilization would take place and where food, clothing, and medical care were to be furnished. However, the Resistance soon repudiated the Toncontín Agreement and demanded a total disarmament of the Sandinista Army as a condition for ending the war and retreating to the security zones.

After a new round of negotiations, new ceasefire agreements were signed on April 18 under which government troops began to retreat 20 km beyond the limits of the security zones, and humanitarian aid to Resistance troops was delivered. The disarmament began April 25 and the total demobilization on June 10.

The UN Central American forces (ONUCA), the OAS International Commission for Assistance and Verification (CIAV), and Cardinal Obando, Archbishop of Managua oversaw the implementation of these agreements. Within days of the demobilization, the Resistance renewed its demand for the simultaneous disarmament of the Sandinista Army, and the government guaranties for its own disarmament and demobilization were accepted. The head of the Resistance Command was offered by President Ortega a position as Vice Minister in the newly formed Ministry for Repatriation. Under the agreements, disarmament was to begin on May 8 and conclude by June 10, 1990, under the supervision of ONUCA and CIAV.

By June 10, President Ortega had proposed a program to reduce the size of the Sandinista Army. Furthermore, under the agreements, the Contras would receive legal assistance in order to set up a political party, once the disarmament had been completed, and development enclaves were set up where the demobilized fighters could work.

After some arms had been turned over to UNCA forces, the resistance made a new demand as a condition for disarmament and demobilization: a 16,000 square km area along the San Juan River to be used as a sort of free zone in which its supporters could work in guaranteed safety and where they would create a rural police force of former resistance members. However, this proposal was rejected by the San Juan River population, particularly by the Sandinistas in that region.

The Sandinista Army began to carry out the peace agreements; on May 12, it confiscated and destroyed the weapons that had been in the hands of Sandinista agricultural cooperatives near the security zones where the Resistance first began to turn in its arms. Finally, in August 1990, the disarmament of the Resistance was completed once approximately 20,000 Contras turned over their weapons.

A rough appraisal of the results of the national and international efforts for the return of the refugees reveals positive trends despite the true difficulties surrounding repatriation. The programs have been particularly successful in encouraging the Miskitos and Sumus to return to their home communities; almost 80 percent of the ethnic group members had been displaced either domestically or as refugees. Nevertheless, the programs implemented prior to 1990 were unable to induce a massive return of Mestizo refugees.

In the absence of accurate figures, it is estimated that 400,000 people fled Nicaragua during the 1980s, of whom tens of thousands remain in other Central American countries. In spite of a number of lingering problems, the process of repatriation now appears to be irreversible so long as external forces do not intervene. In other words, if Nicaraguans are allowed to resolve their differences with international cooperation, but without foreign imposition, the vast majority of Nicaraguan refugees will repatriate.

As of this writing it is still not clear that the existing set of agreements and policy measures will be successful in inducing massive voluntary repatriation. The reluctance of so many Nicaraguans to return prior to the inauguration of the government of President Violeta Chamorro indicated the presence of factors influencing the decision to repatriate. In addition to the requisite physical and social safeguards, one must also consider such other factors in the refugees' lives as the social, economic, and political motives that condition the refugee's existence, their access to information on repatriation and the sources thereof, the distinct political culture of the countryside, and the organizational structures and dominant ideology among the groups of refugees.

Two other critical factors in the decision to repatriate will be explored in this chapter: the political forces that take advantage of the refugees' situation for their own particular political agenda; and the impact of long-term refugee projects organized by humanitarian organizations, which offered refugees safe and stable alternatives to the uncertainty of repatriation.

Given the unpredictable nature of the decision of refugees to seek repatriation, the fundamental objectives of our research were to identify and define the following factors:

a. The different elements that encourage or inhibit voluntary repatriation, especially the impact of the regional agreements;

b. The patterns in the return of individuals, families, and communities, as well as their initial places of settlement;

c. The role of repatriation in the drop or increase in the levels of violence in the country of origin;

d. The coordination among different government and humanitarian agencies that provide assistance to repatriated refugees.

The focus of this research was on the refugee groups in Honduras and Costa Rica, with a particular emphasis on the comparative differences between the experiences of the majority Mestizo population and the ethnic groups; i.e., the indigenous Miskito and Sumu peoples. Points of contrast include their relations with the receiving society and with the government agencies and nongovernmental organizations that provide them with assistance, particularly the impact of these agencies and organizations on refugee attitudes toward voluntary repatriation.

Another important element to consider was whether an individual or group enjoyed official refugee status and was included under the mandate of the United Nations High Commissioner for Refugees (UNHCR).

Not included in the focus of this research are the relatively few refugees or repatriated Nicaraguans who resided in other countries. (For example, there were 355 Nicaraguans in El Salvador who received assistance and were officially recognized as refugees.[1] Refugees outside of camps were not studied due to the logistical difficulty in locating them. There is little information on refugees who repatriate outside official channels; furthermore, they usually do so in small groups. These characteristics increase the level of complexity of their process of reintegration into society, since this takes place beyond the scope of the plans and projects from which they could benefit.[2]

The constraints on obtaining reliable information increase the difficulties of studying the last group. According to the Nicaraguan Institute of Social Security and Welfare, only 50 Nicaraguans repatriated from countries other than Honduras and Costa Rica during the first half of 1989.

Having first defined the population from which our sample was chosen, we moved on to specifying the methodology of our field work, as follows:

a) Analysis of the available literature on Central American refugees and repatriates, particularly Nicaraguans;

b) Eighteen case studies;[3]

c) Interviews with the staff of national and international agencies.[4]

The case studies and the interviews gathered information representing different points of view and various appraisals of the repatriation issue. Information on Costa Rica was derived from such secondhand sources as research and articles on the refugees there.[5]

This report is structured in three major parts. First, we present a characterization of the groups under study, which reflects the refugee process until 1989 in historical and quantitative terms as well as by group and country of asylum. Next, we take up the factors that stimulate and inhibit repatriation, the influence of the regional accords, the impact of other repatriation experiences, the repatriation patterns, the places where the refugees return, and how they are received.

REFUGEES IN HONDURAS AND COSTA RICA

A number of factors facilitated the entry into Honduran and Costa Rican territory of Nicaraguans who left their country to search either for solutions to economic problems or survival in the face of war. These factors include the relative ease in crossing common borders and the close ethnic and commercial ties between Nicaragua and its neighbors. Honduras and Costa Rica became points of reference in the search for asylum or refuge among rural Nicaraguans and particularly for the population in northern Nicaragua. According to the UNHCR, almost 86 percent of the refugees in Honduran camps came from the northern area of the country.

The Mestizo Campesino Refugees in Honduras

Soon after the 1979 Sandinista victory in Nicaragua, some relatively wealthy Nicaraguans began immigrating to Honduras. They were able to purchase property, start businesses, set themselves up successfully, and thus were generally welcomed by their new Honduran neighbors.

The reception was very different for the wave of the poor and the armed Nicaraguans who arrived later.[6] The new arrivals posed a serious competitive challenge to the Honduran population of the border zone both because they constituted a cheaper alternative source of labor and because the organized military groups transformed vast areas of Honduran territory into zones under the control of a foreign army that displaced thousands of small- and medium-scale Honduran farming families. Nevertheless, these Nicaraguans were natural allies of the Honduran government and Armed Forces, which opposed the Sandinista Revolution from the start.

Starting in 1982, two separate currents of Nicaraguan refugees began to enter Honduras. Coming for the most part from the Nicaraguan border area, they tended to settle in and around the city of Danlí in the department of El Paraíso. The majority of these refugees were Mestizo *campesino* families fleeing the war in the Nicaraguan departments of Nueva Segovia, Jinotega, Estelí, and Madriz. Nevertheless, Nicaraguans from the entire country could be found in the camps in the area of Danlí.

These first groups of refugees arrived in waves, consisting of people fleeing the military conflict and others in search of relatives who forcibly or voluntarily had become incorporated into the armed counterrevolutionary units or Contras as they came to be known. From the interviews, we learned that many of these refugees had planned to return soon to Nicaragua. However, both the logic of the war itself and the control over the territory exercised by armed units, who recruited combatants and propagandized the refugees against the Sandinista revolution, led many Nicaraguans to stay in Honduras either from fear or personal preference.

The assistance for these refugees in 1982 was sporadic. The Red Cross played an important role, but systematic assistance was not provided until December 1982, when the UNHCR decided to furnish financial assistance to a group of approximately 400 people ensconced in the Masonic Lodge in Danlí. Though by no means the only refugees, this group was best placed to receive organized assistance quickly.

In 1983, U.S. funding and the internal conflicts within Nicaragua led to an intensification of the war, and the number of refugees receiving UNHCR assistance in the camps rose from 400 to 2,500. The newcomers arrived at Jacaleapa and Teupacenti municipalities, in northern El Paraíso Department. By December 1985, after the wartime momentum had reached its peak, 5,300 people were receiving assistance in these camps near Danlí.

A new camp was set up in July and August 1987, in a place near Teupacenti known as Las Vegas, in order to accommodate the constant influx of new refugees (3,893 were registered at the camps in 1987 and 1988) from Nicaragua as well as an overflow of previous arrivals who had been crowded into the other two camps, far beyond their absorption capacity. The Las Vegas camp was expanded in 1988 to combine two adjoining terrains, La Milpa and El Zacatal, which were leased for new subdivisions. Expansion work on the facilities later increased their capacity and made it possible to accommodate 7,000 refugees in the three subdivisions of the Las Vegas camp.

The increase between 1988 and 1990 in the number of refugees at the camps under UNHCR stewardship resulted mainly from the resettlement of refugees who were already in Honduras, but had not yet obtained official status, resided in camps, or benefitted from any UNHCR programs. There were few new refugees entering Honduras at that time.

Table 1 below is a breakdown by prior residence of new arrivals to the camps. Note that 86 percent of the new arrivals over the last two years had already been residing in Honduras.

TABLE 1

Prior Country Residence of New Arrivals at Refugee Camps
1988-1989

| | Honduras | | Nicaragua | | Total |
	Number	%	Number	%	Number
1,988	1,730	88	237	12	1,967
1,989	1,122	84	213	16	1,335
TOTAL	2,852	86	450	13	3,302

Source: Derived from data of UNHCR-Honduras, 1989.

The 1989 arrivals are shown by month and by camp in Table 2. Note that the vast majority of new arrivals, who totalled 1,967 people in 1988, were received at the Las Vegas camp.

TABLE 2

Refugee Arrivals to UNHCR Camps in Honduras by Month, 1989

Camp:	1988	1989								
		Jan	Feb	Mar	Apr	May	June	July	Aug	Total
Jacaleapa	192	21	41	29	25	34	20	5	6	181
Teupacenti	37	8	12	3	7	15	11	27	4	87
Las Vegas	1,738	108	126	94	171	194	42	202	127	1,064
TOTAL	1,967	137	179	126	203	243	73	234	137	1,332

Source: Derived from data of UNHCR-Honduras, 1989.

As can be appreciated in Table 3, 14,658 Nicaraguan Mestizo refugees were receiving assistance in the three camps by August 31, 1989.

TABLE 3

Total Refugees in Honduras by UNHCR Camp (1986 -1989)

Camp	1986	1987	1988	Aug 1989
Jacaleapa	4,445	6,293	6,125	6,270
Teupacenti	3,746	4,552	4,297	4,370
Las Vegas	0	928	3,005	4,008
TOTAL	8,191	11,773	13,427	14,658

Source: Derived from data of UNHCR-Honduras, October 1989.

The growth in the refugee population at the camps can be explained principally by the disintegration of the Contra forces, which were not able to sustain a permanent presence in Nicaraguan territory.

Moreover, the uncertain nature of the flow of U.S. funds to the Contras led many individuals and families with ties to military units to take refuge in the camps.

Some persons came because of economic difficulties in the military bases; others became tired of the war and sought out relatives who were already receiving assistance in the camps. There were also combatants who retreated to the camps in order to bring a greater counterrevolutionary political presence there and to transfer food, supplied by UNHCR and other agencies for the refugees, to the military units.

Of the population that filled the Honduran refugee camps beginning in 1986, 86 percent had been in the Honduran Department of El Paraíso, mainly around Los Trojes, where the greatest number of Nicaraguan Resistance camps were located. The areas from which the refugees arrived are indicated in Table 4.

TABLE 4

Region of Prior Residence in Honduras
Among New Arrivals at UNHCR Camps, 1988

Trojes	Paraíso	Choluteca	Others	Total
78%	8%	2%	12%	100%
1,539	148	43	237	1,967

Source: Derived from data of UNHCR-Honduras, October 1989.

There were also many people who had left Nicaragua in order to reach the United States, but for a number of reasons, prinicipally economic, were unable to continue their trips. Many of these people who remained permanently in Honduras, then claimed to be victims of political persecution in order to receive UNHCR assistance in the camps.

Nicaraguan Refugees in Costa Rica

The first important influx of Nicaraguan refugees into Costa Rica began in 1982 when the worst fighting of the war was breaking out in the Department of Río San Juan in southeastern Nicaragua along the Costa Rican border.

As part of its tactics in this particularly mountainous region, the Nicaraguan government resettled *campesinos* from the mountains into settlements alongside roads or in areas the army could easily protect. This displacement caused unrest among the population and gave rise to abuses and misunderstandings between the authorities and the *campesinos*. Thus, thousands of persons who opposed the government's decision to resettle them far from their homes sought refuge in Costa Rica.

In the ensuing years refugees from around Bluefields and the Departments of Chontales and Nueva Guinea arrived in greater numbers. As had those before them, these people had become directly affected by the war.

After 1984, refugee flows of other Nicaraguans began arriving from the Pacific region, especially the largest urban areas—Managua, Masaya, Granada, Rivas, Carazo, León, and Chinandega. Most were young men fleeing the draft.[7] Many people also began arriving in search of better living conditions and claimed political persecution in order to win refugee status.

The refugees in Costa Rica came from varying backgrounds, both Mestizo *campesinos* and people from urban areas who had no rural traditions. Most camp dwellers were either from the first group or the ranks of the urban poor.

Thus, in Costa Rica the refugee situation developed quite differently than in Honduras, where almost all the official refugees received assistance in camps. By contrast, in Costa Rica in 1989, only 35 percent of the refugees lived in camps, and the remaining 65 percent of the official refugees lived in urban areas.

The figures on Nicaraguan refugees in Costa Rica are quite controversial (as indeed are the Honduran figures). The Costa Rican Ministry of Government estimated the number of official refugees at just over 30,000 and of clandestine ones at approximately 200,000. Others give 21,675 as the official number.[8]

Indigenous Nicaraguan Refugee Groups in Honduras

According to UNHCR sources in Honduras, some 1,500 indigenous Nicaraguans sought refuge within Honduran territory in the first few months of 1981; in January 1982, there were already 2,000 ethnic Nicaraguans, by July the number had reached 10,000. The majority was resettled in a large camp known as Mocorón. However, the number of ethnic refugees that received UNHCR assistance was only a portion of the total. It is estimated that by January 1982, 15,000 Miskitos had already crossed the border to take refuge in Honduras and flee the military activities that were taking place in and around their communities in Nicaraguan territory.

In 1983, another 3,500 Miskito refugees were registered with UNHCR. In April 1984, a group of 1,500 people settled at the Tapamlaya camps. In April 1986, 7,741 entries were registered. This brought the total of Nicaraguan indigenous Nicaraguans under UNHCR mandate, whether within or outside of the camps in Honduras, to 20,636. By the end of the year, the total number of indigenous peoples who were living in UNHCR camps had reached 14,288.

TABLE 5

Ethnic Nicaraguan Population Living in Honduras Under UNHCR Mandate

Camp	1986	1987	1988	1989
Tapalwas	625	798	686	318
Tapamlaya }	1,397	776	796	819
Prumnitara		500	479	432
Koko	868	822	646	611
Patuca	5,053	4,325	3,185	3,026
Mocorón }	5,759	2,097	1,890	1,891
Río Mocorón		2,268	1,951	1,844
Sixatigni	586	434	97	112
TOTAL	14,288	12,020	9,730	9,047

Source: UNHCR, September 1989.

The ethnic community has traditionally treated the territory of Mosquitia as a single entity without regard to the Nicaraguan-Honduran border that it straddles. Thus, many ethnic refugees settled with friends and relatives in the Miskito communities on the Honduran side of the border beyond the purview of the UNHCR. There were estimated to be a total of 30,000 indigenous Miskito and Sumu refugees living in Honduras by 1986.

In that year, the UNHCR coordinated a repatriation movement of the Miskito people, the majority of whom returned to Nicaragua. By the end of September 1989, there were 9,047 ethnic refugees registered in camps or under UNHCR protection. The majority lived in settlements along the banks of the Patuca, Warunta, and Mocorón Rivers, the main waterways of the area.

THE PRINCIPAL MOTIVES FOR REPATRIATION

Before the elections the rate of voluntary repatriation among Mestizo refugees in Honduras did not grow significantly during 1988 and 1989. However, the ethnic repatriation, which is discussed below, was significant.

Between 1983 (the year that voluntary repatriation to Nicaragua first began) and August 1989, the number of repatriated refugees totaled 1,424, a very small figure in comparison with the number of refugees in Costa Rica who repatriated over the same period. (See Table 6.)

By the end of 1989, a total of aproximately 3,000 Nicaraguan refugees staying in Honduras repatriated to Nicaragua, according to information provided by the UNHCR. This was approximately twice as many as the number who repatriated from Honduras over the previous seven years.

TABLE 6
Nicaraguan Repatriations From Honduras
(1983-1989)

1983	93
1984	185
1985	375
1986	85
1987	113
1988	243
1989 (through 9/19)	330
Total	1,424

Source: UNHCR-Honduras

In general, the repatriation from the Honduran camps was not significant, although it was greater from Jacaleapa and Las Vegas than from Teupacenti. Despite the efforts of the Central American presidents in 1989 to encourage migration, August was the only month of the year that saw more than an insignificant level of repatriation. However, an undetermined number of repatriations, outside the scope of the UNHCR, took place without being recorded.

In the agricultural areas near the border, where the war began to level off in 1988, officials, agrarian associations, and religious groups assisted hundreds of individuals who returned to their former homes. Among the returnees were internally displaced and former rebels and their families who were returning from Honduras. However, it was impossible to determine the proportion of the two groups among the returnees. Normally, the families returning to areas where the war was winding down represented all three of the previously mentioned categories of repatriates.

Repatriation was stimulated by a set of factors that can not be ranked by order of importance. Factors in favor of repatriation were the tenuous or nonexistent link between refugees and the armed groups, and the general desire to avoid involvement in the military conflict. The people interviewed who had returned prior to 1990, and the majority of those who returned under UNHCR auspices had spent relatively little time in Honduras and, in general, either had few ties to the armed Resistance or wished to terminate those that existed.

For the majority of these people, the frustration of the expectations that had led them to leave Nicaragua (better living conditions, immigration to the United States) impelled them to seek repatriation as a more viable alternative to life in the camps.

Moreover, a significant number had been kidnapped or had gone to the camps in search of relatives kidnapped by the Contras at some point during the war. Many refugees of this type were originally from towns bordering Honduras, or they had been unskilled workers from cities in northern Nicaragua; in other words, people of a more urban background with few *campesino* traditions.

From the interviews in the camps, it appears that many from this group of repatriated refugees could not adapt themselves to the majority of the camp residents, the *campesinos* from the hills who made up the bulk of the armed resistance and its sympathizers. These *campesinos* always had closer ties and a greater political commitment to the Contras than did the urban refugees. Repatriates interviewed before 1990 indicated that the militant *campesino* Contras had regarded them with suspicion and distrust.

The insecurity pervading the camps was another factor favoring repatriation. Many who repatriated from the camps and many who were considering it, but had not yet done so, felt they were languishing in a limbo that held a past and a present, but presented no future. The nationalist sentiment and lack of acceptance in Honduras reinforced this feeling. For example, there was great concern over their children's future because the kind of education they received under Honduran programs of study prevented them from learning about their own country.

The training received in the camps also acted as a stimulus for repatriation. Those who learned trades such as carpentry or sheetmetal work felt more capable of facing the prospects of return with the thought of going to live in urban areas of Nicaragua where they believed a better opportunity to develop would exist.

Communication with others who had already repatriated, particularly relatives, contributed to greater repatriation. However, there were few effective channels of communication between those who left and those who stayed in the camps, in part because of the pressure the Contras exerted against contacts between people in Nicaragua and Honduras.

We believe that the measures the Nicaraguan government took to facilitate repatriation (i.e., the Amnesty Law, the completion of the Electoral Process, the winding down of the war, the assistance programs, and the international protection for repatriated refugees) had little impact on the Nicaraguan Mestizo refugees. The government's offers were met by a prevailing distrust of Sandinista promises and became mired in the pressures imposed by the wartime conditions themselves.

The underlying factors that motivated Nicaraguan repatriation at this time were very different in Honduras than in Costa Rica. In general, the differences involved a series of situations that had the net effect of either motivating or discouraging the decision to repatriate. However, no one factor stands out as having made the greatest impact, and it is very difficult to rank such factors in order of importance. Clearly, the war played an important part in all the decisions to repatriate, but this fact alone does not explain the decisions.

It appears that the refugees in Costa Rica were less apprehensive about returning since the war had virtually ceased as of 1985 in their home territory, particularly around the San Juan River near the border. Moreover, the armed groups attempting to prevent repatriation from refugee camps had considerably less influence in Costa Rica than in Honduras.

Mestizo refugees in Costa Rica were able to repatriate freely without pressures or threats because the war had virtually ended in their communities of origin. Thus, the UNHCR and Nicaraguan and Costa Rican agencies did not have to engage in strenuous efforts to convince these refugees to repatriate.

The anti-refugee tenor of the Costa Rican media, which portrayed Nicaraguans as undesirables, also spurred repatriation. Surveys of three major Costa Rican daily newspapers demonstrate their impact in creating a negative image of the refugees. Between 1981 and 1983, 70 percent of the articles on refugees published by *La Nación* projected a negative image, as did 67 percent of those in *Universidad*, and 57 percent in *La República*.[9] The same study shows how local dailies repeatedly portrayed "the assimilation of the figure of the refugee with the methods of political terrorists, the guerrilla struggle, psychosomatic irregularities, and pathologies."[10]

The treatment of refugees was not impervious to the play of political interests that opposed the Sandinista revolution. Aware of this contradiction, the Costa Rican press maintained an ambivalent attitude toward the refugees. On the one hand, Sandinista endeavors were considered to be "against geopolitical interests, politically illegitimate, and economically infeasible....In these terms, (the refugees) are applauded and welcomed with understanding....Nevertheless, the daily litany in the tabloids emphasizes problems that threaten the physical, and sometimes even the moral, health of the Costa Rican population."[11]

In the interviews carried out with repatriated Nicaraguans who had been in Costa Rica, concern was expressed about the way Nicaraguans had been treated in Costa Rica. Thus, it is significant that they felt humiliated there, like second-class citizens. Costa Rican law and the general treatment they received as refugees, served to remind them constantly that their future was limited to life within the camps, without the rights of Costa Rican citizens.

The difficult economic situation of the refugees, in particular that of the camp inhabitants in Costa Rica, and the offers they received of land guarantees from the Nicaraguan government were factors that encouraged the repatriation of the *campesinos*.

Communication between the refugees and their relatives was another element that facilitated repatriation. For example, all the refugees we interviewed indicated that they had made contact on at least one occasion with their families. Some were able to establish direct personal contact because officials of both countries issued special permits so that relatives could meet for a few hours at the border; others stayed in touch through letters or messages broadcast over radio stations in Nicaragua and Costa Rica.

However, there appeared to be little motivation to repatriate among the non-rural refugees. Some persons who repatriated complain that they did so because they missed their home country, but that better work opportunities had been available in Costa Rica than were to be found upon returning to Nicaragua.

Ethnic communities in Honduras, who had taken refuge in the Department of El Paraíso on the Honduran Atlantic Coast, experienced a high level of voluntary repatriation prior to 1990.

The fundamental factors behind the repatriation of these Miskito and Sumu groups stemmed from their relationship to their communities, which were not only their places of birth but also the places their ancestors were laid to rest. The burial grounds furnish the atavistic link to the past that is a persistent traditional element of indigenous cultures throughout Latin America and is in no way unique to the ethnic or indigenous people in Nicaragua.

The war, which had uprooted them from their communities, and the living conditions in ethnic Honduran territory prevented these refugees from finding the necessary space to reproduce their way of life. They had to live as nomads; several different communities would be mixed in one camp or be dispersed among several communities with whom scarce affective ties existed.

The limited resources that the Honduran government directed toward its own Atlantic Coast and the ethnic groups living there led to extremely difficult living conditions, food scarcity, and consequent competition between the ethnic minorities of the two countries. So it was that by 1986, when the military conflict began to lose steam, the refugees participated in the repatriation programs.

There were two principle conditions at work in the process. First, the government presented viable alternatives to the armed ethnic rebels. It recognized the status of their soldiers as combatants in a just cause. (It must be remembered that the Miskito and Sumu soldiers represented heroic figures to their communities of men who instill pride in belonging to one ethnic group, one culture, and one single unifying ethnic spirit.)

Second, as of 1985, conversations got under way between the Sandinista government and the main armed groups to discuss terms that would permit the ethnic territories to become autonomous regions. Thus, as can be appreciated in Table 7, the repatriation became a massive movement in which the majority of ethnic refugees returned in less than a year. This table only reflects repatriation figures for those who returned under UNHCR auspices; it excludes the several thousand who either returned on their own or as members of armed units.

TABLE 7

Repatriation by Year of Ethnic or Indigenous Nicaraguans Who Repatriated Under UNHCR Auspices

YEAR	1984	1985	1986	1987	1988	1989	TOTAL
NUMBER	57	586	1,714	3,724	7,948	1,098	15,127

Source: UNHCR-Honduras, October 1989

After the Sandinista electoral defeat in February 1990, the conditions for voluntary repatriation changed substantially, leading thousands of Nicaraguans to repatriate from Honduras, Costa Rica, and other countries.

This repatriation, in which almost 30,000 Nicaraguans returned home in fewer than six months, revealed the consistency of the motivating factors that stimulated repatriation in the past. According to the majority of repatriated Nicaraguans we interviewed, the decision to repatriate reflected the persistence of economic difficulties, the end of the war and of compulsory military service, and the expectations of a new political situation after the Sandinista electoral defeat.

Monthly repatriation levels between January and October 1990 can be seen in Table 8. Between January and April, aggregate levels tended to grow, although they remained relatively low. After April, with the new government in office and the Contra demobilization under way, repatriation levels, especially from Honduras, burgeoned into the thousands.

There are considerable indications that the refugee phenomenon in Costa Rica was of an economic nature, disguised as political, whereas the majority of persons in Honduras were affected directly by the war in some way.[12] Once the war had ended, the main trend among the refugees in Honduras was to return. In Costa Rica, however, where official efforts to encourage repatriation met fewer impediments, the flow of repatriated persons remained lower because the economic conditions that motivated refugees to enter Costa Rica persisted. Moreover, Nicaraguan refugees in Costa Rica were from rural and urban areas in roughly equal proportions; whereas, the great majority of refugees in Honduras were Mestizos of rural origin whose ties to the land made them more inclined to return.

TABLE 8

Nicaraguan Monthly Repatriation in 1990

| | Honduras | | Costa Rica | | Other | |
	Mestizos	Ethnics	Mestizos	Ethnics	Countries	Total
Jan	112	81	80	0	1	274
Feb	53	124	46	0	0	223
Mar	41	161	172	1	32	407
Apr	47	567	183	0	47	844
May	97	2,250	269	0	227	2,843
June	1,967	2,525	432	6	213	5,143
July	1,481	1,663	678	0	409	4,231
Aug	3,406	472	1,192	3	53	5,126
Sept	3,122	877	1,084	14	181	5,278
Oct*	770	1,543	701	1	25	3,040
Total	11,096	10,263	4,837	25	1,188	27,409

Figures run only through October 20, 1990.

Source: UNHCR-Nicaragua

As can be appreciated in Table 8, as of May 1980, with a new Nicaraguan government in office and the demobilization process well under way, the rate of repatriation accelerated greatly.

The end of the large military conflicts and the signing of peace agreements clearly played a significant part in the decisions to repatriate, although small skirmishes between Contras and Sandinistas still persist. In addition, when the peace agreements were signed, promises were made that those who laid down their weapons would get resettlement assistance in the form of land to work, credit, and health care.

Eleven thousand repatriated Miskito and Sumu refugees had been registered in Nicaragua as of September 1989, although the number of ethnic refugees barely rose above 10,000 in the refugee camps. However, not all resided in the camps, in fact the majority may not have had any contact with the UNHCR.

It is clear from most estimates on the number of refugees in Honduras and Costa Rica that thousands of Mestizo *campesinos* as well as people of urban origin continue to reside there. (And many, especially the urban refugees, have probably become assimilated.) The ethnic refugee phenomenon, however, is effectively over.

FACTORS IMPEDING REPATRIATION

Constraints Prior to Elections

UNHCR and other agencies mistakenly anticipated that the August 1989 signing of the agreement by the five Central American presidents in Tela, Honduras would result in an immediate and significant increase in repatriation requests.

The fulfillment of the Tela Agreement was to bring an end to the war, which had been the main obstacle to repatriation. However, the refusal of the Contras to demobilize and the support it continued to receive from the U.S. government became barriers to the peace for which the regional governments were striving. Thus, the Agreement notwithstanding, a number of factors continued to discourage repatriation. Among them were the disinformation campaigns that took place in Nicaragua. The Contras accused the repatriated refugees of being traitors and said they would be murdered by the Sandinistas when they returned. At the same time, the Nicaraguan government reported that people who had decided to quit the conflict were being persecuted and murdered by the Contras. In fact, some Sandinista groups did persecute returnees. The fact that the government had a clear interest in promoting repatriation and safeguarding the security of those who returned did not prevent the outbreak of violence against repatriated Nicaraguans by Sandinista militants and army soldiers. Other disinformation circulated about the fate of those who repatriated

concerned the Oscar Robelo Welcome Center in the northern
Nicaraguan city of Estelí, where repatriated refugees from all over the
country were received before continuing home. The Center was
portrayed as a concentration camp similar to those of the Nazis during
the Second World War.

After July 1989, there was an open campaign against repatriation
undertaken in the refugee camps by the resistance in cooperation with a
human rights organization of their own creation. People interviewed in
Honduras and repatriated Nicaraguans at home indicated that the
campaign was conducted by people who had been trained for this
purpose in short courses that were periodically conducted by the
Contras on their military bases. (These courses were referred to by the
refugees as "seminars at the base," a Spanish play on words which also
means "grassroots seminars.")

This campaign responded to the need of the Contras to keep the
refugee camps as ongoing sources of military recruits. Under the logic
of the campaign, even the financial problems of the UNHCR were
portrayed as an additional pressure for a forced return to Nicaragua
and as "assaults against their refugee status."

Political factors were also important impediments to repatriation.
Many of the refugees were very close to the Resistance. In fact, they
constituted its base of social support. Moreover, for a long time, almost
until 1989, the refugee camps were open to the Resistance forces
without constraint on their efforts to recruit combatants. The political
control in the camps was so extensive that no one could identify him- or
herself as a victim of war or as a Sandinista sympathizer. All had to be
identified as victims of the Sandinista government.

This political influence in the refugee camps nullified the efforts
of the Sandinista government and the international agencies to put an
end to the war and encourage repatriation. The situation became so
difficult that the condition being demanded for repatriation was "the
departure of the Sandinista Front from the government." This argument
had never been used until the end of 1989. Prior to the August 1989
Tela Agreement, the condition demanded for repatriation was "the
holding of free and democratic elections and the fulfillment of the
Esquipulas Accords."

In general, there prevailed a Manichaean vision of political
relations that boils down to the question members of the Contras would
pose to those whose motives they doubted: "Who are you with, the
Piricuacos or us?" (*Piricuaco* was a term of denigration formerly used

by members of the National Guard under Somoza to refer to the Sandinistas.)

The rejection by the Contras of any attempt at mass repatriation led to tensions in the camps. In late 1989, a visit to the camps by a working group of the Tripartite Commission degenerated into a confrontation. The visitors included representatives of the Nicaraguan Red Cross, the UNHCR Nicaragua, the Nicaraguan Consulate, and the Honduran government. The confrontation created problems for the UNHCR which was later unable to obtain accurate information on repatriation.

The media heard in the camps consisted of anti-Sandinista broadcasts from Honduras. The most popular radio stations were HRN, Radio America, the Voice of America, Impacto, and stations run by the Contras. To listen to the Voice of Nicaragua, the official radio station of the Nicaraguan government, was to court the mistrust of the rest of the refugee population and even to run the risk of being accused of working as an informer for the Nicaraguan security services. The most frequently read publications were *La Prensa* and *El Heraldo*, both of which were daily papers with strong anti-Sandinista positions. However, the print media in general had less impact due to the high rates of illiteracy among the refugees.

An additional factor discouraging repatriation was the mentality of dependency that developed in the camps. Many of the refugees were from the dry zone within the area bordering Honduras, where their own farm production was too small to sustain the family, and therefore the men would work as seasonal migrant laborers to earn salaries in the cotton fields and the coffee harvests. These wage-earning activities have decreased greatly in recent years as cotton production fell 70 percent from its 1978 level and the coffee harvest was also hurt by the war. Thus, many of these *campesino* families looked to the refugee camps for their survival.

However, salaried work in Honduras resulted in smaller real income than the grants and assistance received in the camps. One refugee's response was all too typical: In seven years in the Honduran camps, he had only worked for one month. He preferred not to work outside the camp even when he earned as much as Honduran workers because he did not believe his salary was helpful. Thus, he decided "not to leave the camp, but to receive assistance from the agencies."

This dependence on assistance is a sensitive point among the agencies and one for which they have no response. Officials tend to feel that they are accomplices to the dependency of the refugee population.

When interviewed, UNHCR officials point to the refugees' dependency as a serious constraint. There was little interest in work, especially activities to benefit the community in the camps. It should be noted here that, as a result of the ideological influence of the Contras among the refugee population, any participation in community activities was associated with Sandinismo.

Thus, the refugees preferred to avoid the uncertainty and risk that repatriation represented in favor of life in the camps, where they did not have to make personal efforts to assure their families' basic needs and where they enjoyed basic infrastructure and services superior to what was available both near the camps themselves and at home.

The refugees in the camps were under the impression that the conditions under which they generally lived were superior to what they could hope to attain through their own efforts. According to health personnel in the area, the population in the camps located in the Department of El Paraíso enjoyed higher rates than the local population for such social indicators as infant mortality and nutrition.

Although the standard of camp housing was minimal, it was still superior to what the population had had at home, where, according to the interviews, the population had lived in wooden shacks without drinking water or nearby access to schools or health centers. By contrast, housing in the camps was constructed of wood with zinc roofs, and there were schools, health centers, drinking water, and other community services available such as the opportunity for a patient to be transferred to a hospital should such treatment become necessary.

These are some of the reasons that many of the same people who complained that their condition as refugees was denigrating to them and that thus they wanted to return home, still preferred to remain as refugees in the security of the camps rather than face the uncertainty of repatriation. In the case of the indigenous groups, those who remained in Honduras did so because of their particularly difficult conditions at home, where they had been abandoned by the Nicaraguan governments and international solidarity. Nevertheless, it must be emphasized that a traditional practice of the Miskitos and Sumus is to cross the border regularly to take advantage of what nature, or international assistance, offers. This makes it more difficult to have confidence in assertions about the refugee characteristics of the ethnic groups, since in practice they may be refugees at a given moment and the next moment they are not. What is unquestionable is that thousands of ethnic or indigenous people remained in Honduras until after the 1990 elections.

Another factor that tended to reduce the level of repatriation was the expectation of immigration to the United States or another third country where life was believed to be better than in Nicaragua. This hope was nourished among the ranks of the Contras in order to discourage repatriation. Nevertheless, this aspiration was more widespread among people of an urban background, particularly among the military leaders. These leaders, who were not formally camp residents and were not in Honduras as refugees, nevertheless had greater access to the camps than anyone else, including UNHCR officials. The operational networks of the Contras in the camps was more flexible and effective than those of the international and nongovernmental organizations.

The constraints on repatriation in Costa Rica were quite similar to those in Honduras, although more intense. There was some doubt that what was being offered repatriates would be delivered; a number of rumors circulated about poor treatment of repatriates by the police, lies told, incidents of persecution, and other incidents that supposedly occurred to repatriated Nicaraguans back home.

Nevertheless, social and economic factors posed a greater barrier to repatriation. Costa Rica offers greater opportunities for better paying long-term work, education, and health care. Costa Rica enjoys by far the best economic conditions of any Central American country. Of these distinct factors, the superior education was particularly important to Nicaraguan families outside the camps; their children would not receive the same quality education in their own country.

Constraints After the Elections

As of mid-1990, uncertainty over the economic future was the biggest break on repatriation to Nicaragua. The new government's promises of land and agricultural credits to those returning were sidetracked by the government's own ideological distaste for promoting the transfer of lands to returning *campesinos*. A further limitation was the insignificant level of international assistance, particularly from the U.S. government of whom much was expected.

Thousands of *campesinos* returned from Honduras and Costa Rica or agreed to lay down their arms, because they trusted in the prospects of finding land to farm, only to have this expectation frustrated. Thus, those who were reluctant to return experienced much confusion over their prospects in Nicaragua.

The new government has been of two minds regarding the land issue, which is vital to an understanding of repatriation. A moderate sector has attempted to respond to demands among the repatriates for land by distributing land from state enterprises. Nevertheless, this position has met strong opposition among extreme sectors that are also part of the government. These sectors are led by the Vice President, the Superior Council for Private Enterprise, and some of the leaders of the Resistance, in particular, those from urban areas.[13] They have been pressing for a privatization program and the return of properties confiscated from Somocistas, policies which are in conflict with the interests of *campesinos*, who demand that these same lands be allotted to them to farm.

The influence of the extreme sectors at first led the government to propose that repatriated Nicaraguans be located in development enclaves in the mountainous regions where little productive or social infrastructure exists. This alternative would have permitted negotiations over the confiscated lands to take place with the Somocistas and other capitalists who are returning to the country after ten years of exile. However, in the wake of skirmishes between Sandinistas and ex-Contras, the government has created an Agrarian Commission that is made up of Ministers of State, the Head of the Armed Forces, Resistance representatives, and Sandinista-affiliated *campesinos* and workers. This measure is intended to clarify the government program of support for the *campesino* sector, especially among the repatriated refugees.

THE INFLUENCE OF INTERNATIONAL AGREEMENTS AND PREVIOUS REPATRIATIONS ON THE DECISION TO RETURN

Influences Prior to the Elections

There was scant awareness among the refugees of the agreements of the Central American presidents and of other international agencies to promote the repatriation of Nicaraguans from Honduras. Thus, in the camps managed by the UNHCR, the expectations over the content and possible advantages of the agreements were barely perceptible.

On the contrary, the goals and scope of the agreements were manipulated or at best reinterpreted in order to present the agreements as a Sandinista ploy to consolidate power. The scarce credibility that the decisions of the Central American presidents had within the camps responded to the military interests of the Contras. By contrast, the measures of the U.S. government were viewed with respect, to the degree that they guarantied the survival of the military alternative. In spite of this, one can appreciate in Table 9 that the number of repatriations under UNHCR auspices grew year by year, albeit at a rather insignificant rate.

TABLE 9

Voluntary Repatriation of Refugees in Honduras
1987,1988, and (through August) 1989

Camp	1987	1988	1989								
			Jan	Feb	Mar	Apr	May	Jun	Jul	Aug	Total
Jacaleapa	70	166	8	9	4	16	0	18	30	25	110
Teupacenti	15	15	0	0	4	5	4	0	0	5	18
Las Vegas	28	62	26	28	30	28	15	14	8	53	202
TOTAL	113	243	34	37	38	49	19	32	38	83	330

Source: Based on figures from UNHCR-Honduras, October 1989.

The influence of the former refugees who repatriated on those who remained outside the country appears quite diffuse. Not only were there relatively few who repatriated, but there were only extremely limited opportunities for communication between the two groups. In general, the refugees in Honduras complained that they received very little information from those who had repatriated. However, they believed that the latter were hunted down and murdered when they returned from Honduras. They also expressed concern over the economic situation in Nicaragua, which they supposed was unbearable because of lack of employment and general scarcity throughout the country.

The possible influence of repatriation programs of other countries also carried little weight. In this regard, the important differences should be pointed out between the Nicaraguan refugees in Honduras, particularly the Mestizos, and the Salvadoran refugees there. The Nicaraguans displayed a series of particular characteristics that distinguished them from the others in Honduras.

Unlike the Salvadoran refugees, who did not have the opportunity to leave their camps, the Nicaraguan refugees were treated with tolerance by the Honduran authorities. The Nicaraguans were allowed to enter and leave their camps as often as they cared to. This free movement, conceived to allow the Contras a broad margin to recruit and carry out logistical operations, was restricted under the Tela Agreements through stricter supervision in the camps by the international agencies. Nevertheless, the mobility of the Contras was not eliminated, nor was the operation of its internal networks. The constraints imposed by the Honduran authorities on the Nicaraguan refugees were more *de jure* than *de facto*, since it was an open secret that those closest to the Contras could enter and leave with few problems.

There was far greater margin for discussion and greater access to information in the Salvadoran camps, in contrast to the Nicaraguan camps where only the Contras had a real chance to keep the refugees informed.

The internal changes initiated by the Nicaraguan government in 1984 in its treatment of the ethnic or indigenous groups, in particular the process of autonomy in the indigenous regions, were very positive because they generated a massive process of repatriation.

Among the most important of these changes were the creation in 1984 of the National Autonomy Commission, the start of a dialogue with the armed indigenous rebels in 1985, and the cease-fire agreements. In 1985 the Peace and Autonomy Commissions were also created to foster an end to the uprising and encourage repatriation; in 1987 the National Assembly passed the Autonomy Law, which contributed to the encouragement of voluntary repatriation among the indigenous groups.

By comparison, the agreements later reached by the Central American presidents and the international organizations had very little influence on the indigenous groups.

The first indigenous people who repatriated faced economic and logistical difficulties. Nevertheless, their reception attracted many who had yet to decide to return. The willingness of the government to address political, cultural, and economic demands opened the door to an irreversible process of repatriation.

The governments of Costa Rica and Nicargua, international agencies, and even various armed groups agreed to promote repatriation. The Central American agreements and the changes undertaken by the government in Nicaragua were broadcast widely throughout the camps and among the refugee population in general.

Beginning in 1989, some leaders of the counterrevolution based in Costa Rica agreed to return to Nicaragua and participate in the national political process. Their decision led refugees in Costa Rica to consider the possibility of repatriation, and a few did decide to return right away.

Thus, considering that approximately 3,000 people repatriated to Nicaragua in 1989, we can assert that the regional agreements and the conditions that the Nicaraguan government established helped stimulate repatriation, although not to the degree that had been anticipated.

Post-Election Influences

The electoral process that led to the Sandinista defeat at the polls and the agreements reached between the government and the Resistance in April 1990 under UN and OAS supervision were two of the most important factors that stimulated the process of repatriation. As the elections approached, repatriation accelerated. The repatriation levels of refugees for the period from January to October 20, 1990 is indicated in Table 10. One can appreciate the great increase over the 1989 level of repatriation that was seen in Table 9.

TABLE 10

1990 Repatriation

MONTH	NUMBER
Jan	274
Feb	223
Mar	407
Apr	844
May	2,843
June	5,143
July	4,231
Aug	5,126
Sept	5,278
Oct*	3,040
Total	27,409

* October figure runs only through October 20.
Source: UNHCR-Nicaragua

After April, when the new government was inaugurated, repatriation became a massive movement. The UNHCR coordinated the return of thousands of refugees, while as many as 20,000 Contra rebels returned from outside the country to rejoin civilian life in Nicaragua.

This massive repatriation was made possible by the talks between the government and the Contras, to which the UN and the OAS lent assistance. Although the international organizations acted as guarantors, the agreements had more of a national character as both parties to the agreements were Nicaraguans. By contrast, the previous commitments under the Tela Agreement that set the stage for national accord were reached in a multilateral regional forum and were taken less seriously.

REPATRIATION PATTERNS: INDIVIDUAL VS. COLLECTIVE DECISIONS

The Pre-Election Pattern

Repatriation from the refugee camps in Honduras was an extremely complicated decision, whether it involved an individual or an entire family or whether the refugee originally had been motivated by economic or political factors. The specter of the war posed a radical change for anyone who decided to return, particularly in his or her relationship to Sandinismo and the counterrevolution.

Thus, repatriation became fundamentally a political decision. As has been described above, there was no opportunity to remain neutral or to oppose the armed Resistance in the refugee camps, certainly not in a public fashion. Whoever wanted to oppose the leadership of the counterrevolution had to do so either secretly or at great risk to his or her life. Thus, people or families who wished to return from the camps had to make their decision in secret, lest they be thought of as traitors or pro-Sandinistas. Secrecy was vital, especially among families with male members of fighting age.

The potential repatriate was a person willing to break the model of control exercised by the Resistance in the camps. Such a person represented a challenge to the prevailing military power. Moreover, this was a challenge from someone who had no certainty about his or her future upon returning to Nicaragua.

The decision to repatriate under these circumstances required one to break with the war, with those who encouraged it from Honduran territory, and to, willfully, become an element isolated from a political movement that favored the military option. This decision had to be made with the knowledge that there was no possibility in Nicaragua of running from either the war or the political alternatives.

These conditions forced repatriation to be a personal decision of a single individual or family. This pattern of return did not reflect the characteristics of collective decision-making. Families in the camps tended to follow a pattern in which one of the members, usually the woman, returned on her own, to be followed later by the rest of the family. This was a clandestine form of repatriation, in which those who returned had to flee the camps.

Neverthless, this pattern was less extreme among female-headed families who could offer no potential male combatants for the counterrevolution. Such families had fewer problems in making their intentions known and returning openly under UNHCR auspices.

The indigenous groups, on the other hand, generally made the decision to repatriate in a collective fashion after agreements were signed between those of them in revolt and the Sandinista Army. Thus, the implications of their decision were different from the case of the Mestizo refugees.

Even today, the repatriation process among Miskitos and Sumus is almost always made through collective decisions involving assemblies of the refugee communities under the direction of the Councils of Elders and the spiritual guides, often in coordination with the UNHCR. The Council of Elders has a communal socio-political structure that carries much authority among the Miskitos and the Sumus.

Most indigenous people recall that their decisions to return were made at community assemblies in Honduras, where they were free to express their own opinions.

The returnees from Costa Rica followed the same model as the Mestizos from Honduras. Repatriation was mainly an individual decision there.

For some people from urban areas who went into exile for economic reasons, repatriation became a kind of business, since all

personal belongings could be brought home without customs tariffs
being charged. Thus, many individuals, in effect, engaged in
contraband in which the UNHCR covered the transportation costs.

The Post-Election Pattern

There have been three repatriation patterns since the Sandinista
electoral defeat: (1) those who returned with the troops who laid down
their arms; (2) those who came on their own, without waiting for
UNHCR coordination; and (3) those who came with the assistance of
the UNHCR.

Prior to the elections, it was estimated that there were 12,000
armed individuals in the ranks of the Resistance, but closer to 20,000
people turned in weapons under the disarmament program, which
offered a reward of between $350 and $400 per weapon.

Outside the scope of the UNHCR, many people returned to
search for relatives who laid down their arms. Nonetheless, the bulk of
the repatriates returned under the auspices of the UNHCR, UN, and
OAS programs. They tended to have made their decision collectively.

REFUGEES REPATRIATE

Repatriation and the return of internally displaced Nicaraguans
occurred as parallel phenomena. It is not often possible to distinguish
between the two types of returnees. Clearly, far more people returned
to their homes who had been displaced within the country than had
been refugees outside it. The study of the return issue is complicated
by the fact that few *campesinos* repatriated under the auspices of the
UNHCR, whose flows were documented. Far more returned or laid
down their arms on their own.

Repatriation and return, in general, were still of an exploratory
nature. The returning *campesinos* came from urban areas, refugee
camps outside the country, and from settlements.

Many of those who repatriated went to their home communities
in order to verify the prospects of remaining in Nicaragua. Some did,
however, openly declare their intention of settling down. The internally
displaced who returned did so to re-establish their farms.

The general trait of the repatriated refugees that we encountered in the course of our work is that they did not tend to be heads of households, but rather dependent members of family units. Generally, the head of the family stayed in charge of the family outside Nicaragua, and a son, who had either joined the ranks of the counterrevolution or had become a refugee in Honduras, would return.

Areas of Resettlement Prior to the Elections

In the course of our field work we visited all of the war zones in the country. These are precisely the places where the phenomena of displacement and the subsequent return of refugees and the internally displaced most often took place.

According to government sources in the regions of Matagalpa and Jinotega, between six and eight thousand repatriated and formerly displaced families were expected to return to their communities there.

We did field work in areas where the return phenomenon occurred quite early on, so by way of example we will briefly elaborate on what occurred there.

Pantasma in Jinotega is an area where approximately 5,000 families live. The uprising and displacement there were among the most severe in all Jinotega and Matagalpa. About 900 *campesinos* are estimated to have joined the uprising there, another 300 or so were press-ganged by the Contras and several thousand were relocated to the settlements for the internally displaced by the government.

Beginning in 1987, the fighting began to stop in the area and the displaced from the settlements and the refugees from Honduras started to return. The inhabitants began to converge, regardless of where they had last been, and without any efforts made by anyone to find out.

The people there have now resettled in the same areas where they had lived when the region was at peace. Others took up residence close to the sites of their original homes as they waited for the time at which they could live in safety; that is, until they felt sufficiently reassured that the fighting would not break out again. Generally speaking, these were people who owned property, such as farmers who were not demanding land, but needed credits to produce and reconstruct their farms and houses. On an organizational level, they joined service cooperatives in order to request credits to farm and rebuild their houses.

The war was also very intense in Yalí, a municipality in Jinotega with a population of about 10,000. Peace was also re-established there prior to the electoral process. When massive displacements occurred in 1984, the population from the hills in this area were displaced in different ways. Some were resettled inside the country, others moved to the town of Yalí itself, and most of the families of those who took up arms left the country. Toward the end of 1989, between 350 and 500 families were expected to return as well as a good portion of those who had been resettled. However, many among the resettled were likely to remain in the settlements where they now have access to land, health services, and education.

It was estimated that some 400 young men in Yalí had taken up arms. The majority did not demand land after returning since they tended to return to the family unit under the authority of their fathers. Nevertheless, entire families sought refuge in Honduras when their sons took up arms. The process of return was gaining strength in several rural communities, and in the short-term the trend was accelerating.

The communities had deteriorated significantly: roads were in disrepair, farm facilities and houses had been destroyed, coffee orchards and pastures went unattended or were destroyed. As of late 1989, the government institutions had not implemented any assistance programs for the repatriates, with the exception of the food-for-work project of the World Food Program. Nor had the government come up with a plan of action. However, a few comprehensive projects requiring international assistance had been roughly drawn up, such as PRODERE and the Refugee Assistance Project (PAR), which is supported with funds of the European Economic Community. Then again, government agencies and offices were promoting a number of half-measures to mitigate the situation. The Central Bank offered some small short-term credits for returning farmers, some health care was made available in the settlements, a program was undertaken by which the members of the community could rebuild the schools, and the normal taxes on lumber were lifted so people could cut trees to rebuild their homes.

In the region of Boaco and Chontales return took place in an exploratory fashion. The *campesinos* decided not to return to their former farms since the war, which persisted in that area, did not permit any short-term stability. Many *campesinos* who had stayed in towns or settlements went back to look around and do some repairs on their farms and homes. Very few decided to resettle and begin full reconstruction. However, there is clearly a resettlement trend among the displaced and refugees originally from this area. The main reason for returning is due to the misery they had to face in the outer-lying city slums and the refugee camps. Thus, the majority who returned were the poor *campesinos* whose living conditions deteriorated further and who obviously require special assistance to re-establish their farms with any degree of success.

In the San Juan River area, the wartime displacements began in 1983. Those who were not resettled near towns or urban areas took refuge along with thousands of Nicaraguans in Costa Rica. As the fighting ground to a halt, a few hundred people returned in 1986, the vast majority without any assistance from the UNHCR. By January 1990, 500 families were making preparations to return, and were expected to do so after the harvest in Costa Rica.

The repatriation process displayed similar characteristics. The household head would return to Nicaragua to evaluate the existing conditions, in particular, to see whether it was possible to return to the farm to work and rebuild the family home. The displaced and repatriated persons who were demanding the return of the lands that had been confiscated from them and delivered to the cooperatives under the Agrarian Reform were offered parcels on other cooperatives or settlements by the government.

Furthermore, a restructuring of cooperative lands was being considered in order to establish a land fund in partial response to the demands of those who were returning. Should the lands prove insufficient, consideration was being given to using 12,000 acres of land from state enterprises. As a last resort, a five kilometer wide swath up into the hills could also be partitioned.

There was a loose relationship between the demands of those returning and the land zones considered for reallotment:

a) Landless Repatriates: Those who had lived in the network of settlements set up under the revolution generally demanded the return of their original parcels. These demands, not surprisingly, have caused conflicts between this group and the cooperatives.

The position of the state institutions and the *campesino* organizations was to allow the cooperatives and the returnees to resolve the issue among themselves. The cooperatives were often flexible and returned original parcels when it did not adversely affect the members of the cooperatives or hurt their efficiency. However, in several cases cooperatives would not return land because the transfer would be detrimental.

b) Repatriates With Land: Those who returned whose land had not undergone changes in the system of tenure were from communities that had not been evacuated. Their initial demands were for building materials to reconstruct their homes, credits, clothing, and food until after the first harvest.

c) Immigrants: Some repatriates went to new areas instead of their original communities. Their main demand was for land. Those in this group are particularly distinguished by their abject poverty as they sought better living conditions than in their original communities.

Their needs were basic and wide-ranging: food, housing, land, credits, health care, and education.

The government and *campesino* associations believe that the principal areas of return and repatriation are in Chontales, in the central part of the country; in and around the North Atlantic Autonomous Region, Matagalpa, and Jinotega; and in the area of the San Juan River toward the southern border with Costa Rica. All of these areas are mainly agricultural areas.

According to both the National Union of Farmers and Ranchers and the government, the principal receiving areas are in: Nueva Guinea, El Almendro, Muelle de los Bueyes, El Rama y Santo Domingo, Río Blanco, Waslala, Yalí, Pantasma, el Cua-Bocay, and the entire San Juan River area. These are therefore the places where efforts to assist repatriates and formerly displaced persons must be focussed.

Here it must be pointed out that by the end of 1989 no programs to assist those who were returning had been implemented by any institutions, whether official or private. There was no coordinated plan of action, although some programs were in the formulation stages.

The nongovernmental organizations that operate in these areas continued to dedicate their attention to the same efforts they had been engaged in before the mass return began.

Areas of Resettlement Since the Elections

Many thousands of repatriated refugees and internally displaced persons have been returning to these areas since the Sandinista defeat at the polls.

Since April 1990, thousands of persons each month have been returning to Chontales (El Almendro, Nueva Guinea, and along the road to el Rama); Waslala and Río Blanco in Matagalpa; Yalí, Pantasma, and el Cua-Bocay in Jinotega; and to San Miguelito and San Carlos in the San Juan River area.

The majority of returnees tended to proceed to their places of origin. However, many had to go elsewhere because the uprising and subsequent displacement in their original communities were followed by the organization of cooperatives there under the Sandinista Agrarian Reform.

Different zones were set up in national territory where the ranks of the Resistance would turn over their arms. Often these same troops and their families remained where they were without returning home.

The entire process of repatriation has become quite disorganized; promises of land have not been fulfilled, and this has led to a spontaneous relocation of many former troops who have proceeded to their original homes and communities. The entire process is in flux, making it extremely difficult to guage its scale with any degree of certainty.

THE ROLE OF REPATRIATION IN THE
LEVEL OF VIOLENCE

The Pre-Election Period

The repatriation of Mestizo *campesinos* until 1989 had little effect on the reduction of violence. If anything, it increased tensions. Rather, political factors, such as the international pressure brought to bear and the inability of the counterrevolution to achieve its objectives on the battlefield, are what led to the pacification of the large areas of the country.

By contrast, among the indigenous groups, the massive repatriation of thousands of people and the opposition in their communities to continuing the fighting were the determining factors in the pacification. Beginning in 1986, when the ethnic repatriation got under way, the size of the armed groups continued to diminish until only small groups, unrepresentative of the ethnic uprising, remained.

After the Elections

The panorama has changed dramatically since the Sandinista electoral defeat. Now, repatriation is contributing to pacification, despite the areas of tension and the occasional outbreaks of violence between the repatriates and Resistance fighters on one side and the Sandinista *campesinos* on the other. On occasions, the military authorities have also taken part.

These disturbances, however, are sporadic, not widespread, and related to the government's failure to fulfill promises to turn over land. (After all, the majority of repatriates have relatives among the former Contra fighters, and often it is practically impossible to distinguish between one and the other.

In the various areas visited, the desire for peace among both Sandinistas and repatriates is almost palpable. In Yalí, Pantasma, and el Cua-Bocay as well as most of Jinotega and Matagalpa, coexistence has largely supplanted conflict. It is not uncommon for Sandinistas, returnees, and former Contra fighters to work and live in the same area; in some cases, even in the same cooperatives. These are areas in which great barriers do not exist to rebuilding the economic and social infrastructure, where the land is richest, and where extremists from either side have had the fewest confrontations and the least influence. Sandinismo in this area has been most successful in achieving peaceful coexistence with the repatriates and former Resistance fighters.

On the other hand, in Waslala and Río Blanco a climate of great tension prevails. Contra fighters have even taken over rural communities, and blood has been spilled. These are areas in which the soil is poorest and the economic and social infrastructure is weakest.

The situation is similar in the Department of Chontales and in the area of San Juan River, although the incidence of violence has been less serious.

Moreover, small bands of rustlers and thieves have preyed on returnees and upset the stability in some areas of repatriation. Fortunately, these incidents have had little impact on the general climate of relative peace that has returned.

CONDITIONS FOR RECEIVING REPATRIATES

Repatriation Conditions Prior to the Elections

Before repatriating to Nicaragua in 1989, the UNHCR delivered to every recognized refugee the sum of US$50 per adult, $25 per minor, up to a maximum of $450 per family, and the basic food provisions to last a month. Once in Nicaragua, the individual or family was received by the National Refugee Commission, which financed the return to the home community.

The repatriation program was coordinated by the UNHCR and the Nicaraguan Institute for Social Security and Welfare.

Once they arrived at the border, repatriates were then sent to the Oscar Robelo Welcoming Center in the city of Estelí, until conditions were made ready for the final return either home or to another mutually agreed place. Repatriates from urban areas could proceed directly to their communities.

Other reception sites were later opened in Peñas Blancas, near the Costa Rican border; and near the Honduran border at Las Manos and in the North Atlantic Autonomous Region. At these sites, assistance and rehabilitation programs were available to repatriated and internally displaced people alike. Upon arrival, individuals would receive blankets, shoes, household utensils, mosquito netting, tools, and materials for home construction, including 25 sheets of zinc roofing material per family.

The European Economic Community donated tools and other productive inputs as part of a housing construction program it sponsored in Jinotega, Matagalpa, Boaco, and Chontales. The government made credits available to the returnees through the National Bank of Development.

Projects for the construction of schools and health centers were also started in all of the repatriation areas. Even so, none of these programs were sufficient to meet the needs of those who repatriated. And further complications resulted because repatriated and internally displaced persons returned to the same areas at the same time, overwhelming the government's ability to provide assistance.

Repatriation Conditions After the Elections

The assistance program before the elections, notwithstanding scarcities and problems, was at least manageable and relatively simple, in particular because of the low level of repatriation. However, after April 1990, the situation became extremely difficult as resources ran out and repatriates returned in massive proportions. Furthermore, repatriates, former internally displaced returnees, and former Contra fighters are not three distinct groups; they are all part of the same phenomenon and must be dealt with as such.

The physical facilities of the reception sites are generally the same. The Institute for Repatriation (at the ministerial level), which was created by the Pan American Health Organization in coordination with the OAS International Commission for Assistance and Verification, receives repatriates at different reception sites and provides minimum living conditions until the people can proceed to the places where they will settle.

The levels of assistance provided by the UNHCR have diminished appreciably; in some cases, individuals have received no aid whatsoever. Thus, the conditions of repatriation are becoming ever more dire. The U.S. government donated $30 million for the repatriation of former Contra fighters. However, this was insufficient to cover their needs. Thus, given the economic constraints and an ambiguous government response under the strain of interests favoring privatization and the return of property to Somocistas and capitalists who have recently returned to the country, there is a constant threat of crisis or, at best, the gnawing erosion of the national economy and, along with it, the peace that has been achieved to date at the cost of great sacrifices to all.

INSTITUTIONAL FRAMEWORK
AND COORDINATION

The institutional framework within which the refugee and repatriation problem has been handled under the government of Mrs. Chamorro remains essentially the same as under the Sandinista government.

During a six-month period in 1979 and 1980, three international agreements concerning human rights and refugees were ratified. Furthermore, the 1987 Nicaraguan Constitution also provided refugees with special legal protections.[14]

The National Office for Refugees was created in 1981 as an agency of the Nicaraguan Institute of Social Security and Welfare (INSSBI). Among its duties, this office must determine the refugee status of migrants in coordination with the Immigration Office. It is also responsible for the design and implementation of policies and projects for refugees at the national level as well as for fulfilling international guidelines and agreements entered into by the government with the UNHCR.

In addition to the legal and institutional framework, the Nicaraguan government has implemented political measures to handle the needs of refugees and repatriated persons. Prominent among these measures was the Amnesty Law issued in April 1983. The law offered amnesty to all Miskitos, Sumus, Ramas, and Creoles imprisoned for having committed crimes countervening public order or security. It provided for all such persons to be immediately freed. The Amnesty Law was translated into three indigenous languages and read in the communities.

As of 1986, Peace and Autonomy Commissions (PACs) were organized to promote Miskito and Sumu repatriation. The PACs became mediating channels for constant communication between the refugees in Honduras and national government officials.

The efforts of the Sandinista Government to resolve the issue of the indigenous refugees also included the first and only process of indigenous autonomy and rights in the American continent.

Moreover, two chapters of the Nicaraguan Constitution concern the "Communities of the Atlantic Coast." Article VI guaranties equality between Atlantic Coast communities and others in Nicaragua. It also guaranties the ethnic communities "the right to preserve and develop their cultural identity within the national unified nation," the right to free speech, and the preservation of their languages, art, and culture. For its part, the state is required to pass laws to ensure that there be no discrimination on the basis of language, culture, or origin.

The communities are also guaranteed "the form of social organization corresponding to their tradition, the benefit of the natural resources, the legal recognition of their communal property, the free election of their officials and representatives, and the preservation of their cultures, languages, religions, and customs."

The Autonomy Law was the result of a thorough process of discussion that culminated in the Multi-Ethnic Assembly held in April 1987 in Puerto Cabezas (on the Nicaraguan Atlantic Coast). The draft of the law was presented to the National Assembly three months later. In addition to reaffirming the rights guarantied under the Constitution, it established an administrative structure that divides the Atlantic Coast into two regions; one, headquartered in Puerto Cabezas, and the other in Bluefields. The Law also reaffirms cultural economic, educational and social rights as defined and determined by the members of the communities.

Other important agreements were those reached through the Tripartite Commission in which Nicaragua, Costa Rica, Honduras, and the UNHCR all took part. Nicaraguan representatives to the Commissions were from the INSSBI, the Chanceries, and the Immigration Office.

In its agreements with the refugees living in Costa Rica, the government of Nicaragua agreed to facilitate the free flow of information so that refugees could decide whether or not to return and so that those interested could do so on the basis of an informed decision. The Nicaraguan Government also guarantied non-discrimination against returning refugees, respect for human rights, and offers of land and credit for *campesinos*. A public awareness campaign was undertaken by the official Costa Rican agency handling refugee assistance, DIGEPARE, so that the refugees understood the details of the guaranties being offered those who would return.

In late 1989, the Commission visited the refugee camps in Honduras, where it was assisted by the official Honduran National Commission for Refugees (CONARE) in making known to the camp inhabitants what guaranties they could expect upon returning, the plans for assistance for the repatriated refugees, and the legal procedures required to repatriate.

The Mestizo *campesinos* promoted many commissions to mediate between the expatriated Nicaraguans and the Sandinista government. Among the most prominent was the National Reconciliation Commission with representatives of the Catholic Church and several political parties. In contrast to the case of the ethnic groups, however, these commissions were largely ineffective until the new government took office.

When the new government took office, it created the Nicaraguan Repatriation Institute (INRE) in order to coordinate repatriation reintegration activities. INRE worked with the UNHCR, the OAS-CIAV, INSSBI, Agrarian Reform, and the Nicaraguan Resistance Civic Association (ACRN). However, due to INRE's lack of resources, its role in repatriation has been limited to attending to technical legal and economic issues (e.g., obtaining tax waivers, driving permits and business permits, compensation for confiscations and job dismissals, helping apply for U.S. visas, giving attention to prisoners and human rights).

In contrast, the UNHCR and the OAS-CIAV have played major roles in organizing the repatriation and reintegration process and channelling resources for economic assistance.

The ACRN has been active in assisting children, widows, and the wounded throughout the repatriation process; in cooperation with the government, it has also coordinated the social and political organization of the former Contra fighters.

ASSISTANCE PROGRAMS

The problem of the repatriated, demobilized, and displaced *campesinos* who either return to their original communities or seek land elsewhere is an extremely complex issue that requires international cooperation. The problem of urban refugees is equally complex, although its dimensions are not as great.

The two governments have dealt with the problem under different conditions. The Sandinistas attempted to foster repatriation in the midst of the war, when there were few repatriated, demobilized, or displaced persons returning to their homes, and small promises were the only resources available to ease their resettlement.

Under the Chamorro government, thousands of people have returned to their former homes in every corner of the country. Like its predecessor, the current government does not have the resources to devote to resettlement, although the prospects for assistance are much brighter.

Neither of the two governments has offered returning urban residents more than political promises. Whereas the Chamorro government has committed itself to returning confiscated properties, the fulfillment of this promise would not affect the majority of urban returnees who never were property owners.

Agrarian reform has been a keystone of the assistance policies under both governments. In each case, the thrust of the policy has consisted of land distribution. Under the Sandinistas, the distribution of state-owned properties in the traditional agricultural areas of the country was a major priority, followed by the opening up to agricultural exploitation of previously uncultivated lands on or beyond the so-called agrarian frontier (i.e., the perimeters of the traditional farming areas). Under the Chamorro government the emphasis has been reversed; uncultivated land in the mountains comprises the bulk of that being redistributed, and land on the perimeters of state enterprises is allotted to a lesser degree.

A number of specific programs were proposed and a few were implemented in 1990. The Special Plan of Cooperation for Central America (PEC) was created under UN auspices in support of the August 1987 Esquipulas II Agreements. PEC sought to identify measures that would have an immediate short-term impact. The 150 proposed projects included under the Plan were meant to be established on the basis of an emergency plan for immediate action to reactivate the economy and social and institutional development, with measures for implementation and follow-up.

PEC and the UNHCR have concentrated their efforts in the special zones of Region I and the border area. Whereas UNHCR gives priority to repatriated persons, PEC provides most of its assistance to the internally displaced. The liaison between the two programs is coordinated by the United Nations Development Program (UNDP).

One of the first projects conceived within this framework has been the Refugee Assistance Project (PRODERE) which, among the development services it is set to undertake, will construct 500 housing units, brickworks, and a saw mill.

In addition, the Repatriate Assistance Program was established through an agreement between the San Juan River Regional government and the UNHCR in order to provide assistance to 300 families in the region, in particular the victims of Hurricane Joan. The bulk of the assistance consists of providing the materials necessary for the 300 families to reconstruct their homes.

The 1989 International Conference on Central American Refugees (CIREFCA) has served as an important channel for Central American countries seeking international assistance for projects.

Nicaragua requested more than $188 million for projects through the CIREFCA process and received almost $97 million in pledges.[15] Of the amount requested, 61 percent were intended for productive rural projects and 35 percent were for demobilization and repatriation activities. The entire amount pledged has not been received, however, and Nicaragua has yet to receive a response on the other $91 million requested.

It is unclear from the information provided to the author exactly what amounts have been dispersed within the total pledged through the CIREFCA process. The general opinion of Nicaraguan and international officials involved in refugee-related assistance holds that just over one-half of the near $97 million pledged for Nicaragua had been received as of January 1991. Most of the disbursements support the repatriation, demobilization and disarmament of the Contras; little has gone toward reintegration and development.

REFERENCES

[1]Segundo Montes, **Refugiados y Repatriados: El Salvador y Honduras**. (San Salvador: Departamento de Sociología y Ciencias Políticas, Instituto de Derechos Humanos (IDHUCA), Universidad Centroamericana José Simeón Cañas, 1989), 13.

[2]Ricardo Stein, **The Spontaneous and Planned Return of Repatriates and Displaced Persons, in 1989 Central American Refugees** (Washington, D.C.: Hemispheric Migration Project, Center for Immigration Policy and Refugee Assistance, Georgetown University and the Consejo Superior Universitario Centroamericano [CSUCA], 1989).

[3]Twelve case studies were carried out in Nicaragua, six in Honduras. Two case studies were carried out in each one of three Nicaraguan Mestizo refugee camps in Honduran territory, at Jacaleapa, Teupacenti, and Las Vegas. In Nicaragua, there were six case studies of Miskito 'campesinos' and six of repatriated Miskitos and Sumus.

[4]Structured interviews were held with the following:

(a) repatriates from Honduras and Costa Rica; (b) Honduran government officials from CONARE and the General Office for Migration; (c) UNHCR officials in Nicaragua and Honduras; (d) officials from Non-Governmental Organizations; (e) Officials from the Ministry for Agricultural Development and Land Reform (MIDINRA), the Nicaraguan Institute of Social Security and Welfare, the Sandinista Front for National Liberation (FSLN), the Evangelical Council for Development Assistance, the Center for 'Campesino' Development, officials of regional governments, and the National Union of Farmers and Ranchers; and (f) people displaced by the war.

[5]Gilda Pacheco, **Nicaraguan Refugees in Costa Rica: Adjustment to Camp Life** (Washington, D.C.: HMP-CIPRA, Georgetown University, 1989).

[6]Montes, **Refugiados y Repatriados**, 32.

[7]Pacheco, **Nicaraguan Refugees in Costa Rica**, 4.

[8]Ibid.

[9]Mario A. Ramírez and Flor E. Solano, **La política general para los refugiados y la repatriación de los refugiados nicaragüenses en Costa Rica: presente y perspectivas** (San José, Costa Rica: Centro de Análisis Sociopolítico, 1988).

[10]Mario A. Ramírez, **La problemática del refugiado y las perspectivas de integración socio-económica; el caso de Costa Rica**, Revista de Ciencias Sociales 36 (1987): 81, in which he cites Krysia Muñoz Jiménez, The Mass Media and the Image It Presents to Costa Rican Society Regarding the Institution of Refugee Reception, Chapter VI, 194-227, in **Los refugiados en Costa Rica en el proceso coyuntural-político: período 1978-1984** (thesis in Political Science, Universidad de Costa Rica. San José, 1985).

[11]Ramirez and Solano, **La política general para los refugiados**.

[12]Mario A. Ramírez, **Refugee Policy Challenges: The Case of Nicaraguans in Costa Rica** (Washington, D.C.: HMP-CIPRA, Georgetown University, 1988).

[13]The Vice President, Virgilio Godoy, has been shunted aside by the new government to the point where he no longer exercises any official duties. No office has been assigned him in the presidential palace, and the National Assembly has denied him the power that traditionally corresponds to his position to exercise presidential authority when the President is absent from the country.

[14]The Inter-American Convention of Human Rights, also known as the San José Pact, was ratified in September, 1979; in January 1980, the International Convention on Economic, Social and Cultural Rights was ratified; as was the following month the 1951 UN Convention on Refugees and the 1967 Protocol.

[15]The figures presented here were calculated on the basis of data provided the author by the UNHCR/UNDP CIREFCA Joint Support Unit, January 1991.

YUCATAN

QUINTANA ROO

• Campeche

• Quetzal Edzna

YUCATAN PENINSULA

Maya Tecún •

Rancho Uno

Los Lirios •

CAMPECHE

Chetumal •

MEXICO

Belize City •

* Belmopan

BELIZE

San Cristóbal de las Casas •

GUATEMALA

CHIAPAS

PETEN

Lacuntun

• Las Margaritas

Barillas •

Ixcan

• Chisec

Xalbal •

HUEHUETENANGO

ALTA VERAPAZ

Paso Hondo •

QUICHE

IZABAL

Tapachula

SAN MARCOS

Chichicastenango •

HONDURAS

QUEZALTENANGO

* Guatemala City

EL SALVADOR

CHAPTER III

REPATRIATION OF GUATEMALAN REFUGEES IN MEXICO:
Conditions and Prospects

by Adolfo Aguilar Zinser

INTRODUCTION

This chapter examines the spontaneous repatriation of Guatemalan refugees, returning from Mexico to a homeland still experiencing conflict and turmoil.[1] It attempts to assess the significance of this form of return, the refugees' motivations for repatriation, and the importance of spontaneous repatriation for future return movements.

In using the term "spontaneous," I do not wish to imply that these repatriations have taken place without forethought or planning, the term is simply used to differentiate them from "official" repatriations. The major distinction between the two is that the spontaneous form of return is initiated and managed by the refugees themselves, whereas official repatriations can only take place after a process of discussion and negotiation among the two involved governments and the office of the United Nations High Commissioner for Refugees (UNHCR). Spontaneous repatriations may benefit from official governmental and UNHCR support and assistance, but they often occur with little or no such aid. Official repatriations are characterized by considerable outside logistical, financial, and technical support, which can begin in advance of the actual move and continue for a period of time after reintegration into the home communities.

The Mexican Commission for the Assistance of Refugees (COMAR) refers to spontaneous returns as "unofficial repatriation," while the Guatemalan Special Commission for the Assistance of Repatriated and Displaced Persons (CEAR) uses the term "repatriations outside the program." CEAR includes in this category refugees who were not transported to the border and presented to Guatemalan government authorities by Mexican or UNHCR officials, even though the refugees who returned on their own may have presented themselves as returnees to military or civilian authorities at a later date.

ORIGINS OF THE SOCIAL CONFLICT

The internal conflict in Guatemala, which remains at the root of the refugee problem, can best be understood in the broader context of the political and social crisis in Central America. After achieving independence in the early nineteenth century, Central America experienced a profound concentration of economic wealth and political power. This concentration of wealth continued even during periods of rapid economic growth, such as between 1950 and 1980, when regional exports of such crops as coffee, cotton, sugar, and meat grew 16 times. The majority of the people did not benefit from increased economic opportunities or expanded social services, nor did they see an improvement in their minimum standards of living. This situation was compounded by an expanding population in Central America which grew from 9 to 26 million people between 1950 and 1980.[2] The expanding population placed such intense social pressures on narrowly based and utterly inflexible institutions that a violent uprising was inevitable.

Throughout Central America the most vivid manifestation of economic inequality is the concentration of land. Guatemala is an extreme example of this situation. Seventy-two percent of all its arable land belongs to only 2.1 percent of the landholders, while 14.3 percent of the agricultural surface must be divided among 88.4 percent of the rural landholders. It is thus not surprising that 82 percent of Guatemala's eight million people are illiterate and that most of these people are living below subsistence levels.[3] The coexistence of a very few families and individuals who possess huge landholdings, *latifundios*, alongside millions of mostly indigenous people, who own either no land at all or just tiny farms, *minifundios*, has been maintained through fierce political control, economic exploitation, and brutal military repression.

Thus, it is not surprising to find that according to the United Nations Economic Commission for Latin America and the Caribbean (ECLAC), two and a half million Guatemalans suffer conditions of extreme poverty in the rural areas, and that 56 percent of the rural Guatemalan population was illiterate as of 1986.[4]

There were attempts at reform in Guatemala in the 1940s and early 1950s, and the 1970s saw the emergence of an incipient democratic electoral movement. However, all such attempts at institutional and peaceful change were nullified, usually through violent repression. As a consequence, an enduring and highly motivated guerrilla movement emerged in rural Guatemala, with a strong presence at times in urban centers, particularly in Guatemala City. Although the guerrillas have not been able to challenge the existing power structure, they have demonstrated sufficient strength to generate fear amidst the military and oligarchy and trigger the singularly violent counterinsurgency campaign of the army and security forces of Guatemala.

The objects of this campaign, first launched in 1976 and intensified after 1980, were the rural, indigenous population and the Ladino *campesinos*. (The former comprise the majority of the country's population of eight million, and the latter are Mestizo or indigenous people who have abandoned traditional native language and customs.) This campaign was aimed at eradicating support for the guerrillas as well as non-violent forms of protest in the indigenous communities. Following the classic counterinsurgency model refined during and since the Vietnam War, the specific objective of these military campaigns was to "dry up the water in which the fish swim," that is, to eliminate the possibility of civilian support for the guerrillas. These military campaigns were carried out under three consecutive military governments: Romeo Lucas García (1978-1982), Efraín Ríos Montt (1982-1983), and Oscar Mejía Víctores (1983-1985).

The direct targets of the Guatemalan army's large-scale operations were not the skillful, well-hidden, and mobile guerrilla fighters, but rather the vulnerable inhabitants of towns and villages in a vast area of the northern highlands. This area included the departments of Quezaltenango, San Marcos, Huehuetenango, Quiché, Alta Verapaz and Baja Verapaz, El Petén, Sololá, and Chimaltenango. Six of these nine departments border Mexico. Some of the rural villagers attacked by the army as part of its scorched earth strategy may have been direct or indirect supporters of the guerrillas. Others were attacked in an attempt to curtail the spread of sympathy for the revolution, to establish firm authority by instituting a regime of terror in the countryside, or simply to disperse the population so as to destroy any potential for developing social and ethnic networks of support for the opposition.

The majority of human rights violations that forced the refugees to flee Guatemala were committed by the army. In some instances the guerrillas might have targeted civilians, but those were direct strikes against specific individuals rather than random attacks on the general population. A few communities might have been caught in the cross fire; nevertheless, ample evidence indicates that the vast majority of Guatemalans who fled to Mexico did so to escape indiscriminate army raids.[5]

Human rights organizations estimate that the Guatemalan army inflicted more than 30,000 deaths and forced over one million people into internal exile. Over 200,000 persons sought international refuge, with the majority fleeing to Mexico and others entering Honduras and Belize. The fact that the majority of refugees ended up in Mexico was more a matter of circumstance than of choice. Over centuries of persecution and plunder, the indigenous people of Guatemala have been expelled from the rich valleys and fertile coastal lands and forced to colonize remote mountain and jungle regions, many of which border Mexico. Victims of army attacks often fled in great haste, and sometimes unaware of their destination, found themselves in Mexico after covering a relatively short distance.

By the mid-1980s the immediate military objectives of the scorched earth campaign were attained. The army regained control over the countryside and isolated the guerrillas in the mountains. However, the highly unjust social and political structures that gave rise to the conflict remained and even worsened as Ladino *campesinos* and indigenous people were further segregated from the rest of the Guatemalan population.

At the same time that the leading Guatemalan army officers were beginning to feel confident about their military achievements, they were becoming uneasy about the task of administering the government at a time of mounting economic problems and growing international isolation. They decided to hand the government back to the civilians in order to regain international acceptance. In 1985 General Mejía Víctores sponsored an electoral process, in which only those parties recognized by the military participated and that resulted in the election of Christian Democrat President Vinicio Cerezo Arévalo.

After Cerezo assumed office in January 1986, political violence decreased, especially in the cities. However, the general abuse of human rights in the country, particularly in the countryside, did not change substantially. Random killings and massacres decreased, but abductions, disappearances, and death-squad kidnappings and executions persisted. There is no evidence that the government has made a sincere effort to crack down on the armed groups responsible for the killings.

Although Guatemala has a civilian government, the dominant role of the army has not diminished. It enjoys undisputed authority concerning most major decisions and all security matters. The armed forces are absolute masters in the countryside, particularly in the sensitive border departments where the refugees had resided and to which they return. In those devastated areas, soldiers control all aspects of every community's daily life, in what is essentially a military occupation. *Campesinos* living in these areas are called upon at all times to demonstrate their absolute loyalty and obedience to the military or risk being characterized as "guerrilla collaborators."

MEXICAN GOVERNMENT RECOGNITION OF GUATEMALAN REFUGEES

The migration of Guatemalan refugees escaping military violence against their communities must be distinguished from other forms of Guatemalan migration to Mexico. These other forms of migration include: the search for asylum by political leaders, trade unionists, intellectuals, journalists and professionals; the seasonal migration of agricultural workers to the coffee plantations in Soconusco, the coastal region of Chiapas; and the migration of other workers who look for jobs in southern Mexico or continue on to the United States. Since many of the Guatemalans who enter Mexico are motivated by a combination of political and socioeconomic factors, the entire migration process might be considered in large part a refugee phenomenon.

Despite the international prestige Mexico enjoys as a country open and generous to people suffering from political persecution, Mexican immigration laws are highly restrictive. Until new legislation was approved in July 1990, the Mexican General Population Law recognized only one specific category of asylum: political asylum. Political asylum is granted only to those individuals escaping direct individual persecution in their countries of origin because of their political activities, beliefs, or opinions.[6]

Very few Guatemalan refugees qualified for asylum since persecution was not directed against them as individuals. After an initial period of time during which a number of Guatemalans were deported and others tolerated but not legally admitted, some refugees were granted a special immigration status as Local Visitors under Mexican law. Under this status, the refugees received personal identification documents which restricted their movement to the border region and which were valid for a limited period of time. Renewal of the documents was left to the discretion of local immigration authorities.

Since 1980, no more than 46,000 Guatemalans have been accorded refugee status in Mexico. (This figure does not include the approximately 10,500 children born in the refugee camps nor the few Guatemalans that have been granted political asylum.) There are an estimated 150,000 other Guatemalans in Mexico, who most likely also fled violence in their homeland and have never been recognized as refugees.

The Mexican authorities distinguished between refugees and other migrants based on the circumstances under which they crossed the border, the characteristics of their settlements in Mexico, and the types of communities to which they belonged. Almost all of the Guatemalans who obtained refugee status arrived in the state of Chiapas between 1981 and 1985. They were allowed to settle in improvised camps along the border by the local *campesinos*, members of *ejidos* (public lands used communally), and settlers of remote jungle areas. For the most part, those Guatemalans who left their country as an ethnic and linguistic group and preserved their social cohesion in Mexico gained the status of refugees. On the other hand, refugees who fled into areas of Mexico other than the state of Chiapas and scattered in search of jobs rather than establish refugee camps were denied official refugee status. The major factor in acquiring refugee status was residence in an official camp.

By 1984 there were about 10,000 recognized refugees in Paso Hondo, 9,000 in Tziscao, and 9,000 in Las Margaritas, most of whom arrived from Huehuetenango. There were some 18,000 recognized refugees in Márquez de Comillas and the Lacandón jungles, most of whom came from the cooperatives of the Ixcán region in Quiché, El Petén, and Alta Verapaz. The majority of refugees were from diverse Mayan groups, including the Kanjobal, Mam, Cakchikel, Chol-Lacandón, Jacalteco, Chuj, Ixil, Quiché, and Kekchi. Some were also Ladinos. Approximately 49 percent spoke Spanish, in addition to their own language. Women and children predominated, many of whom became widows and orphans as a consequence of the conflict. Most of

the refugees suffered from diseases, hunger, and exhaustion after weeks
or even months of hiding from the army in the mountains.

The estimated 150,000 Guatemalans considered by the Mexican
government as undocumented workers received neither assistance nor
protection from UNHCR. If they repatriated, no special treatment was
provided. One study refers to these Guatemalans as "the other
refugees."[7] Included in this category were some victims of earlier
deportations who had returned to Mexico. Also included were many of
the approximately 20,000 seasonal workers who in 1983 and 1984
decided to stay in Mexico for fear of persecution in Guatemala.
Indigenous and Ladino families from the departments of San Marcos,
Huehuetenango, and Quetzaltenango were among the nonrecognized
refugees. These seasonal workers had arrived or settled in the more
densely populated, economically active coastal region of Chiapas. Fear
of deportation and economic necessity forced them to disperse and hide
from authorities.

The most important source of protection for these individuals not
recognized as refugees was their anonymity. In Mexico they hid from
the immigration authorities, and upon return to Guatemala they
avoided being identified as former refugees. Yet the same anonymity
that offered protection also hindered their identification as a vulnerable
group in need of assistance. It made them easy targets for abuse and
repression on both sides of the border. Because they could not be
located in Mexico nor traced back to Guatemala upon return, this
chapter does not address their experience in detail. Nonetheless,
certain observations are made in the course of this chapter on the
repatriation of nonrecognized refugees.

In July 1990, after considerable national and international
pressure, the Mexican government incorporated into law the category of
refugee, defined as someone who, "to protect his life, security, or
freedom, threatened by generalized violence, foreign aggression,
internal conflicts, massive violation of human rights, or other
circumstances that have seriously disturbed public order in his country
of origin, is forced to flee to another country."[8] However, it was not
clear if this new refugee category was designed to apply only to those
refugees living in camps and already receiving official protection and
assistance, or if it was meant to be extended to the thousands of
Guatemalan refugees in Mexico who have not received official
documentation.

GENERAL FINDINGS REGARDING
SPONTANEOUS REPATRIATION

The overwhelming majority of Guatemalan refugees in Mexico want to return to Guatemala. However, most of them are convinced that if they return they will be subjected to very serious personal threats, particularly if the army labels them as guerrilla sympathizers for having fled the country.[9] Furthermore, they fear that their return could place their communities as well as their very ethnic identity and culture at risk. There is a general concern that the omnipotence of the army in their places of origin seriously jeopardizes any possibility for the refugees to reorganize their lives, prosper, and find peace in Guatemala.

Repatriation Data

Both COMAR and CEAR maintain data on return movements of officially recognized refugees, whether they returned on their own or enrolled in the formal repatriation program initiated in 1987 with the establishment of the Tripartite Commission (UNHCR-CEAR-COMAR). According to their data, most of the 46,000 Guatemalans who originally settled in camps and were recognized as refugees remained in Mexico at the end of 1989. COMAR calculates that slightly more than 5,000 refugees returned to Guatemala from 1984 until the end of 1989. Of those 5,000, approximately 25 percent, or 1,188, returned spontaneously between 1984 and 1986, that is, prior to the establishment of the Tripartite Commission.[10] CEAR counts 4,801 returnees, with 21 percent, or 1,056, returning outside the official program.[11] Repatriates, both official and spontaneous, thus constitute around ten percent of the original official refugee population. If a significant number of other Guatemalans have returned, they were nonrecognized refugees and therefore not reflected in these figures.

In addition to the official statistics maintained by CEAR and COMAR, I have obtained from a field officer of UNHCR-Guatemala a copy of what appears to be a comprehensive, unofficial UNHCR listing of refugee participants in the UNHCR-CEAR return assistance program, since its inception in 1987 until April 1989. This computer print-out (referred to hereafter as the UNHCR-Guatemala list) contains a total of 811 families totalling 3,876 persons. Of this number, 309 families of 1,491 persons (38 percent of the total) are spontaneously repatriated refugees who enrolled in the UNHCR-CEAR program after their return.[12]

Differences Between Official and Spontaneous Repatriates

The UNHCR-Guatemala list reveals no major demographic differences between returnees who entered the program in Mexico and those who enrolled after returning home. Fifty-four percent of both the official and spontaneous return populations were comprised of families with an average of 4.7 and 4.8 members respectively. Seven percent of both categories of repatriates were single men or women. Slightly more women heads of family entered the program following a spontaneous repatriation to Guatemala (13 percent) than did those who enrolled while still in Mexico (8 percent).[13]

The destination of both categories of returnees is also similar. Although repatriated refugees are found in at least 122 communities in ten of the 22 departments in Guatemala, most of the refugees returned to Huehuetenango, El Quiché, Izabal, and El Petén. A large portion of both spontaneous and official returnees went to three municipalities: 26 percent went to Barillas and 16 percent to Nentón, both in Huehuetenango, and 13 percent went to the municipality of Ixcán in Quiché. Three factors account for the high concentration of returnees to these three municipalities. First, many of the refugees went back to their places of origin in these areas; second, the army tended to concentrate returnees in the enclaves known as "development poles" in these areas; and third, those who were landless or had lost their properties could find greater opportunities to acquire land in these municipalities. The only clear distinction between the two categories of returnees was their place of settlement in Mexico. This resulted from the Mexican government's decision in 1984 to relocate the camps, over the opposition of many refugees, to the states of Campeche and Quintana Roo in the Yucatán Peninsula. (This forced relocation is discussed in further detail later in this report.) The vast majority of spontaneous repatriates came from Chiapas. In contrast, the UNHCR-Guatemala list (supported by data from UNHCR-Mexico) revealed that a disproportionate number of participants in the official program came from the resettlement communities established by the Mexican government in the Yucatán Peninsula. Fifty-six percent of the official repatriates came from the state of Campeche, where, according to Mexican government figures, only 28 percent of the refugee population lived and 22 percent came from Quintana Roo where only 16 percent of the refugee population resided, whereas 22 percent came from Chiapas which was home to 53 percent of the refugee population.

More recent UNHCR-Mexico figures demonstrated that this pattern continued to hold throughout 1989. All of the 68 spontaneous repatriates came from the camps in the state of Chiapas; none were from the resettlement communities in the Yucatán Peninsula. In contrast, 61 percent of that year's 902 official repatriates originated in the Yucatán Peninsula and only 39 percent in Chiapas. The reasons for these differences in participation in the official return program are taken up later in this chapter.

Refugee Mobility

The first important decision any refugee makes affecting his or her refugee status is whether or not to abandon the refugee camp. Such a move does not necessarily involve a return to Guatemala. Since official Mexican policy holds that only those Guatemalans living in established camps can receive refugee status, the individual runs the risk of losing refugee status by leaving the camps for other parts of Mexico. Some camps do not physically stop residents from leaving, but if the refugees do leave without proper authorization – especially if they travel long distances – they can run into serious trouble with immigration authorities. Sizable numbers of Guatemalans found outside the camps are routinely taken to the Tapachula/Talismán border post to be deported as undocumented migrants. When the refugees leave the camps, they lose material assistance and official protection. Upon return to Guatemala, they lose their legal refugee status.

While the mobility of refugees in Mexico is highly restricted by the authorities, many refugees, especially young males, manage to move around with or without the authorization of COMAR. They move from one camp to another, work in other parts of Mexico and in the United States, and even travel back and forth to Guatemala. While most of this travel is economically motivated, the government of Guatemala insists that movements back and forth across the border with Guatemala – especially from the Chiapas camps – are politically motivated. The Guatemalan government maintains that in this way the guerrillas receive logistic support.

Even without specific supporting data, the pattern of movement of Guatemalan refugees in Mexico indicates that it is in response to economic conditions.

Refugees who do not want to return home and are not prepared to look for work outside their settlements remain in the camps where their minimum subsistence needs are met by agencies such as COMAR, UNHCR, and the Catholic Church. The most dependent are typically the elderly, mothers with young children, widows, and disabled persons.

Refugees, generally young adult males, go outside the camps to work for relatively short periods of time, leaving their families in the camps.

Refugees leave the camps for extended periods, some even permanently, to work in other parts of Mexico or in the United States. They also travel back to Guatemala to visit relatives or to tend their land. They send money to their families left behind in the camps, and they occasionally return to the camps for a visit.

Refugees repatriate to Guatemala, generally as a complete family unit. In some instances the repatriation might occur in stages, as when family members opposed to the return remain for some time in Mexico before joining the rest of the family. In other cases the head of the family returns to assess conditions for repatriation; he can return to Mexico to bring the rest of the family, or he can wait for them in Guatemala. In this case, the head of the family usually travels to Guatemala on his own, rather than as part of an official repatriation group.

Phases of Repatriation

Repatriations of Short-Term Refugees – Before 1984 there were virtually no voluntary repatriations. Refugees continued to enter Mexico, and the situation in Guatemala was not safe. However, a few refugees remained in Mexico for only a very short time, returning home after concluding that the situation in their particular town had improved. These repatriations of short-term refugees involved Ladinos working for rich or influential employers, well established merchants, and other more advantaged members of the community. These individuals felt compelled to seek refuge in Mexico to escape the indiscriminate violence, confident that they could return soon. A few had connections in the army or the government and returned under their protection.

The First Repatriations, 1984 to 1986 – The first significant repatriations took place in 1984 and 1985 in response to the Mexican government's attempt to move the Chiapas refugee camps to the Yucatán Peninsula. There are considerable discrepancies regarding how many refugees left during this relocation period, there is general agreement that thousands left the camps and very likely the country because they opposed the relocation. According to unofficial UNHCR and COMAR estimates, between the time the relocation began in 1984 and 1986, the number of refugees living in camps may have dropped by 6,000. CEAR affirms that more than 7,000 refugees returned to Guatemala on their own after the relocation.[14]

The repatriations tapered off in 1985 and 1986; that they continued at all was presumably due in part to the negative environment created in Mexico after the relocation and to improving conditions in Guatemala. Although during this time there was no established repatriation program, refugees who wanted to return could notify UNHCR and Mexican authorities and be taken to the border. Once they crossed over, they were completely on their own, as UNHCR was practically banned from operating within Guatemala until the establishment of the tripartite repatriation program in 1987.

From 1983 to 1987 the official Guatemalan repatriation policy consisted of an amnesty program whereby returning refugees were compelled to apply for amnesty and be relocated by the army. Under this program, the returnees were forced to declare themselves as former terrorists, regardless of their experience, and they were not necessarily resettled in their home communities. Many were sent to "development poles" and "model villages" under military control. Refugees who wanted to go home thus had no real incentive to use official channels for their return. Once in Guatemala, however, many were eventually forced by military authorities to present themselves to have amnesty papers signed.

The Second Stage of Repatriations, 1987 to 1990 — All available figures indicate that the establishment in 1987 of the tripartite repatriation program, under which UNHCR, CEAR, and COMAR rendered assistance and protective services and gave impetus to the return process. The creation of this program may also explain the decrease in spontaneous repatriations after 1987.

According to COMAR, repatriations in 1987 increased 212 percent over 1986 return figures, with repatriations in 1988 increasing by 215 percent over 1987 returns. CEAR figures indicate a 200 percent increase in repatriations in 1988 over 1987 figures. In spite of this substantial increase in the relative proportion of repatriations after 1987, the absolute number of returnees under the official program was no more than 3,000. This represented less than 10 percent of the total official Guatemalan refugee population in Mexico. Official repatriations decreased substantially during 1989, when, according to CEAR, fewer than 1,000 refugees returned home. This is substantially fewer than the 10,000 repatriates that CEAR had earlier predicted would decide to return.

After UNHCR opened an office in Guatemala in July 1987, many of the early spontaneous returnees voluntarily enrolled in the program, attracted mainly by the material assistance provided by UNHCR and distributed through CEAR. According to the UNHCR-Guatemala list, of the 309 families enrolled in the program as spontaneous repatriates, 16.1 percent had returned in 1985, 23 percent in 1986, and 51 percent in 1987. Only 5 percent of the families returned spontaneously in 1988, with an equal percentage returning spontaneously in the first four months of 1989.

Clearly, the official repatriation program did not trigger a large-scale repatriation of Guatemalan refugees from Mexico. Nor did it convince the general refugee population that it was safe to go home. Rather, the program has facilitated the repatriation of refugees already inclined to return for personal, family, or economic reasons. Aware that the situation in Guatemala has not improved substantially, these refugees view the program as their best option for reducing the risks involved in returning.

Other Findings

The decision to return to Guatemala is influenced by various factors. One crucial element is the time factor: attitudes towards repatriation change over time, responding to varying circumstances. For instance, following the 1986 change in government in Guatemala, the refugees noted a slight decline in the level of violence. For those individuals who were inclined to return, such marginal changes represented sufficient grounds to consider going home. The majority of refugees, however, did not regard the changes as sufficient to warrant a return under the terms being offered by the government.

One type of spontaneous return taking place independent of the decisions of the larger community is repatriation to areas under guerrilla control. As noted later in this paper, at one point the government of Guatemala alleged that most unofficial repatriations were in fact illegal entries of refugees returning to help the guerrillas. While there is no proof that the refugees serve as a social base for the guerrillas, it is known that some of the internally displaced people live in the mountain regions outside the control of the army where the guerrillas have their hideouts, especially in northern Quiché, Huehuetenango, and the jungles of El Petén.

Some refugees may have belonged to these communities, known as "populations in resistance," since many of them spent weeks and even months hiding from the army before crossing into Mexico. However, the number of refugees repatriating who join insurgents does not seem to be great enough to count as meaningful experiences of repatriation. At any rate, there would be no trace of them; the Guatemalan guerrillas — unlike their Salvadoran counterparts — have not established control over a sizable amount of territory where they can organize and protect a sympathetic population.

In general, the decision to return to Guatemala is heavily influenced by the assessments and deliberations of the larger Guatemalan refugee community, which thus far has decided to stay in Mexico. The following sections of this report analyze this collective decision-making process as well as factors influencing individual decisions to return. They also examine the "push and pull" factors behind repatriation; that is, the motivations resulting from experiences in Mexico as well as those based on considerations regarding the home country.

ATTITUDES OF REFUGEES TOWARDS THE REPATRIATION PROCESS

Land and Indigenous Culture

You order us to abandon our lands to have them free for coffee crops. In exchange for those lands you offered us 2,500 hectares on the coast. We know how to cultivate coffee; we do it for the plantation owners on their estates. But we want the land of our fathers and grandfathers to produce corn. It has always been ours. We came to talk to President Carrera and we told him, "Here are the titles." Later we came to talk to President Cerna and we paid once again for those lands and they gave us new titles. Here they are. Later President Barrios demanded the same thing. Here are the titles we got from him. We have here the money. How much do you want us to pay this time for our land?" (Guatemalan Indian leader speaking on behalf of hundreds of Indians from the region of Nahuala before President Manuel Lizandro Barillas [1885-1892]).[15]

Most of the refugees who fled to Mexico are *campesinos* belonging to one of the 22 ethnic communities that exist in Guatemala; few are Ladinos. The possession of land is crucial to the indigenous peoples' sense of individual and collective identity, to community cohesion, and to their very cultural survival. The land is their bond with their ancestors and deceased relatives, and the land provides the underpinning for their myths and spiritual beliefs. They practice vivid cultural rituals, dress in ornately woven and embroidered clothing charateristic of their group, and speak their own languages; all of these traditions sharply differentiate them from the rest of the population of Guatemala.

Guatemalan indigenous peoples have traditionally maintained a very weak sense of identification with Guatemala as a nation where they comprise 55 to 60 percent of the entire population. Rather than considering themselves as Guatemalan citizens, they think of themselves as a part of a large and diverse ethnic community. When asked in an interview about his country of origin, a refugee in Chiapas said, "I don't come from Guatemala. I come from Nentón (a town in Huehuetenango)." Extending his arm towards the south he added, "Guatemala is far away, in that direction; Nentón is just ahead and I am from Nentón."

The refugees are aware, however, that legally it is in Guatemala where they reclaim or otherwise obtain a plot of land, which they can then leave to their children. This notion of "leaving land to my children" was repeated again and again by refugees and returnees as the only guarantee of survival and security for the future. It was this hope of regaining control over their land and reuniting with family members that provided the impetus for most of the repatriations thus far.

The desire to return to the land is shared by the refugee community at large. To date, however, the actual decision to return has come more from the individual than the community. It is, therefore, not unusual to find among repatriates Ladino *campesinos* or indigenous people who are less interested in larger community matters than in simply recovering their land.

Many of the Guatemalans who remain in Mexico have achieved a high level of political awareness from their refugee experience. They have also become more politically sophisticated from their interactions with Mexican *campesinos*, religious workers, government personnel, staff of international organizations, and Mexican and foreign press representatives. As a result, what some refugees refer to as "the sense of indigenous citizenship," has developed among the refugee population. Those sharing this political consciousness view recovery of their land not in terms of individual survival but as the basis for the construction of a new Guatemalan nation, one which fully encompasses all the diverse indigenous peoples. They see their sacrifices as part of a historic struggle to liberate all Natives of the Americas. For them, the return to Guatemala is a collective endeavor that must be undertaken only after certain basic conditions have been met.

The Religious Factor

The majority of Guatemalans are Catholics. The indigenous Guatemalans, however, have historically maintained an ambivalent approach to Catholicism, adapting the Catholic rituals to their traditional religious practices and beliefs. The appearance in the Guatemalan highlands in the 1960s and 1970s of missionaries professing the new "liberation theology" marked a significant change in the traditional relationship between the Catholic Church and the indigenous communities.

The traditional Catholic teachings emphasized the need to accept poverty and sacrifice in the hope of achieving a better life after death. The missionaries, preaching the new "option for the poor," instead promoted social awareness, the need to struggle for individual and collective rights, and the improvement of material conditions. Much of the social consciousness of the Guatemalans in Mexico grew out of their earlier participation in Christian Base Communities. These study groups were promoted by the liberation theology priests as a mechanism for encouraging the people to analyze critically their communities and their society.

Following the spread of liberation theology, Protestant evangelical sects began to penetrate the indigenous communities. The evangelists preached the need to improve material conditions, but as an individual effort to acquire personal wealth rather than as a community effort. In contrast with liberation theology, these teachings did not denounce the concentration of wealth and power, economic exploitation, and political repression. They instead encouraged political passivity and respect for the property and wealth of others.

The evangelical sects were supported by the Guatemalan army as counterweights to the perceived dangers of liberation theology. They gained considerable influence during the presidency of General Efraín Ríos Montt, himself a minister of the Church of the Word. Evangelicals gained considerable influence in the indigenous communities, particularly in the Ixil Triangle in the department of Quiché and in Huehuetenango, where many of the refugees originated.

Despite its sympathy for evangelicals, the army did not differentiate between them and Catholics when attacking villages. Thus, followers of both liberation theology and Protestant evangelism were forced into exile together. In Mexico tensions grew and the evangelicals segregated themselves from the larger refugee communities. When the possibility of repatriation arose, the evangelicals were more inclined to return, since they were not at odds with the government and army.

Repatriation of the evangelicals served as a natural process of self-selection and social accommodation, separating out individuals not in tune with the majority. The political and cultural cohesion of the larger refugee community was strengthened, thus favoring the decision of the community to stay in Mexico until conditions existed for a collective return.

Organization and Political Representation of Refugees

The issue of repatriation has served to enhance the process of political mobilization and to strengthen internal cohesion among the refugees in Mexico. The propaganda campaign and other efforts of three consecutive Guatemalan governments between 1983 and 1990 to induce the refugees to return to military-controlled model villages and development poles reinforced this process. Following the establishment of the Tripartite Commission, the issue of repatriation helped to consolidate new forms of organization and decision-making in the refugee community, which led to a collective determination to refuse repatriation until certain demands were met by the government and the army of Guatemala.

Before considering further these new forms of decision-making, it would be useful to first understand the evolution of leadership structures in the refugee camps in Mexico. Internal forms of political organization of the camps were the result of a combination of circumstances. In many cases, community authorities in Guatemala continued to exercise their leadership in exile. In numerous other cases, however, a new leadership had to be quickly established. In other situations, the diaspora brought together different communities and even different ethnic groups. Conflicts over authority arose, but were resolved by either splitting up the community or accommodating themselves to new forms of internal political organization.

The extraordinary conditions in the refugee camps favored a rapid erosion of the authority of the traditional leaders and the rise of new leaders more in tune with the needs of the communities. Teachers, catechists, and health workers assumed many of the leadership roles, since they were often among those members of the community who could communicate in Spanish with the outside world. In exile, Spanish became a vital instrument for the Guatemalan indigenous people as the vehicle for seeking help from Mexican *campesinos*, Church representatives, and government officials and for denouncing human rights abuses to the press and to international organizations.

Under the new camp leadership, decisions were made only after an assembly of refugees discussed every issue affecting the community.

No outside presence or interference, with the exception of some trusted church officials providing material assistance to the refugees, was allowed at such assemblies. This procedure was largely an effort to protect the identity of the leaders. The indigenous peoples' traditional suspicion of outsiders was exacerbated by the hostility of many Mexican authorities towards the refugees and by fears of Guatemalan army incursions into the camps to kidnap or assassinate the leaders.

This tendency to protect the anonymity of the leaders led Mexican authorities to suspect that the camps were being run clandestinely by guerrillas. Whereas in some instances the guerrillas may have attempted to exercise direct leadership or to influence the elected leaders, it is unlikely that the refugees surrendered entirely to such control. This kind of direct authority was not exercised by the guerrillas in Guatemala, even in villages sympathetic to the revolutionaries. An important step in the development of leadership structures was the Esquipulas II peace agreement signed by the Central American presidents in August 1987. The agreement stated:

> *The governments of Central America are committed to assist with a sense of urgency the flows of refugees and internally displaced people caused by the regional crisis . . . as well as to facilitate their repatriation, resettlement, or transfer. This must always be done voluntarily when that wish is manifested individually.*

The refugees saw this statement as an invitation to express their own views on repatriation in an organized and representative fashion. At the end of 1987 the refugees created the "Permanent Commissions," a representative body elected by direct vote of all refugees living in camps in Chiapas, Campeche, and Quintana Roo. Each camp elected six permanent and two supplemental representatives to the Commissions. An election procedure developed by the refugees was strictly observed. It included a written description of the process, endorsed by all refugees. In most cases the election was carried out in the presence of a Mexican government representative. The Permanent Commissions have not replaced the internal organizational structures in the camps nor supplanted the authority of the leaders who administer the internal affairs of the community. They are, however, gaining considerable power.

Until the establishment of the Permanent Commissions, the refugees in Guatemala had no country-wide representation. Each individual camp was represented by the same leaders who exercised internal authority. The Permanent Commissions enjoyed greater leeway for representing the interests of the refugees before the outside world than did the traditional camp leaders. This was a departure from the traditional process of decision-making through assemblies, a change which held both positive and negative consequences. On the one hand, it eroded the purity of the traditional democracy practiced in the camps and led to a rivalry between the permanent representatives and the internal camp leadership. On the other hand, it facilitated the development of camp governments based on consultation with representatives of the larger refugee community in Mexico.

Prior to the establishment of the Permanent Commissions, the refugees consistently opposed repatriation on the grounds that the Guatemalan army only wanted them back in order to place them under strict military control in the model villages. The inauguration of the elected government of President Cerezo and the creation of CEAR in 1986 did not alter this stance. The establishment in February 1987 of the tripartite mechanism for voluntary repatriation, however, created a new environment for return. The refugees felt compelled to respond to this new situation.

In early 1989, following an elaborate process of discussion and consultation, the Commissions formulated conditions for the return of the Guatemalan refugees to their homeland. That spring three members of the Permanent Commissions traveled to Guatemala to participate in the National Dialogue, a forum which grew out of the Esquipulas II agreement. They presented six points that repatriation would require:

° The return must be voluntary, collective, and organized;

° The refugees must receive full guarantees that they will recover their land;

° The refugees must have the right to organize and freely associate;

° The refugees must receive guarantees regarding respect for their right to life

° The return must be witnessed by accompanying members of solidarity groups, foreign government officials, and representatives of nongovernmental organizations; and

° The Permanent Commissions must have the right to organize internally and internationally in order to ensure the presence of refugees in the National Dialogue and in other national or international deliberations regarding their future.

The most controversial and crucial of the six points is the demand for a collective and organized return, which assigns a key role to the refugees' political representatives. The refugees note that once their conditions have been met they will not necessarily return *en masse.* They insist, however, that the integrity and cohesion of their communities be respected so that upon return they can be better prepared to defend their cultural identity and their indigenous forms of organization.

The government of Guatemala rejected these demands and the claims of the Permanent Commissions to represent the mass of refugees in Mexico.[16] Military authorities in Guatemala consider the concept of a collective return a plot to reestablish a base of popular support for the insurgency in communities outside military control. CEAR officials claim that they will be unable to cope with all the logistic, administrative, and political problems that a collective return would create. Instead, the Guatemalan government and military prefer a gradual repatriation consisting of small groups that can be controlled easily and that provide the returnees minimal opportunities to organize politically. Many refugees see this proposal for a gradual, piecemeal repatriation process as a threat to the safety of the individual returnee and a ploy against the community.

CONDITIONS IN MEXICO

The precarious economic conditions for Guatemalans in Mexico provide an important incentive for some refugees to repatriate, even though Mexico benefits from a higher level of socioeconomic development than Guatemala, as measured by such indicators as income, infrastructure, social services, literacy, nutritional level, and infant mortality. While many Guatemalans have experienced an improvement in some aspects of their lives as a result of access to health and educational services in the camps, most of them have suffered greatly in Mexico.[17]

General economic and social conditions in Mexico have been poor, and the violence experienced by the refugees has seriously affected their psychological status. Many refugees lost their possessions during their escape, and then found themselves living in an extremely difficult physical environment in Mexico. They had to build their camps in areas lacking water, roads, arable land, fuelwood, and any kind of social services. They made their houses of reeds and palm, instead of the more durable adobe that they had in Guatemala.

Assistance Provided by the Catholic Diocese of San Cristóbal de las Casas

The Catholic Church in Mexico, especially the Diocese of San Cristóbal de las Casas in Chiapas, played an influential role in shaping Mexico's response to the Guatemalan refugees. From the beginning of the refugee influx, the Church provided assistance to the Guatemalans and displayed particular sensitivity to their special needs.

Many of the fleeing refugees crossed into the jurisdictions of either the Diocese of San Cristóbal, headed by Bishop Samuel Ruiz García, or the Diocese of Tapachula, closer to the coast. Refugees who entered the region of Tapachula travelled in small groups and settled in more densely populated areas of Mexico. As a result, they scattered in search of jobs and sought assistance on an individual basis. On the other hand, the refugees who entered areas under the Diocese of San Cristóbal arrived in large, ethnically coherent groups. There were fewer inhabitants in this region, which motivated the refugees to remain together as a group. In addition to these circumstances, the response of the Church as well as the attitudes of the authorities in both regions had an influence on the type of refugee settlement that developed. The Diocese of San Cristóbal is one of the most progressive dioceses in Mexico. It is well known internationally for its work with the Mayan Quiché Indians, one of the largest remaining Indian communities in the country. The close relationship between the Diocese and local Catholics allowed the Bishop to learn of the presence of the refugees before government authorities were alerted. As a result, when government officials arrived on the scene, the refugees were already under the very active protection and assistance of the Church. The Bishop, priests, and nuns of the Diocese became strong advocates on behalf of the refugees, which created a difficult and at times highly conflictive relationship with the government.

In contrast, the dispersion of the refugees in Tapachula gave the local authorities the opportunity to refuse the establishment of refugee camps and ultimately to deny the Guatemalans refugee status. The local Church, in turn, reacted cautiously. This combination of factors explains why all of the 46,000 refugees officially recognized by Mexico were originally located in the Diocese of San Cristóbal.

The Bishop of San Cristóbal instructed the parishes to work directly with the refugees and to provide food, clothes, medicine, and shelter. Large quantities of material aid for the refugees arrived, partly

in response to the Church's directive and partly as the result of the
spontaneous generosity of many Mexican organizations and individuals.
As the aid piled up and as new groups of refugees continued to arrive,
the need for a special organization responsible for the distribution of
aid was recognized.

In 1982 the Dioceses of both San Cristóbal and Tapachula
created special committees to perform this task. Committees to collect
material aid for the Chiapas refugees were formed by the Dioceses of
Tehuantepec and Cuernavaca, the latter of which was headed by Bishop
Sergio Mendez Arceo, the leader at that time of the progressive wing of
the Church in Mexico. The Dioceses of San Cristóbal, Tapachula, and
Cuernavaca, together with an ecumenical Christian committee founded
in Mexico City, established the Christian Coordinator for Aid to
Guatemalan Refugees. All of these assistance activities were carried
out independently of the government and before the authorities could
decide upon a policy and plan of action for the refugees.

Nongovernmental Organizations and the Catholic Church

At the same time these assistance structures were being created,
a number of international nongovernmental organizations (NGOs),
particularly from Canada, Europe, and the United States, were
searching for mechanisms to deliver funds and material aid to the
refugees. Some wanted to work directly in the refugee camps. The
government of Mexico, however, feared that it would lose control of the
situation if it allowed NGOs to participate in the relief program. Some
government officials believed that international espionage agencies
could use NGOs as fronts to infiltrate Mexico's southern border, or that
funds could be channelled to subversive Guatemalan groups, which
could pose ramifications for Mexico. More importantly, the Mexican
government feared that NGOs would scrutinize the human rights
situation of the refugees in the country.

The government used various tactics to persuade the NGOs that
their help was neither welcomed nor needed. Officials set up their own
refugee assistance organization. They forbid foreigners from visiting
the camps without written permission from federal authorities; and they
asked other governments to pressure NGOs to stop interfering in
Mexican refugee policy. All of these activities made the presence in
Mexico of most international NGOs almost impossible.

In an effort to overcome government restrictions, many NGOs,
especially those with church connections in their own countries,
decided to provide financial assistance through the Christian
Coordinator for Aid to Guatemalan Refugees. These close links

between international NGOs and the Church in Chiapas annoyed the Mexican government, but it did not take any action out of fear of creating an international controversy. With the help of these international resources, the Church instituted an honest and efficient system to administer and distribute aid to almost all refugee settlements in Chiapas. This assistance program has been crucial to the ability of the refugees to maintain their autonomy in the face of pressures from the governments of Mexico and Guatemala.

Disputes between the Church and government of Mexico over the treatment of the Guatemalans intensified as refugees continued to arrive. The initial controversy was over massive deportations occurring in 1981. Subsequent disputes concerned corruption and abuses of authority as well as policy and programmatic decisions. The government prohibited improvements in housing for the refugees, refused to install small machinery in the camps, to train or employ refugees. It resisted the introduction of any significant improvements in camp life and refused to authorize the relocation of camps to safer sites away from the border. Progressive bishops around Mexico joined with the Bishops of San Cristóbal and Tapachula to issue statements supporting the refugees in the face of government abuses.[18] Tensions between the Church and Mexican government reached their highest point in 1984 when the government tried to relocate the refugees against their will.[19]

After the government quietly abandoned its forced relocation strategy, relations with the Diocese of San Cristóbal improved substantially. The Mexican government's policy regarding repatriation has not been a source of significant friction with the Church to date. There have been disagreements, but no acute controversies, mainly because the government has not actively promoted repatriation.

The Treatment of Guatemalan Refugees by the Mexican Government

Mexico has a long tradition of granting asylum to victims of political persecution, especially Latin Americans. Egregious contradictions and conflicts in the case of the Guatemalan refugees have tarnished these traditions. These inconsistencies in Mexico's refugee policy have influenced many Guatemalans to go home even though conditions in Guatemala are less than optimal for return. In particular, many of the early spontaneous repatriations can be attributed to Mexican government actions.

Guatemala has applied pressure on Mexico to adjust its refugee policy to respond to the interests of its military. In having control established over the refugee population or having it as far away from the border as possible in order to neutralize whatever influence they might have on political events in their homeland.

It is possible to identify five phases in the official Mexican policy towards Guatemalan refugees. The refugees have responded differently to each phase.

First Phase: Denial of the Problem

The first phase began in late 1980 and lasted until early 1982. This phase can be described as a period of denial of the problem during which many refugees were deported. Mexican authorities were surprised by the initial influx of refugees in late 1980 and early 1981. They assumed that it was a temporary phenomenon that could be ignored and handled by deporting the refugees. According to conservative estimates, some 3,000 Guatemalans were expelled in 1981 alone.[20]

Second Phase: Benign Containment

The second phase, lasting from 1982 to 1984, can best be described as a period of benign containment. Undeterred by the deportations, refugees continued to arrive in Mexico in growing numbers through 1984. The public outcry in Mexico and strong international reaction to the early expulsions and other government abuses prompted the Mexican authorities to discontinue deportations and permit refugees to remain in Mexico under a general policy of asylum with no firm legal status. The government feared that if it offered explicit refugee status, the country would be overwhelmed by refugees and dragged into a dangerous political and possibly military conflict with Guatemala.

Only those Guatemalans already living in camps along the border were treated as refugees. The rest of the refugees, an estimated 150,000 people, were considered to be undocumented economic migrants subject to deportation. Probably one-half of the original 150,000 nonrecognized refugees, mostly indigenous ones, decided to remain in Chiapas until they could return safely to Guatemala. A large number of Ladinos who entered Mexico through Tapachula probably moved on to the north of the country. Many others, however, were likely to have returned to Guatemala. Since they were never counted as refugees in

Mexico, and cannot claim former refugee status on their return home, it is difficult to locate and enumerate these repatriating refugees.

Mexico is not a signatory to the international conventions on refugees. After a bitter inter-agency struggle within the Mexican government, UNHCR was officially admitted into Mexico in January 1982; this step signaled the government's willingness to adopt a more generous approach to the refugees. However, Mexico remained uneasy about events in Guatemala and the flow of refugees, so its refugee policy was more a component of the country's incipient national security strategy than a reflection of true humanitarian concern.

While reluctantly accepting the presence of refugees along its southern border, Mexican authorities allowed them to stay only in assigned camps and prohibited them from leaving the camps without permission. This decision was taken out of concern that the refugee presence would result in a *de facto* "Guatemalization" of the rich tropical forest area of Chiapas. They were also concerned that the refugees might "contaminate" the political environment of that volatile state, which is one of the poorest in the country, and increase social tensions by interacting with the local population.

Encompassing constant harassment from immigration authorities, this policy of "benign containment" persisted until the end of President José López Portillo's administration. In 1983, under President de la Madrid, the containment policy was refined. Refugee assistance was upgraded with the support of UNHCR, but, as an official of COMAR put it in an interview, "The government wants to help the refugees but without attracting the bees to the honey." Submerged in a deep economic crisis, the government also felt that the refugees should not receive more attention, better services, and opportunities than those available to the Mexican people of the impoverished and isolated regions of Chiapas.

Around this same time, immigration controls were tightened to reduce the flow of all Central American immigrants to Mexico. In June 1983, this containment approach led to the appointment of Mario Vallejo as Coordinator of COMAR. Vallejo was already the head of the Immigration Bureau where he oversaw the strict enforcement of Mexican immigration laws. This policy anomaly disappointed international assistance and refugee advocacy organizations. Tensions between UNHCR and COMAR escalated and in October 1982 the UNHCR representative in Mexico was declared virtually *persona non grata* and recalled to Geneva. During this period relations between the refugees and the Mexican government grew more tense and were characterized by mutual suspicions and recriminations. Meanwhile, new refugees continued to enter the country, although at a lower rate. The Guatemalan army maintained an overwhelming presence in the border region and made regular incursions into the refugee camps in Mexico.

Third Phase: Relocation to Campeche and Quintana Roo

During the third phase from 1984 to 1986, the refugee camps were relocated and spontaneous repatriations began. This period is crucial to the understanding of the phenomenon of the spontaneous repatriation of Guatemalan refugees.

Beginning in the fall of 1982, as part of its scorched earth campaign, the Guatemalan army carried out a number of attacks on the refugee camps across the border. Through the end of the year, those incursions increased in number and in the level of violence. The Mexican authorities interpreted those events as provocations intended to undermine Mexico's foreign policy initiatives in the Contadora peace process. While resisting pressures to militarize the border, Mexico became increasingly impatient with the presence of the refugees in Chiapas. Then in April 1984, 200 Guatemalan troops attacked the refugee camp of El Chupadero, five kilometers from the border. Mexican authorities announced that in order to avoid further tensions along the border and to protect the refugees, all 46,000 refugees living in camps in Chiapas would be relocated to the states of Campeche and Quintana Roo in the Yucatán Peninsula.

Although many refugees had long requested to be relocated further away from the border for security reasons, the majority did not see this relocation proposal as a gesture of goodwill and refused to move their camps. This brought them into direct and bitter confrontation with government authorities. By mid-August 1984, 10,632 refugees had been relocated to Campeche, some voluntarily, others by force. Over the next four years, the government used a combination of persuasion, threats, and confrontation in order to relocate 12,000 refugees to Campeche and 6,697 to Quintana Roo; by the end of 1988, 22,429 refugees remained in Chiapas.

The number of refugees transferred out of Chiapas plus the number of those who stayed in their camps did not add up to the original figure of 46,000 refugees. UNHCR sources calculated a gap of 6,000; CEAR estimated a gap of 7,000. The gap may be partially explained by an incomplete census; regardless of the specific figures, however it is clear that the trauma of the relocation caused many refugees to disperse within Mexico or return to Guatemala.

According to one refugee who now lives in Chacaj, a municipality in Nentón, Huehuetenango:

> *When the government came to Las Delicias to take the*
> *Guatemalans to Campeche, I moved with my family to another*
> ejido. *A campesino we knew let us stay, but life was difficult.*
> *Later (early 1985) I came to Guatemala to see if I could recover*
> *my land. Later my family came. My son found work in Mexico*
> *and stayed until this year (1989).*

Following the controversy over the relocation, the government of Mexico decided to punish the defiant refugees and force them to relocate. Thus, it reduced the level and quality of its assistance to those refugees who remained in Chiapas. This action caused further deterioration of conditions in many camps that had already lacked adequate assistance due to their remote location.

The refugees relocated to camps in Campeche and Quintana Roo enjoy housing and basic services superior to those available in Chiapas. Since the relocation camps are administered directly by COMAR, more attention and resources are devoted to them as a matter of policy. Mexican authorities want to demonstrate that refugees in the Yucatán Peninsula have improved their situation and that COMAR can efficiently administer a refugee assistance program. One aspect of the relocation policy was the investment in workshops and other productive activities that would allow the refugees to become self-sufficient, a goal the government had opposed in Chiapas.

The self-sufficiency policy was also designed to permit gradual reductions in food rations. However, the Campeche camps are all located in very poor and difficult terrain that requires an immense investment of hard labor prior to farming. Lack of water and other problems have contributed to poor productivity and constant crop losses. The local economy of Quintana Roo is precarious, with a high cost of living, significant risk of crop failures, and a scarcity of alternative sources of income.[21] Administrative, managerial, and financial obstacles also undermined the goal of self-sufficiency. In June 1987, the refugees of Quintana Roo asked the government to postpone the reduction in basic food assistance that was to take place between 1987 and 1989.

The problems in achieving self-sufficiency and the lack of jobs available to the refugees left them highly dependent on outside assistance. The poor diet contributed to a high incidence of tuberculosis and other diseases in the camps. The poor economic situation, arid landscape and hot climate in most of Campeche and

Quintana Roo, as well as the sense of isolation and lack of hope for the future have all been incentives for some of the refugees to leave the Yucatán. This explains in part the high number of official repatriates coming from Campeche and Quintana Roo.

Fourth Phase: Official Repatriation

The fourth phase of Mexico's refugee policy, the sanctioned repatriation phase, began in 1986 with negotiations that led to a tripartite agreement between COMAR, CEAR and UNHCR, which was signed in 1987. Ever since the first arrivals of the refugees, Mexico has been eager for them to return home at the earliest possible time. In 1983, however, after the controversy over the massive deportations of Guatemalans, Mexican government officials made a commitment to respect the right of refugees to repatriate strictly on the basis of voluntary, individual decisions.

Mexican officials, supported by UNHCR, quietly initiated discussions with the military regime of President Efraín Ríos Montt regarding the possibility of a joint program for voluntary repatriation. In the course of these discussions, Guatemala presented a plan for massive repatriations with no real security guarantees. This approach was not acceptable to Mexico. Although Mexican officials did not want to publicize the repatriation discussions, reports of the talks surfaced and gave rise to considerable suspicion among the refugees, many of whom perceived the terms presented by Guatemala as a threat. Talks continued until 1984, when border tensions escalated and Mexico decided to move the refugees further inland.

When the elected government of President Marco Vinicio Cerezo took office in Guatemala in January 1986, repatriation became the first priority on Mexico's agenda for the new administration. The new head of COMAR, Ambassador Oscar Gonzales, visited Guatemala in April and began formal discussions on conditions for repatriation. During his state visit to Mexico in June, President Cerezo spoke of repatriation as a key issue, and despite the absence of bilateral agreements, President Cerezo made a commitment to create a repatriation agency. In October, CEAR was established. The following month the head of CEAR, Carmen Rosa de León, and the President's wife, Raquel Blandón, visited the camps in Mexico and told the refugees that the new democratic government was preparing conditions for their safe return. Later that month the UN High Commissioner for Refugees, Jean Pierre Hocke, visited Guatemala and offered President Cerezo assistance for any official repatriation program.

In January 1987, COMAR, CEAR, and UNHCR officials met in Guatemala to prepare the final draft of the tripartite agreement, which laid out the ground rules, procedures, and logistics for the repatriation. The agreement was signed the following month, and UNHCR opened an office in Guatemala in June. In November, COMAR announced that the first group of 500 people, or 90 families, was preparing to return from Campeche to Guatemala under the official program.

The expeditious manner in which the repatriation program was negotiated, agreed upon, and put into action created a whole new dynamic for the refugees. As noted earlier, the collective decision of the majority of refugees was to remain in Mexico until certain conditions were met by the Guatemalan government. A number of refugees, however, saw the change of government in the country and the establishment of a formal mechanism for return sanctioned by UNHCR as an opportunity to go home. According to COMAR figures, 840 refugees were officially repatriated in 1987 and 1,808 in 1988. CEAR lists 1,407 returnees for 1987 and 2,838 for 1988. However, the latter figures include a number of refugees who returned on their own prior to 1987 and who applied for assistance once in Guatemala.

The initial apparent success of the repatriation program gave Mexican officials hope that most refugees would leave during Cerezo's tenure and that the problem would soon be over. With this in mind, Mexico practically froze all new initiatives for improvements in the camps, and contingency plans were made to redirect toward other purposes the use of some of the facilities created for the refugees. However, three years after the signing of the formal agreement, it is clear that the repatriation program has not resulted in a significant return movement and that short-term prospects for mass repatriations are not good.

The Fifth Phase: The Institutionalization of Refugee Status

Mexico's new government under President Carlos Salinas de Gortari (1988-present) made some improvements in its refugee policy, at least as far as the 46,000 Guatemalans settled in camps are concerned. The Mexican government apparently learned from its mistakes, miscalculations, and false assumptions. In 1980, the year COMAR was founded, fewer than two percent of its beneficiaries were Guatemalans. Currently the government recognizes as refugees 176,000 of the estimated 400,000 Central Americans who have sought refuge in Mexico from the region's conflicts. Guatemalans form the core of this population of recognized refugees.

From the mistakes and abuses of the Mexican government against the Guatemalan refugees these positive developments emerged. The government's actions helped to focus international awareness of the problem of indigenous Guatemalan refugees in Mexico and to give them greater public visibility. Furthermore, the refugees' interactions with the hostile though not brutal, Mexican government forced them to develop political and organizational skills and to learn to resist, negotiate, and even compromise. Out of this experience the refugees are now better prepared to take charge of their own destiny. For its part, the Mexican government has learned that refugees may be vulnerable and naive, but when collectively organized, they are neither helpless nor incapable of recognizing and defending their interests.

In 1989, COMAR was placed under the jurisdiction of a newly created Office of Human Rights in the Ministry of Interior. The head of that office is Luis Ortiz Monasterio, who, as a COMAR coordinator in the early 1980s, played a crucial role in convincing higher Mexican authorities to stop deportations, establish a regular system to deliver food and other basic assistance to the refugees, provide a stable immigration status (the F-8 border residence permit), and sign a cooperation agreement with UNHCR. COMAR is headed by Estevan Gariz, a conscientious, well trained, and honorable former administrator of social assistance programs for the poor. Evidence of the new attitudes instilled by this team came in May 1989 at the International Conference for Central American Refugees held in Guatemala. The Mexican Under Secretary of the Interior, José Limón, announced the government's commitment to include the status of refugee in its population laws, and he announced that Mexico will sign the UN Convention on the Status of Refugees.

Repatriation continues to be the first priority of current Mexican refugee policy. However, COMAR officials acknowledge that the repatriation process is slow and will become more so in the future. Mexico could attempt to accelerate the repatriation process by working more closely with the Guatemalan authorities than they already do, by intensifying the propaganda effort to convince the refugees of the virtues of the repatriation program, or by making the lives of the refugees in Mexico even more difficult than they are now. However, COMAR officials realize that those tactics would have little impact and could erode the credibility and prestige that the organization is trying to re-establish.

COMAR has announced plans to place the refugee camps under the jurisdiction of local Mexican authorities, to develop a stable relationship between refugees and surrounding communities, and to integrate the refugees into the local economies. This new policy has several components: a) to promote voluntary repatriation as a solution to the situation of the refugees; b) to assist refugees in Campeche and Quintana Roo, who do not yet want to repatriate, in achieving self-sufficiency on a par with the local population; c) to redress the situation of the refugees in Chiapas who refused relocation by integrating their dispersed settlements into established communities there; and d) to regularize the refugees' legal status and to provide birth certificates to all refugee children born in Mexico.

Mexican officials claim that this so-called "Mexicanization" process is not an attempt to take full control over the social and political life of the camps nor to destroy the ethnic, cultural, or linguistic identity of the refugees. However, the Mexican government has always been concerned with the degree of freedom the refugees have had to govern the internal life of the camps, especially those in Chiapas. Well entrenched cultural barriers and the refugees' profound distrust of Mexican authorities reduced the government's participation in the decision-making processes within the camps. The new COMAR administration wants to reverse this situation and to bring the refugee communities under the jurisdiction of local authorities in such matters as law enforcement; civil registry of births, deaths, and other changes of civil status; national vaccination campaigns; and supervision of educational programs.

Experience suggests that some aspects of this policy, such as relocation to "refugee towns" under local jurisdiction, could face opposition from the refugees. For example, refugees have been reluctant to register their children born in Mexico.[22] Their fears, which lack substance or any legal grounds, are that Mexico will claim these children as Mexican nationals and not allow them to return to Guatemala with their parents.

A crucial element of the new approach has been to recognize the legitimacy of the Permanent Commissions and to discuss and negotiate refugee policy issues with the Commissions' representatives, thus conferring on them the status of legitimate interlocutors.

If the new policy were to achieve success, it would lead to the creation of a firmer base for the refugees to remain in Mexico. However, since this is not at all the purpose of the Mexican government, the new program has been implemented with ambivalence and insufficient resources. In any event, if the refugees' situation improves as a result of this new policy, and if at the same time the situation in Guatemala continues to deteriorate, the repatriation process could diminish significantly.

There are nonetheless important obstacles to upgrading life in the camps. The most critical impediment is the lack of resources. COMAR has always had to operate largely on international, that is, UNHCR, resources. Given Mexico's economic situation and the multiplicity of social demands on the government, it is highly unlikely that the government will allocate significant funds for the refugees. UNHCR has confronted serious financial problems of its own since 1988. The 1988 budget of US$6 million for the Guatemalan refugees in Mexico (an amount insufficient to meet all the refugees' needs, much less to increase their productive capacity) was cut in 1989. This in turn resulted in deep cuts in COMAR's staff.

THE GENERAL SITUATION IN GUATEMALA

Almost all repatriations to date have been undertaken on an individual or family basis, against the judgment of the larger refugee community. The entire refugee community, including both refugees who decided to return and those who decided to remain in Mexico, had access to the same information about events in Guatemala upon which to base their decisions. Both groups prefer to use their own sources of information rather than trust versions of events disseminated in media reports or public statements, which they view as misinformation. The two refugee groups also receive news directly from visiting journalists, UNHCR officials, church representatives, and Mexican government authorities.

In addition to these "formal" communications, the refugees use "informal" communications through contacts with family members and friends in Guatemala. These communications can be in the form of audio cassette tapes passed from hand to hand or direct oral testimonies of refugees who travel back and forth to Guatemala. The refugees have used all available resources to develop these informal means of communication. In fact, one of the most persistent requests of Mexican and Guatemalan repatriation officials is the development of more expedient means of communication with family and friends. A private mail service has been established between Mexico and Guatemala using the personnel and transportation resources of COMAR and CEAR.

Individual mobility is also essential to the collection, dissemination, and exchange of information within and among the camps. Although they rarely discuss their movements with outsiders, it is widely believed that refugees travel secretly to Guatemala to take care of personal matters. A refugee's absence is concealed by the rest of the community and so is rarely noticed even by the authorities who maintain a daily presence in the camps.

In addition, since the formal repatriation process began, the refugees have insisted that their representatives be allowed freedom of movement to confer with refugees in other camps, to talk with national and international officials, and to see for themselves the conditions in Guatemala. They insist that the representatives be allowed to travel home under the sponsorship of the repatriation agencies, but without government escorts. When the representatives do return to Guatemala, they usually carry a full load of letters from fellow refugees. After three years of spontaneous and official repatriations, during which more than 5,000 refugees returned home, the Guatemalans in Mexico have well-established ways of learning about the experiences of those who have chosen to repatriate.

When the tripartite repatriation program was established, Guatemalan government officials visited the camps in Mexico and talked directly with the refugees. While such visits served obvious propaganda purposes, they nevertheless offered government officials and refugees the opportunity to meet each other face to face for the first time on neutral ground. As noted, in November 1986, the wife of President Cerezo, plus other members of the new regime, visited the camps. In March 1987, municipal and other departmental authorities from Huehuetenango went to the camps to report on conditions and to discuss the situation regarding land ownership in certain towns. In May 1987, for the first time a group of refugees made an official public visit to their country. Again in October 1989, refugees from Quintana Roo went to Guatemala with the specific objective of assessing the land situation in the cooperatives of Ixcán.

All these exchanges helped the refugees to evaluate conditions in their homeland. However, the encounters stirred up emotions on both sides and created controversy. In general, meetings between refugees and Cerezo administration officials have built very little trust. Refugee representatives have accused CEAR officials of deceit and manipulation, and CEAR officials have refused to recognize the Permanent Commissions as representatives of the community.

Security and land tenure are the two major concerns of returning refugees. Two aspects of the security situation are particularly worrisome to them: the prospect that on their return they could again become victims of military campaigns of the type that forced them into exile; and the control the army would have over their lives when they returned home.[23]

Both concerns relate to the overall counterinsurgency strategy of the Guatemalan army. The refugees demonstrate remarkable awareness of the basic mechanisms and logic of this strategy, and they clearly differentiate between its two facets; the implications of actual violence and those of military control. Thus, the refugees are not worried simply about the degree of physical violence they could encounter in Guatemala, but about the extent to which the counterinsurgency strategy of the army has become the institutional framework around which communities may organize and relate to one another and the state. In other words, the refugees see the presence of the army not only as an immediate physical threat to their existence, but also as the agent of bondage imposed upon them.

This distinction between actual military violence and military control explains why the majority of refugees have decided collectively not to repatriate, although some individual refugees have returned. The larger community has no guarantees that it will have an opportunity to resume community life upon return, much less fulfill any cultural or political aspirations. On the other hand, some individuals perceive an easing of the physical danger of being murdered and seriously consider going home.

Guatemalan Government Perceptions of the Refugees

Refugees in Mexico pay particular attention to three factors that serve as warning signals of what is really happening in Guatemala. First is the number of new refugees crossing the border and entering the camps; such flows have almost ceased since 1984. Second is the observation of Guatemalan army activities in the vicinity of the border.[24] Third, and at present the most significant factor, are accounts of specific experiences of repatriates.

According to most reports, the majority of the repatriates who have returned under the official program have not suffered serious human rights violations. Nonetheless, many refugees feel that they would be singled out for repression and harassment because of their social awareness and cohesion. Several concrete factors make the refugees particularly fearful of returning: government accusations that they are associated with the guerrillas, suspicions harbored by the local population in communities to which they wish to return, and land disputes with other *campesinos*.

The military and, to some extent, the civilian government of Guatemala view the refugees as guerrillas or at least as dangerous groups of people who have lived in Mexico under the influence of seditious ideas. Consequently, during the military regimes of Ríos Montt and Mejía Víctores, repatriation policy consisted of a series of amnesties offered to "terrorists." In May 1983, President Ríos Montt sent a message over the radio to the refugees in Chiapas: "To the guerrillas in Mexican territory—if within one month you do not return to apply for amnesty, we will go inside to get you."[25] For a long time the refugees saw the invitation to return as an ultimatum. Although the attitude that refugees were guerrillas has changed somewhat, refugees continue to be characterized in official Guatemalan circles as being closely associated with the insurgency.[26] A detailed study of Guatemala's repatriation policies prepared by the Guatemalan Church in Exile points out that the official view of the armed forces, even under President Cerezo, is that at least some of the refugees have rebel connections. President Cerezo himself once said that the refugees abroad have been fed with "permanent disinformation" by groups "interested in keeping them out of the country or very close to a political position against the democratic regime."[27]

Based on this perception, there is obviously a strong tendency within the military to see the repatriation as a security threat. A Guatemalan army officer assigned to Huehuetenango was quoted in 1987 as saying, "The increase in violence in Huehuetenango, where up to now most of the refugees have returned, has been explained by security experts as the result of the infiltration of guerrillas among the refugees.[28]

In a 1988 study of the Guatemalan repatriation process, Beatriz Manz quoted an army document which noted that in four municipalities in the department of Huehuetenango (Barillas, Nentón, Husta, and Jacatenango) the presence of repatriates coincided with increases in guerrilla activity. In that document refugees were described as people who have "Marxist-Leninist ideology," taught by the "Red Bishop," Samuel Ruiz García from San Cristóbal de las Casas. Those ideas, according to the document, were clearly manifested in "the degree of hate injected into the consciousness of children and youth against the security forces of the country."[29]

The fact that the Guatemalan military associates refugees with the guerrillas has serious consequences for the kinds of controls to which the refugees might be subjected upon their return. The association of refugees with the opposition also has a strong impact on the relationship between the returnees and the rest of the population. The experiences of a widow interviewed in a refugee camp in Chiapas serve as a representative account of repatriate life in Guatemala. This woman had returned to her village twice since 1987.

> *I went to Nentón to see the land my husband had cultivated before we came to Mexico as refugees. After I had spent ten days with my father, who is taking care of my husband's land, the military commander sent for me. He told me, "The situation in Barillas, where I wanted to visit relatives, is very dangerous because the refugees that have returned are fighting with the people. That is why we don't want the refugees to come back." At first, the people of my village were very happy to see me. But later they called a meeting and they told me never to come back because I was bringing trouble. When something happens, they blame the people that have returned. The military commissioner told me to leave and never come back because they would kill me. My brother also told me to leave.*

The experience of this woman shows how volatile the situation can be for returnees. [30]

Some repatriates have been detained or harassed by army authorities upon return. Many more returnees have been harassed by the civil patrols or military commissioners. There are even reports of some killings, such as the 1989 killing in Ixcán Quiché, supposedly by the army, of repatriate Juan Baltazar as he returned from a meeting of the National Reconciliation Commission in Guatemala City. In October 1989, the Guatemalan press reported that eleven repatriates had been killed in Ixcán, allegedly by the guerrillas. Eleven other returnees died in the cooperative of Xalbal, three in the Resurrection Cooperative, and one in Mayanda. Some of these killing may have been related to the bitter land disputes that took place between refugees and new settlers in the Ixcán region of northern Quiché.

The Land Issue, Cooperatives, and the Repatriation Process

As we have already seen, the dispute over land is the cornerstone of Guatemalan social history and the source of the most crucial struggles within the society. The landed aristocracy is the most powerful and influential economic group in the country, and their opposition to land reform is implacable. It is widely recognized by aid agencies and international organizations that Guatemala's land distribution is more unequal than in any other country in Central and South America. [31] This problem of unequal access to land is exacerbated by a variety of difficulties the refugees confront in attempting to regain control over the small plots of land they may have owned or worked cooperatively.

Many regions of the country have been placed off-limits by the army on the grounds that they are located in a highly disputed area where the guerrillas maintain a strong presence. The most notable of such areas include the northern part of the Quiché region known as the Ixil Triangle, sections of Ixcán in both Huehuetenango and Quiché, and parts of El Petén.[32]

Upon their return, many refugees are also likely to find that their land has been occupied by others, mostly internally displaced *campesinos*, but also army officers and large landholders. Some individuals took advantage of the refugee's absence, but many of the internally displaced people had little choice and were relocated to those lands by the army.

Of particular concern in this regard are those lands that were formed into cooperatives and that became the center of conflict in the 1960s. In 1965 the Catholic Diocese of Huehuetenango responded to the growing number of landless *campesinos* by obtaining authorization from the government to buy land and to promote rural cooperatives. These were established in the remote, rich, but unexplored tropical forest region of Ixcán in Huehuetenango and northern Quiché.

The cooperatives were highly successful in the production of traditional corn and rice crops as well as export crops such as citrus fruit, cacao, and coffee. Success led other landless *campesinos* to move to the area and form cooperatives. It also drew land speculators, ambitious army officers, and the former owners who wanted to retake the newly productive land. When the *campesinos* refused to sell the land, selective violence, followed by massive repression were used to gain control over the cooperatives. In 1982, the military launched a massive attack against the cooperatives, entailing aerial bombing raids, massacres, and destruction of houses and crops which forced the cooperative members to flee their homes.

As a result of this history, which includes some of the bloodiest massacres in the country, former cooperative members living in Mexico are reluctant to return to those areas where the army continues to maintain an overwhelming presence. On the other hand, they are under considerable pressure to rejoin the cooperatives or lose their right to the land. While CEAR has obtained a commitment from the Guatemalan Institute of Agrarian Transformation (INTA) to honor the cooperative rights of the refugees, CEAR is encouraging the refugees to return now or risk losing their membership.

Some refugees who have returned to either cooperatives or their own plots recovered the land with little difficulty. In some instances, the land had remained idle and abandoned due to the ongoing conflict. In other cases, the refugees had rented their land or left it in the care of friends and relatives. However, in still other cases, the occupiers of the land contended that they had acquired legal rights to it. Other areas were turned into development poles under the jurisdiction of the army.

Development poles and model villages were established by General Oscar Mejía Víctores in 1984 in an effort to secure absolute military, political, economic, cultural, and even religious control over restive rural populations in the conflictive areas. Development poles were also meant to establish control over refugees who returned home.

One of the original development poles was located at Chacaj in the municipality of Nentón, Huehuetenango, which was conceived mainly to serve refugees returning from Mexico. In the absence of sufficient numbers of returning refugees, the army has relocated there internally displaced people and given them possession of the refugees' land. The development pole of Playa Grande, Quiché, was to have absorbed both internally displaced people from the remote Ixcán areas and refugees who fled to the region of Márquez de Comillas, Chiapas. The pole of Chisec, Alta Verapaz, was created to receive people displaced within that same department, and the pole of Ixil, Quiché, was to serve the people who fled to the mountains in that part of the country. In some cases, the army has not only extended possession of these lands to the internally displaced, but also granted them titles of ownership.

Problems in recovering land are often exacerbated by the lack of legal documents to prove ownership, even though land may have been cultivated by a family for many generations. Many other refugees lost their titles during the conflict, or the public records in towns and municipalities, including those of communal lands, were destroyed. To make matters worse, a law that converts into state property all lands that were "voluntarily abandoned for more than one year with no justified cause" is being applied to the refugees. The refugees presented their own account of the difficulties they have confronted on their return to the National Reconciliation Commission created to comply with the provisions of Esquipulas II. Repatriated refugees from Ixcán and other parts of eastern Guatemala noted that the land question, and in particular the application of the "abandoned land" decree, was their major problem.[33]

THE REPATRIATION PROGRAM

The tripartite program of organized return offers only a modest amount of material assistance and a tenuous level of protection to returning refugees; even so, it represents an improvement over the previous situation. Even though spontaneous repatriation of Guatemalan refugees from camps in Mexico diminished after the initiation in 1987 of the official program, the total number of repatriates under the program has not been great. In general, the repatriation program only serves to facilitate the return of those individuals already inclined to go home and allows them to take advantage of the formal repatriation process rather than returning on their own.

By all accounts, the refugees in Mexico have no trust in the agencies of the Guatemalan government, whether military or civilian. This lack of trust is shared equally by both refugees who do not want to return as well as those who decide to repatriate. The establishment of the tripartite program helped to attenuate, but not alter, this basic distrust. Without the multinational dimension, a return program would not have attracted even the modest number of refugees now enrolled. Refugees already inclined to return can be more flexible in their contacts with the Guatemalan government, because the participation of UNHCR and, to a lesser extent, the involvement of Mexico, signify that they are not completely at the mercy of Guatemalan officials. Even though the refugees are aware of the limitations of UNHCR and other international organizations in providing them adequate assistance and protection, they feel that such a modest measure of protection is better than none at all.

To evaluate the program endorsed by COMAR, CEAR, and UNHCR in February 1987, it is important to compare objectives with actual results. The program is based on certain shared interests of its three sponsors. However, each sponsor has its own institutional objectives and its own views on the results that the program should deliver. Mexico's refugee policy and approach toward repatriation have already been addressed in this report, so this section will therefore concentrate on the positions of the Guatemalan government and UNHCR as well as the responses of the refugees to those positions.

There are two ways to look at the repatriation program: as an instrument for actively promoting return or as an instrument for assisting and protecting refugees who choose to return. It could be said that Guatemala sees the program in terms of actively promoting return in an effort to rebuild its international human rights image and to gain international legitimacy.

CEAR was originally created by Christian Democrat President Vinicio Cerezo as an instrument for reshaping the human rights image of his elected government. Its mandate is to "assist Guatemalan refugees, mainly those found in Mexican territory, in their return from abroad."[34] Existing data on repatriations indicate that CEAR was not created in response to repatriations already in progress, since the numbers were minimal at that time. Rather, CEAR was founded in order to encourage the repatriation process--a political objective of the Cerezo administration in order to support its claims to be genuinely respectful of human rights and concerned about the refugees' welfare. This objective was clearly stated in an official document:

> *With the change of political regime in the country in 1986, the government of the Republic of Guatemala expected the flow of repatriations to increase because of the environment of social and political tranquility created under the constitutional regime.*[35]

UNHCR's objectives were to assist refugees in their return and to facilitate and promote repatriation. However, since the security situation in Guatemala did not show a definite improvement with the Cerezo administration, the refugees were highly suspicious of anyone actively promoting their repatriation. Neither the Mexican government nor UNHCR could show that they were too eager to induce refugees to go back. In order not to undermine their own credibility, both COMAR and UNHCR distanced themselves from Cerezo's propaganda campaign to convince the refugees to return.

Conditions in Guatemala and the Promotion of Repatriation

Following its first two years of operation, during which official repatriations more than doubled, CEAR predicted that at least 6,000 refugees would return in 1989. Contrary to that prediction, by the end of 1989 no more than 900 people had repatriated, and the immense majority did so during the first semester. The total number of repatriates registered under the program—around 4,500 through the end of 1989—demonstrated that the tripartite program has not been as successful an instrument of return as expected by Guatemalan officials. Both UNHCR and CEAR acknowledge that repatriations have decreased substantially in 1990, if not ceased altogether.

Two major factors help to explain this decline. One is the sharp decline in expectations of the refugees, given the disappointing performance of Cerezo's administration in both economic and political areas. The other is the reappearance of incidents of political violence

in Guatemala. A third, though less critical factor, is the limited
capacity of the repatriation program itself.

Economic and Political Situation Under President Cerezo

The economic and political situation in Guatemala continued to
deteriorate as the Cerezo administration entered its final phase.
Growing inflation, economic stagnation, the reappearance of visible
guerrilla activities close to urban centers, and the proximity of the
presidential elections were all factors contributing to the reemergence
of acute social and political tensions in Guatemala.

In 1986, the Christian Democrat government inherited a country
already in serious economic decline. According to Cerezo's own
estimates, by that year capital flight had depleted the economy by two
billion dollars.[36] Armed with a strong popular mandate and challenged
by high public expectations, Cerezo implemented several economic
plans: the Economic Reorganization Plan of June 1986, the National
Reorganization Plan of July 1987, the Guatemala 2000 Export Plan of
the summer of 1988, and the 500 Day Plan of August 1989. The main
objectives of the administration's economic policy were to control
inflation and cut the fiscal deficit, while attempting at the same time to
increase salaries, stimulate employment, build up the infrastructure,
and expand social services for the poor.

These economic plans were given a boost by the renewal of
capital inflows, consisting mainly of foreign loans and donations by
various governments and international organizations to the new
democratic government. During the first three years of Cerezo's
tenure, the economic program yielded modest results. The Gross
National Product grew by between 2.5 and 3.5 percent, at approximately
the same rate as the 3 percent growth in population. In spite of this
progress, no perceptible social gains were achieved, income distribution
worsened, and social welfare programs steadily deteriorated.

Open and disguised unemployment continues to affect 45 percent
of the population, real incomes have fallen 60 percent since 1980, and
50 percent of the population is completely illiterate, and another 25
percent is functionally illiterate. According to the Ministry of Public
Health, 98 percent of the hospitals around the country are unable to
meet the demand for health services in their communities. Inflation
undermines the purchasing power of the people, especially in such
sensitive areas as basic nutrition and medical care. The economic crisis
has severely damaged the government's standing with its own
constituency. Moreover, President Cerezo has been accused of
corruption and of personal irresponsibility.

The major obstacles to the success of President Cerezo's reformist social program have been the concentration of wealth and the entrenched resistance of the local oligarchies to meaningful social and economic reform. Cerezo constantly faced the threat of military coups from the extreme right. He held on to power by forfeiting his social program and accepting the effective military control of the political system.

Human Rights Situation Under President Cerezo

Despite an initial decline in the level of human rights abuse, President Cerezo has not been able to eradicate political violence and repression. Particularly controversial and critical to the prestige of the government are the unfulfilled demands of the families of thousands of persons who disappeared during the previous military regimes. The families of the missing persons formed the internationally renowned Group of Mutual Support (GAM). They demanded an investigation into the disappearances and exposed the existence of at least 100 clandestine cemeteries in the department of El Quiché alone. Not only have GAM's pleas for justice been ignored by the Christian Democrat government, but since 1989 many prominent members of the organization have been killed. Frustrated with Cerezo, GAM decided to take its case against the government of Guatemala to the Inter-American Court of Justice of the Organization of American States (OAS).

The human rights situation in Guatemala has deteriorated steadily since the fall of 1989, to the point that some observers compare the current situation with the high levels of repression experienced during the former military regimes. Highly visible political murders include the assassinations in August 1989 of the respected Christian Democrat leader Danilo Barilles, who was critical of the government, and of progressive businessman Ramiro Castillo Love. In November 1989, a group of students were abducted from the University of San Carlos and assassinated. These are clear indications that the horrors of the past are not yet over. The refugees are fully aware of the deteriorating political and economic environment in Guatemala.

Limitations of the Repatriation Program

Also contributing to the decline in the number of repatriations is the fact that CEAR created expectations that it could not fulfill. The political role assumed by the organization, in convincing the refugees that they could safely return, led CEAR to impose impossible standards upon itself.

In general, CEAR's work in assisting the repatriates has been positive. Throughout its history, Guatemala has never created a welfare system. The concentration of government finances in military expenditures and the country's very slim tax base reflect the control of an oligarchy ever alert to any attempt at redistributing wealth. Consequently, the Guatemalan bureaucracy has virtually no experience with social development programs. CEAR is one of the few, and in many places the only, public agency working directly with the poor.

Carmen Rosa de León, the director of CEAR since its creation, shows a genuine concern for the well-being of the returnees. Agency staff include several highly motivated individuals who are truly committed to assisting the refugees. However, the director and agency personnel as a whole are strongly conditioned by the traditional political processes of the country and are sensitive to the concerns of military and security officials regarding the repatriation issue. Bureaucratic quarrels, interagency rivalries, administrative deficiencies, budgetary constraints, staff limitations, and lack of experience all undercut the quality of CEAR's performance.

CEAR operates with a small staff of no more than 50 field officers. They work mainly at the headquarters office in Guatemala City and at the main branch offices in Huehuetenango and Quiché (Ixcán). CEAR's operating budget comes mostly from UNHCR. The food program is supported by the European Economic Community, working through UNHCR.

At the reception center of Huehuetenango, the refugees receive their identity documents and get medical check ups. They are then transported, along with their belongings, to the town or village of their choice. CEAR provides the returnees basic food supplies, some essential tools and building materials to construct simple houses, and seeds for the first harvest. CEAR personnel present the returnees to the local authorities and help them comply with the bureaucratic procedures necessary to regularize their status in Guatemala. It is also within the mandate of CEAR to participate with other agencies in the delivery of health education and other social programs and to assist in the construction of basic services such as schools, water supplies, drainage systems, and electricity for communities hosting returning refugees and internally displaced persons.

Many repatriates complain about delays in food deliveries and about the lack of sustained attention to their needs. This is often the consequence of the lack of staff experience, scarcity of resources, and the virtual lack of communication with the communities where the returnees live. Carmen Rosa de León admits that, even with the far fewer number of repatriates than expected, CEAR is overcommitted. Refugees in Mexico as well as some repatriates have publicly accused CEAR of having lied to them by painting a rosy, unrealistic picture of the situation in Guatemala.

A group of repatriates from the Ixcán region and from the eastern part of the country presented a document to the National Reconciliation Commission denouncing what they called the "legal, moral, and social" problems they face. They accused Guatemalan authorities of "deceit," regarding comments about the availability of land and about the social and economic conditions of the repatriates. They noted that "many of the repatriates are thinking about returning to refugee status." According to the authors of this document, CEAR has a "political character" that contradicts its humanitarian mandate. The repatriates demanded that the government either improve the quality of CEAR's work or allow it to be replaced by a nongovernmental organization.

The appearance of this document created a bitter controversy. The Guatemalan government challenged its authenticity and alleged that the opinions did not represent the genuine views of the refugees. CEAR prepared an alternate text allegedly written by the so-called "Commission of Delegates, Representatives of Repatriates and Communities Affected by the Violence." This alternate statement, which expressed praise and "gratitude" to CEAR, was presented to the National Reconciliation Commission as the "official view of the repatriates." The other, critical document was not admitted. This incident contributed to the climate of distrust and recrimination between the refugees and the government.

The Military Dimension of the Repatriation Process

One of the most controversial issues between CEAR and the refugees is the question of land. During the November 1986 visit of President Cerezo's wife, Raquel Blandón, to the refugee camps in Mexico, Carmen Rosa de León stated that the refugees' land had not been taken over by others. Further, she promised land to landless refugees. It turned out, however, that the National Institute of Agrarian Transformation (INTA) and army officers had redistributed many parcels of land that belonged to refugees.

CEAR has consistently sided with the repatriates in the often bitter land disputes, although with insufficient energy. INTA and the army have tended to favor the new settlers over the refugees. So far, the most serious confrontations between repatriates and new settlers have reportedly taken place in areas such as Nentón, Huehuetenango, and Ixcán, Quiché, where the majority of the refugees still in Mexico had their homes and parcels of land or were members of cooperatives. In order to solve this problem and avoid future conflicts, CEAR officials say they are working hard to purchase or otherwise acquire new land from the government in Nentón, Barillas, Chisec, and Ixcán.

The most obstinate limitation to CEAR's effectiveness is its relationship with the armed forces. The government of Guatemala made a commitment to UNHCR and Mexico when signing the tripartite agreement to demilitarize the process of repatriation. However, in order to gain the approval of the military, the civilian authorities had to assure them that nothing in the agreement contradicted their interests and authority. As a result, the text of the agreement is insufficiently explicit regarding the role of the armed forces in the repatriation process. The document states,

> *For the purpose of their identification, protection, and security, the repatriates will receive a certificate of repatriation issued by the civilian and military authorities. Amnesty will only be given to those who request it voluntarily. As applicable legal and administrative statutes establish, the participation of the refugees in the civil defense patrols will be voluntary.*

This provision of the agreement meant that, contrary to previous military practices, refugees joining the repatriation program did not have to sign amnesty papers, drafted in such a way that the beneficiary would automatically "confess" his or her affiliation with the insurgency. It was also understood to mean that the army should not be directly involved in the process of providing documentation to returning refugees. It was further expected that refugees would not be placed directly or indirectly under the control of military authority. On the basis of this agreement, CEAR was created as a civilian structure responsible for the security and well-being of the repatriates.

In reality, amnesty is still a public law, allegedly only to be applied in a few isolated cases. Refugees are, in fact, no longer forced to settle in model villages, but instead are taken to wherever they request. However, many of the towns and villages where they came from and want to return are under direct military control or have even become model villages.

In any event, the army is still very much involved in the repatriation process, and its decisions usually prevail. The Ministry of Defense is formally a member of the Tripartite Commission and is regularly represented in the Commission's deliberations by the Under Secretary of Defense. Military personnel are present at the reception of repatriating refugees, although maintaining a discreet distance from the proceedings. They do, however, participate actively in the documentation process in Huehuetenango. In fact, the repatriation certificate is filled out, signed, and extended to the refugee, not by a CEAR official, but an army officer. CEAR fully takes charge of the remainder of the repatriation process, providing assistance and protection until the end of one year, when the returnee is expected to become self-sufficient.

While there is no conclusive evidence, it is possible that the involvement of the military in the repatriation process serves as an incentive for some refugees to return spontaneously to Guatemala. Whether or not a refugee uses official return channels, all repatriates wishing to recover their land or to return to their home communities eventually have to be placed under the supervision of a military authority. However, by returning spontaneously, refugees have a better chance of avoiding, or at least minimizing, military control while choosing where they want to settle and under what circumstances they join the official program to obtain material assistance.

The typical process by which families repatriate in stages would be, first, for the head of the family or another member to return spontaneously to Guatemala to explore the situation and prepare for the arrival of the family. Once acceptable security and economic conditions are assured, the individual goes back to Mexico to enroll in the official program with the rest of the family. Alternatively, the refugee could remain in Guatemala, while the family joins an official repatriation contingent. In the latter case, the "scout" registers as a repatriate with CEAR once the family is reunited. In that way, he or she could even evade military interrogation, since such a procedure would only take place at the reception center in Huehuetenango.

NGOs, the Guatemalan Catholic Church, and Repatriation

There is little collaboration between CEAR and NGOs in Guatemala, due to mutual suspicions and disagreements over the use and distribution of resources. Furthermore, the activities of NGOs in the Guatemalan countryside are tightly controlled by the military. In spite of these difficulties, some European relief agencies have managed to establish a workable relationship with CEAR. This is particularly the case with Médecins Sans Frontières (Doctors Without Borders), whose dedicated services reach communities even in the most inaccessible and conflictive parts of the country, such as Quiché and Huehuetenango.

As in Mexico, the Catholic Church is the only national nongovernmental organization capable of influencing the country's behavior towards the refugees and of providing assistance and protection. The Church speaks out on behalf of the refugees, supports their claims, and provides institutional backing to refugee representatives visiting Guatemala. As an institution, however, the Church in Guatemala has not taken a very active role in assisting returning refuges, and it has specifically refused to participate in the repatriation process.

This stance has its antecedents in the historical relationship between the well entrenched conservative leaders of the Church in Guatemala and the ruling oligarchy. The Guatemalan Church never fully adopted the social interpretation of the gospel which emerged from the 1968 Latin American Bishops Conferences held in Medellin and later in Puebla. However, as occurred elsewhere in Central America, the Church did embrace some progressive positions, linking its spiritual and religious mission with the promotion of necessary social changes.

It was the impact of liberation theology and the establishment of many Christian Base Communities during the 1970s that created immense pressures on the Church hierarchy to demonstrate its concern for the poor. Military repression against the Christian Base Communities that resulted in the murder of at least 14 priests and forced the clergy of El Quiché to abandon completely the Diocese and found abroad the Guatemalan Catholic Church in Exile compelled the hierarchy to denounce official violence. Bitter competition with the evangelical churches for the minds and souls of the indigenous Guatemalans and *campesinos* contributed to a more assertive role by the Church.

One example of the Church's stance against social injustice is the letter "The Clamor for Land," issued by the Guatemalan bishops in February 1986. In this document, the bishops denounce the "obsolete and sinful social structures" which compel the majority of Guatemalans to live in inhuman poverty. The letter called for changes in legislation to guarantee small property rights, fair crop prices, access to credit and technical assistance, and minimum salaries for agricultural workers. The letter was a clear departure from the traditional Church position on the issue of land, as expressed in a 1954 Pastoral Letter which denounced the agrarian reform program of President Jacobo Arbenz as anti-Christian.[37] Even though it did not call for radical agrarian reform, "The Clamor for Land" provoked a bitter conservative debate in the country.[38]

The Church's role in promoting peace was seen in its efforts to encourage direct negotiations between the government and the insurgents and in the participation of Monsignor Prospero Penados, the Archbishop of Guatemala, as president of the National Reconciliation Commission, an institution established under the Esquipulas II Peace Agreement of 1987.

In March 1983, Guatemalan Bishops for the first time acknowledged the existence of at least 200,000 refugees abroad as a result of the violence in the country. Again in June 1984, in the "Collective Letter to Build Peace," the bishops denounced the displacement of families in internal and external exile. The issue of repatriation was first addressed by Monsignor Penados in 1985, when he said the Church was opposed to the forced resettlement of returnees in military-controlled development poles and model villages. He further cited the refusal of the government to allow the refugees to return freely to their own communities and land as the reason why so few refugees had decided to repatriate.[39]

The Church's position on repatriation came about in part as a result of contacts between the Diocese of San Cristóbal de las Casas and the Guatemalan bishops. Both the Chiapas and the Guatemalan churches were particularly concerned about the fate of spontaneous repatriates placed under strict military control. Some were believed to have been murdered or disappeared. Furthermore, the military government of Guatemala was exercising pressure on some bishops to support a repatriation program based on amnesty and the creation of model villages.

These pressures on the Church to participate in the government's repatriation campaign greatly increased after President Vinicio Cerezo took office in 1986. The participation of the Church in the repatriation program was considered by the Christian Democrat government not only as a crucial political and moral endorsement of its human rights policy, but also as a very valuable source of material and logistical assistance. However, speaking on Vatican Radio prior to Cerezo's first state visit to Mexico in July 1986, Monsignor Penados reiterated that the refugees should be allowed to return wherever they chose. Furthermore, Monsignor Juan Geradi, the Vatican Envoy to Guatemala, stated that conditions in Guatemala were not conducive to the safe and orderly return of the refugees.[40]

The position of the Church on the issue of participation in the return program is particularly delicate. The Guatemalan bishops, especially those in direct contact with the resettlement areas of Huehuetenango and Quiché, are fully aware of the military dimensions of the repatriation program and do not want the Church to be party to a government program strongly influenced by security considerations. They feel that their participation would be distorted to support government objectives, thus seriously jeopardizing their credibility and independence. Given the disastrous social and economic conditions in Guatemala, particularly in areas hosting returnees, the Church is severely limited in its ability to mobilize resources in favor of a single target group.

On the other hand, Catholic leaders realize that the role of the Church in providing material and moral assistance to returning refugees could be crucial. In any event, thus far the decision of the Church has been to refuse to participate in the tripartite program and instead to concentrate their resources on assisting internally displaced people to rebuild their communities. It is in those communities that receive both internally displaced people and returning refugees where Church social workers come into direct contact with repatriates and provide them assistance.

The Role of UNHCR in Guatemala

The support of UNHCR and the physical presence in Guatemala of its personnel are very important to the repatriation process. Until President Cerezo's assumption of power in 1986, relations between the international refugee agency and the Guatemalan government were very tense. In November 1984, General Mejía Víctores even denied entry visas to a UNHCR mission seeking to visit a group of repatriates.

Under the tripartite agreement and separate accords signed in 1987, President's Cerezo's administration allowed UNHCR to establish an office in the country. International refugee officials accredited to the government can move freely around the country and are allowed to observe the entire repatriation process. While UNHCR does not have the means to deter military and paramilitary abuses, its presence makes a difference.

Travelling in a vehicle with a highly visible UNHCR emblem, the author of this report and two CEAR field officers were stopped by soldiers in Nentón and asked at gunpoint to step out of the car while they searched the vehicle. This small incident illustrates how irrelevant UNHCR presence can be in some circumstances. At the same time, however, a few weeks earlier a UNHCR officer in Chacaj interceded on

behalf of a repatriate accused by civil patrolmen of collaborating with
the guerrillas. The returnee was released unharmed, and UNHCR and
CEAR continue to monitor his case. As was the case in Mexico,
UNHCR often bends over backwards to avoid offending the host
government and quietly tolerates abuses against refugees and
repatriates under its protection.

CONCLUSIONS AND RECOMMENDATIONS

Over the years the Mexico-Guatemala border has developed into
an active crossing point and a place where not only people from these
two countries interact, but people from all over Central America as
well. Violence, repression, social upheaval, and economic necessity
have forced through this gateway the most dynamic stream of migrants
in the Hemisphere and one of the most significant movements of people
in the world. The political situation in Guatemala is especially
influential in shaping the environment of that border region.

Traditionally, migration between Mexico and Guatemala
consisted mostly of people seeking seasonal agricultural employment in
Mexico or better economic opportunities in the United States. Today,
the economic and social exodus can not be clearly differentiated from
the political exodus. In accordance with the United Nations concept of
a refugee and the description recently incorporated into Mexican law,
this border is truly a region of refugees.

During the past decade hundreds of thousands of people have
crossed the border, but few of them have been recognized as refugees,
either in Mexico or in the United States, which is the ultimate
destination of many. Only a relatively small proportion of the refugees
remain in the region, waiting for the opportunity to return home.

This is particularly the case with the Guatemalan *campesinos* and
indigenous peoples who entered Mexico between 1980 and 1984
escaping widespread persecution. With the help of Mexican
campesinos and the Catholic Church, they settled collectively in refugee
camps, which were eventually placed under the official protection of
UNHCR and the government of Mexico. Most of these official refugees
have no intention of remaining permanently in Mexico. However, it has
been almost a decade since the first group arrived. The immense
majority continues to feel that their "lives, security, and freedom" are
threatened; and they are "unwilling to avail themselves of the protection

of their country" (cf. 1951 Convention and 1967 Protocol Relating to the Status of Refugees). Evidence presented in this report demonstrates that less than 15 percent of the original refugee population has returned to Guatemala, either as spontaneous repatriates or as part of the official repatriation program. The creation of an official program designed to promote and assist refugees on their return has reduced the incidence of spontaneous repatriations and created a preference for organized returns among those willing to repatriate. However, the program has not encouraged the majority to return to Guatemala.

Despite all the difficulties encountered by returnees, individual and family repatriations have become a steady, though slender, stream. However, the majority of refugees has decided not to return through this piecemeal process. Curiously enough, the birth rate in the refugee camps has compensated for the reduction of the population resulting from repatriations. Today the total number of refugees registered by UNHCR and the Mexican government is almost identical to the 46,000 counted in 1984.

Throughout their years in Mexico, the refugees have suffered arduous economic deprivation. Some have been forced to relocate away from the border to strange, inhospitable regions with no economic opportunities. To avoid relocation, others have dispersed in the jungle, and many have openly resisted relocation and consequently often suffered harsh treatment at the hands of Mexican authorities.

This has also been a period of time during which important changes have occurred in Guatemala, including a new democratically elected government which claims that the refugees will be safe in their country and encourages them to return. In spite of all enticements to return and the fact that the Mexican government prefers that they go home, most of the refugees maintain a firm determination not to repatriate at this time. They are convinced that if they go back, not only will they face great dangers to their personal security, but also their communities and culture will be destroyed.

In a series of communiqués, the refugees in Mexico have stated that they want to return, but only after certain basic conditions have been met. These include assurances that they will not be placed under military control and that they will be able to reclaim their communal, private, or cooperative lands. They also demand the unequivocal recognition by the Guatemalan government of all their rights as distinctive cultures and communities. The refugees do not feel that these conditions have been met. Thus, they are unwilling to repatriate, a position that has been firmly reiterated by the refugees and their elected representatives for a long time. At the same time, most refugees have not given up the hope that one day the Guatemalan social order will be radically transformed so that they can return to a new life of dignity, freedom, and opportunity.

Carmen Rosa de León, head of CEAR, stated on August 12, 1990, on Mexican government television, that the issue of repatriation had to be continuously analyzed and explored. However, she noted, that the time has come to start thinking about the possibility of the refugees' permanent assimilation into the host country. She acknowledged that most refugees do not have sufficient confidence to return, and she implicitly recognized, that President Cerezo's repatriation program failed to provide that confidence.

It is possible that some of the refugees might decide to settle permanently in Mexico in the future, paticularly those who have developed kinship ties with local Mexicans. According to an estimate made by Church workers at an early stage of the refugee influx, around 33 percent of the refugees had relatives in Mexico prior to their entry. Despite culturally based resistance, marriages between Guatemalan refugees and Mexican citizens are no longer a rare event. It is likely that those mixed families will remain in Mexico.

The following observations and recommendations are offered regarding how the process of repatriation of Guatemalan refugees should be addressed by the international community. These observations and recommendations are based on the experiences of refugees who have already repatriated, spontaneously or officially, on an analysis of the situations in Guatemala and Mexico, and on the views of the various actors involved in the refugee program. These recommendations are addressed to the affected governments, UNHCR, and in particular to nongovernmental organizations wishing to dedicate resources to the repatriation effort.

It is clear that a spontaneous repatriation does not ensure the refugee's minimum protection needs, much less his or her requirements for material support. However, the official repatriation program is not a sufficient alternative, even though it does serve as a realistic option for those refugees wishing to return.

The refugees have proven that they are capable of collecting and evaluating on their own all information needed to decide if they should return. There is very little guidance or information that any organization can provide the refugees that is more relevant than the information they already have. Therefore, specific information should be offered only at their request.

The fact that the return program is almost exclusively the responsibility of the two affected governments and has the support and blessing of the official international refugee agency constitutes both the program's weakness and its strength. It is its strength in that exclusive official involvement creates at least some degree of official accountability for the fate of the refugees. It also makes the process and the participants in it more visible and identifiable. It is a weakness in that the absence of NGOs allows military and national security considerations to predominate. The lack of NGO participation also results in the provision of insufficient and poorly distributed material support.

However, the basic nature and character of the official repatriation program should not be changed. Human rights organizations and other NGOs should scrutinize more carefully the repatriation process within the current framework in order to help the Guatemalan government to identify and correct the program's deficiencies. A special effort should be made to ensure that the Guatemalan government comply with the spirit of the tripartite accord in its call for no military involvement in the repatriation process.

Ensuring compliance with the tripartite agreement should have been the task of UNHCR. However, experiences in both Mexico and Guatemala demonstrate that UNHCR officials are especially sensitive about their relationship with the host government and that they often give highest priority to maintaining it. UNHCR officials tend to avoid conflict with local officials, even when that means tolerating measures clearly hostile to the refugees. NGOs could fill the gap by collaborating more actively in overseeing compliance with all repatriation program commitments and international norms. Beyond these efforts, it would be difficult to ensure the participation of NGOs in the official repatriation process because of the resistance and suspicion displayed by the Mexican and especially the Guatemalan governments toward NGO collaboration. A more useful course for NGOs would be to leave the repatriation process itself to the governments and to define clearly other related areas in which the presence of NGOs would make a difference. COMAR, CEAR, and UNHCR should continue to be directly responsible for the task of bringing refugees from Mexico to the villages in Guatemala of their choice. The role of the NGOs should be to strengthen the ability of refugees to support themselves, whether in Mexico or in Guatemala. This should be done taking the following criteria into consideration:

A. The experiences endured by the refugees have made them particularly receptive to the acquisition of new skills and a better understanding of the world around them. Their communities are highly motivated and eager to institute improvements in such areas as health, education, nutrition, and housing. This receptivity to change could erode with time in Mexico, or it could be completely lost once the refugees return to Guatemala. Therefore, NGOs should concentrate their efforts on providing the refugees with technical, administrative, organizational, and productive skills, which will help them to strengthen their communities and achieve viable local economies.

  B. Economic and social development assistance from NGOs should be provided outside of government programs, yet in a way that is parallel and complements government-sponsored projects.

  C. Support for refugees in the camps in Mexico should be viewed as an essential part of the larger task of integrating the refugees into a better life in Guatemala. NGOs should develop parallel programs in Mexico and Guatemala, not with the immediate objective of inducing refugees to return, but rather with the idea of making the economic environments in both countries more conducive to a participatory economic and social development strategy.

  D. The resources devoted to these development projects should be modest in order to avoid the false impression that conditions of scarcity could easily be reversed. The overall objectives should also be modest, concrete, and immediate. Refugees should be aware at all times that the greatest challenge they face is recovering the ability to sustain their families and communities through their own work and with resources they themselves can mobilize.

  E. Whether or not they return home, many of the refugees will not have land available to them and will have to look for other means of survival. NGOs should help them to identify those opportunities without uprooting the refugees from their communities. This work should serve to strengthen the local economy.

  F. It is absolutely essential that the refugees acquire the skills and confidence necessary to succeed upon return to Guatemala.

REFERENCES

[1]In preparing this report, I interviewed government officials in Mexico and Guatemala, officials of the United Nations High Commissioner for Refugees (UNHCR), representatives of the Catholic Church and other nongovernmental organizations, researchers, journalists, academics, refugees, and repatriates. The interviews were conducted in Mexico City, the Mexican state of Chiapas, Guatemala City, and the Guatemalan departments of Huehuetenango and Quiché, between August and December 1989. This report does not reflect changes which may have occurred later during the Administration of President Serrano.

Substantial information was also gathered from the archives of UNHCR-Guatemala, UNHCR-Mexico, the Mexican Commission for Refugee Assistance (COMAR), the Guatemalan Special Commission for the Assistance of Repatriated and Displaced Persons (CEAR), the Conference of Guatemalan Religious Persons (COFREGUA), the Secretariat for the Assistance of Guatemalan Refugees (SARG), which is now an independent agency originally created by the Catholic Church in Mexico City, and from my own collection of documents.

I wish to express my gratitude to the individuals of the aforementioned institutions whose assistance and advice were essential to the preparation of this report. Leticia Deschamps, who helped with the collection of documents and the analysis of data, deserves special recognition.

[2]Edelberto Torres-Rivas, **Report on the Condition of Central American Refugees and Migrants** (Washington, D.C.: Hemispheric Migration Project, Center for Immigration and Refugee Assistance, Georgetown University, July 1985), 4.

[3]Thomas and Marjorie Melville, **Tierra y Poder en Guatemala** (San José, Costa Rica: Editorial Universitaria Centroamericana, Segunda edición, 1982), 292-304.

[4]**Centro América en Gráficas** (San José, Costa Rica: IICA-FLACSO, 1990), 59, 73.

[5]This pattern of human rights abuse has been amply documented over the years by researchers and human rights organizations. Beatriz Manz is the scholar who has done the best research and analysis of the Guatemalan refugees and their experiences. See Beatriz Manz, **Refugees of a Hidden War: The Aftermath of Counterinsurgency in Guatemala** (Albany: SUNY Press, 1988). See also Beatriz Manz, **Repatriation and Reintegration: An Arduous Process in Guatemala** (Washington, D.C.: Hemispheric Migration Project, Center for Immigration Policy and Refugee Assistance, Georgetown University, 1988). In 1982, four months after General Efraín Ríos Montt assumed office and before the climax of repression had been reached, Amnesty International published evidence of sixty-nine massacres of civilians. See Amnesty International, **Guatemala: Massive Extrajudicial Executions in Rural Areas Under the Government of General Efraín Ríos Montt**, July 1982. By January 1984, Americas Watch had produced three reports with accounts and eye witness testimonies of many more instances of massive violence against civilians. See Americas Watch, **Human Rights in Guatemala: No Neutrals Allowed** (New York and Washington, D.C., November 1982); **Creating a Desolation and Calling it Peace**, May 1983; and **Guatemala: A Nation of Prisoners**, January 1984.

[6]Such protection is extended on a case-by-case basis by immigration officials once the petitioner arrives in Mexico (territorial asylum) or by Mexican diplomats in the individual's country of origin (diplomatic asylum). Mexican authorities can restrict the asylee's freedom of movement and determine his or her place of residence. Asylum is relinquished when the individual leaves the country without a special permit. See General Population Law of 1974 and the Regulations to the General Population Law as amended in 1990.

[7]Luis Raúl Salvadó, **The Other Refugees: A Study of Nonrecognized Guatemalan Refugees in Chiapas, Mexico** (Washington, D.C.: Hemispheric Migration Project, Center for Immigration Policy and Refugee Assistance, Georgetown University, 1988).

[8]See Mexican Population Law, Article 42, Section VI.

[9]Since the first groups of refugees arrived in Mexico, Guatemalan military authorities have alleged that guerrillas were either moving or chasing people across

the border to establish hideouts for the insurgents which were disguised as refugee camps in Mexico. In March 1987 General Gramajo Morales, then Minister of Defense, was quoted as saying, "The return of the refugees could bring to the country and especially to the government a series of problems from family matters to guerrilla infiltration." See Centro de Documentación de la URNG, **Cuatro Años de Gobierno Democristiano** (Guatemala, January 1990), 51. These allegations are discussed in greater detail later in this report.

[10]COMAR lists all returnees, after the establishment of the Tripartite Commission, as official repatriates. Mexican officials acknowledge that statistics on repatriation compiled by COMAR before the establishment of the Tripartite Commission in 1987 are impressionistic and incomplete. They believe that a number of official refugees who were not accounted for have either dispersed inside Mexico or gone to the United States or Canada in search of work.

[11]CEAR began compiling data on repatriation in 1987, but it incorporates information on returnees prior to that date if they can prove residence in a refugee camp in Mexico. This is not a difficult requirement, since Mexican authorities maintain records on most of the refugee camp inhabitants.

[12]Despite discrepancies among the three sources of information, the data nonetheless provide a general sense of the magnitude of the repatriation phenomenon. Although the UNHCR-Guatemala list does not qualify as an official document, it will be used in this report since it offers much more information about the refugees than other available sources. The listing consists of the following information: first name and two last names of the head of the family, number of dependents, date of entry to Guatemala, place of residence in Guatemala by municipality and village or town, and repatriation number. Only those refugees who participated in the official return program and were processed at the Huehuetenango center were assigned numbers. Thus, those refugees who were not assigned a number are considered to be spontaneous repatriates.

[13]Gender was inferred by the given name of the head of family on the UNHCR-Guatemala list.

[14]This number represents the difference between the 46,000 refugees officially recognized by the Mexican government in 1984 and the COMAR figure of 36,677 refugees living in the Mexican camps in 1986, with an assumption that some 2,000 refugees went elsewhere within Mexico. (The 1986 camp population is contained in UNHCR and UNDP, International Conference on Central American Refugees [CIREFCA], **Diagnóstico, Estrategia y Propuestas de Proyecto: Documento de la República de Guatemala** [Guatemala, March 1989, 11]). While not strongly disputed by Mexican officials, the 7,000 figure may be distorted as a result of Mexican government miscalculations of the actual number of refugees in the camps before and after the relocation.

The estimated 2,000 other refugees are believed to have dispersed at the time of the relocation to find other living arrangements within Mexico. For example, around 900 refugees hid for years in the Lacandón jungles in extremely precarious conditions, and, according to Mexican officials, are now being transferred by their own request to Quintana Roo. Some of those who remained in Chiapas on their own may have left the country later, tired of hiding from Mexican immigration authorities and exhausted by their harsh economic conditions.

[15]Melville and Melville, **Tierra y Poder**, 43.

[16]The stated position of the Permanent Commissions appears to represent the views of the majority of the refugees in Mexico. While some refugees interviewed in camps in Chiapas did express privately that they have not returned because of peer pressure, they are clearly in the minority. Those refugees who wish

to return come under considerable pressure not to break with the collective decision to remain in Mexico. They are seen by other refugees as "disloyal" and as indirectly supportive of the government propaganda campaign proclaiming the advent in Guatemala of democratic change, peace, and security.

This peer pressure weighs heavily not only on the decision whether or not to return individually but also on the decision concerning the method of return. Refugees often do not notify UNHCR and COMAR that they intend to repatriate, because such an announcement has to be formalized on a repatriation form signed in front of authorities by each individual family member. The refugees must then wait until a group is formed, a process which could take several weeks. In order to avoid conflict with the community, the refugees may pack up and leave on their own.

[17]Primary education is provided by Guatemalan and Mexican teachers in both Spanish and indigenous languages. Infant mortality has sharply declined, and some diseases endemic to the area have been brought under control.

[18]In February 1982 the five Bishops of San Cristóbal, Tapachula, Oxaca, Huautla, and Tehuantepec issued a joint communiqué that stated, "The Church assumes the defense of the human rights [of the refugees] and expresses its solidarity to all who advance them." Again in 1984, following several attacks on refugee camps by Guatemalan troops and the decision of the Mexican government to relocate the refugees outside Chiapas, the five bishops issued a second statement defending the human rights of the Guatemalans.

[19]Responding to government accusations that he opposed the relocation because he wanted to keep the refugees in Chiapas for political reasons, and under heavy pressure from the conservative Church hierarchy to endorse the relocation, in 1985 Bishop Samuel Ruiz stated, "The Diocese has no right to decide in the name of the refugees those issues that concern them. . . They will have to suffer themselves the direct consequences of the relocation outside Chiapas or if they wish to remain in this state of the Republic, therefore, it is they who have to decide and ponder this issue... We recognize the right of the government to decide the most convenient location for the refugees, but this right is conditioned by respect for the human rights of the refugees as persons. . . The Church rejects any violent measure taken against the refugees and will denounce serious violations of their human rights (Christian Coordinator of Aid to Guatemalan Refugees, **Boletín**, May-July 1985, 5-10).

[20]Americas Watch, **A Nation of Prisoners**, 50.

[21]Christian Coordinator, **Boletín**, No. 16, August 1987, 19.

[22]COMAR estimates that 10,563 children (around 26 percent of the current refugee population) were born in Mexico. Most of them have already received their Mexican birth certificates.

[23]These concerns have been well documented in reports by human rights and academic organizations as well as through interviews with UNHCR officials, NGO representatives, refugees, and repatriates.

[24]Refugees are often disturbed by the heavy presence of Guatemalan army troops, shooting and shelling from the other side of the border. In February 1988, Chiapas camp representatives publicly denounced the fact that since September of 1987, they had witnessed indiscriminate bombings taking place in northern Quiché and Huehuetenango. They also complained about fumigation of the forest with poisonous substances. They cited these occurrences as evidence of the inconsistency of government claims that the situation in Guatemala had changed under President Cerezo.

[25] Guatemalan Church in Exile [Iglesia Guatemalteca en el Exilio], "Guatemala: Refugiados y Repatriación," **Boletín Trimestral**, (Managua, Nicaragua, No. 2, August 1987), 33.

[26]In July 1986, President Cerezo's then military Chief of Staff, General Gramajo, commented on the accusation that the refugee camps in Mexico were guerrilla hideouts, "We know where the bands that infiltrate us are coming from" (**La Jornada**, July 1, 1986). In March 1987 General Gramajo, then Defense Minister and a strong moderating force within the army, explained to a local newspaper his view regarding the origin of the refugee problem: "There were three big flows of refugees to Mexico. The first were those people kidnapped by the guerrillas; the second, the ones running away from subversion; and the third, those people hiding from the army" (**El Gráfico**, March 10, 1987).

[27]Guatemalan Church in Exile, "Refugiados y Repatriación," 52.

[28]Guatemalan Church in Exile, "Refugiados y Repatriación," 53.

[29]Manz, **Repatriation and Reintegration**, 26-28.

[30]In addition to the tensions between the local population and the returnees created by fears of military reprisals, another source of friction in some communities is the fact that repatriates receive outside assistance while those who remained behind receive nothing. This is especially sensitive considering that hundreds of thousands of Guatemalans who did not escape to Mexico also lost their land and their homes during army counterinsurgency operations. While CEAR extends assistance to internally displaced people, it has virtually no international funding (UNHCR funds provided to CEAR can only be used for assisting the repatriation of refugees.) As a result, during 1988 and 1989, only 6,500 people, a small proportion of the total number of internally displaced, received assistance from CEAR. See UNHCR and UNDP, **Diagnóstico**, Guatemala.

[31]See Manz, **Repatriation and Reintegration**, p. 31.

[32]Manz, 1983.

[33]Ponencia Report 1989:1.

[34]CEAR, **Informe de Actividades, Enero 1987 - Mayo 1989**, Guatemala, May 23, 1989.

[35]UNHCR and UNDP, **Diagnósticos** (Guatemala), 15.

[36]**Prensa Libre**, February 9, 1986, 11

[37]See Monsignor Rosell y Arellano, **About the Advances of Communism in Guatemala**, Pastoral Letter, 1954.

[38]**La Iglesia en Centroamérica, Guatemala, El Salvador, Honduras y Nicaragua: Información y Análisis** (Mexico, D.F.: Colectivo de Análisis de Iglesias en Centroamérica, Centro de Estudios Ecuménicos, 1989).

[39]**El Día**, March 19, 1984.

[40]**Excelsior**, July 7, 1986.

Puerto Cortés
Omoa
GUATEMALA
San Pedro Sula
Chamelecón
El Progreso
YORO
CORTES
La Entrada
El Tesoro
SANTA BARBARA
El Paraíso
Florida
El Florido
COPAN
Sta. Rosa de Copán
Santa Bárbara
COMAYAGUA
Agua Caliente
Cucuyagua
Gracias
Siguatepeque
OCOTEPEQUE
Nueva Ocotepeque
Mesa Grande
Comayagua
El Poy
San Marcos
LEMPIRA
INTIBUCA
La Esperanza
La Paz
Guarita
Chalatenango
La Virtud
San Marcos de Sierra
Marcala
Chalatenango Department
Concepción
San Antonio
Colomoncagua
LA PAZ
Lempa River
Buenos Aires
Sumpul River
Morazán Department
Goascorán River
VALLE
EL SALVADOR
El Amatillo
Scale 1:1, 125,000
0   10   20   30   40   50
Nacaome
Kilometers
Usulután

Western Honduras

▲	UNHCR Sub Office
■	Salvadoran Refugee Camp
◪	Guatemalan Refugee Camp
□	Reception Center
○	Repatriation Point
△	Military Base
◖	Immigration Office

CHAPTER IV

EL SALVADOR MOBILIZED AND POOR

by Patricia Weiss Fagen and Joseph T. Eldridge

INTRODUCTION

A History of Struggle and Reprisals

El Salvador is small, poor, and heavily populated. The country has one of the least equal land tenure systems in the world, and its wealth is highly concentrated. During the late 1970s, the urban and rural poor organized to obtain social justice as they often had in the past. Many people took up arms, and reprisals followed. During the 1980s, hundreds of thousands, facing war and repression, fled for their lives.

The situation was reminiscent of the time, almost 40 years earlier in 1932, when *campesinos*, mostly indigenous Salvadorans, working on coffee plantations in the western provinces, had risen up against landholders and shopkeepers. At that time the Salvadoran Communist party had mobilized the insurgents. The government responded with a wide ranging massacre known as *La Matanza* of about 10,000 people. (Some accounts put the figure at 30,000, which would have been two percent of the population. This massacre marked the end of Salvadoran indigenous culture.)[1] Among those executed was the leading organizer of the insurgents, Agustín Farabundo Martí.

Subsequent leaders introduced modest reforms and relatively successful development strategies. Industries were established, and the Salvadoran export sector grew. The country attracted investment, particularly from the United States. Land distribution, however, was not addressed, and so these economic improvements brought few changes to the lives of the rural poor. They remained dependent on subsistence agriculture and plantation labor.

Salvadorans in Honduras

For decades, land-hungry Salvadorans rented or squatted on land in their less densely populated neighbor, Honduras. A large number fled there in the wake of the 1932 massacre. Others migrated to work on Honduran banana plantations. By 1969, more than 300,000 Salvadorans were living in Honduras, often firmly settled and married to Hondurans. As the Honduran economy deteriorated in the 1960s, Salvadorans competed with Hondurans for land and jobs, and Hondurans increasingly resented the settlers. In 1969, the Honduran government expropriated the Salvadorans' property, invoking a virtually ignored provision of the Honduran Agrarian Reform Act of 1962 requiring owners to be Honduran born. Tens of thousands of Salvadorans were forced back into El Salvador, where they no longer had ties or prospects of land or work.

Tension over the land and immigration issues sparked the brief, but bloody "Soccer War" between the two countries in July 1969. Fighting ended under a truce negotiated by the Organization of American States (OAS), but the issues remained unresolved. Most of the remaining Salvadorans had to abandon their Honduran homes. Technically, the two countries remained at war until 1980. The decline in commerce across the border that resulted from the war further impoverished the *campesinos* in both countries. Disputed areas are still claimed by both sides, and the border has yet to be demarcated.

About a decade after the 1969 war, tens of thousands of Salvadorans returned to western Honduras, but this time as refugees. The history of cross-border contact and the legacy of bitterness and distrust generated by the Soccer War were both important factors in the Honduran response to these refugees.

CAUSES OF THE REFUGEE FLIGHT

Polarization and the Rise of Armed Conflict in El Salvador

Government, Armed Forces, and the Paramilitary Right — During the 1970s, the Salvadoran population, long polarized between the left and right, formed battle lines.[2] Defending the government and oligarchy against strikes, protests, and insurgency were the armed forces and the three branches of anti-terrorist special police: the National Guard, the Treasury Police, and the National Police. These three forces were routinely condemned by human rights groups during the 1970s and 1980s for arresting, torturing and "disappearing" civilian opponents. The so-called death squads also operated under such names as the Secret Anti-Communist Army, the White Hand, and, most important in the rural areas, the Nationalist Democratic Organization (ORDEN).

ORDEN was founded in 1967 as a mass organization, most of whose members were recruited from among the peasantry. In exchange for such privileges as jobs for their families and access to land and credit, members monitored and denounced their neighbors. For a time, they even were given the power to arrest those they considered to be subversives. Although ORDEN was formally disbanded in 1979, it continued to operate and inform the military and death squads about the local opposition and its leaders.[3]

Political and Armed Organizations of the Left — The left was fragmented during the 1970s among popular blocs, fronts, and unions, with which were affiliated a number of national and regional *campesino*, labor, student, and professional groups. Although their members operated in the political realm, each of the popular organizations was associated with an armed revolutionary group.

The Christian *Campesino* Federation (FECCAS) operated under one of the major umbrella entities, the People's Revolutionary Army (ERP). FECCAS had a large following in the rural areas of northern Chalatenango, Cabañas, and Morazán, and was allied with the Union of Rural Workers (UTC) that operated in San Vicente. The two groups were active throughout these provinces, which later produced the refugee flow to Honduras. The *campesinos* active in FECCAS-UTC were largely subsistence farmers and landless, or nearly landless, *campesinos* who had suffered gradual impoverishment during the 1970s.

The *campesinos'* philosophy and organizational capacity owed a great deal to the Christian base communities (CEBs) from which most, apparently, were drawn. CEBs had been organized in *campesino* communities by rural priests whose activities reflected the growing influence of liberation theology among Salvador's clergy. Salvadoran Archbishop Oscar Romero, assassinated in March 1980, was the most prominent proponent of the Church's commitment to defending the poor. CEBs met to study the Bible, to relate Christian ideas to their own lives and, in some manner, to live out socialist ideology.[4] In the more remote northern regions bordering Honduras, CEBs represented virtually the only form of community organization among the population of subsistence farmers.

The lay preachers and teachers, called catechists and delegates of the word, were selected by their villages. They became recognized as leaders, capable of expressing the communities' needs. Subsequently, in the refugee camps, some of the FECCAS-UTC leaders, as well as many former delegates of the word and catechists, re-emerged as camp leaders.

FECCAS-UTC increasingly moved beyond problems of land and social justice that directly affected the Salvadoran rural poor, and, to the dismay of some religious supporters of the early movement, it joined the broader struggle. In the words of a prominent Jesuit intellectual, the strength of the masses as an independent force became "diluted" by both "government intransigence and revolutionary urgency."[5]

Although he insisted on the Church's separation from strictly political activity, Archbishop Romero publicly encouraged popular movements, which expanded and became more vocal between 1977 and 1988. After Romero's assassination in 1980, Church leaders continued to criticize government repression, but distanced themselves from leftist opposition groups. Despite government threats and opposition from conservatives in the Church hierarchy to what they considered politicization, some priests continued to "accompany" the popular movements throughout the 1980s. They were prominent among those killed for their involvement and, like Romero, became martyrs of raw repression. Because of this history of church support, organization, and accompaniment – and the legacy of Archbishop Romero – the Salvadoran rural poor, including the refugees, looked to the church for support, and the popular organizations continued to press for greater commitment from the clergy.

Armed Conflict and Refugee Flight

As popular protest grew during the late 1970s, the Salvadoran military, paramilitary and death squads attacked villages and murdered leaders and members of the opposition organizations. People fled from their villages to other parts of the country, especially San Salvador. By January 1980, the targets of these actions were crossing the border into Honduras. In April 1980, the civilian opposition (including political parties, mass organizations, and dozens of *campesino*, student, and professional groups and unions) united to form the Democratic Revolutionary Front (FDR). The following October, the guerrilla groups united to form the Farabundo Martí Liberation Front (FMLN). In 1980, stepped-up repression and murder further reduced the leadership of the popular organizations and political parties in the FDR, driving political activity underground. By discouraging political activity, the repression created numerous recruits for the FMLN.

Ironically, a large number of *campesinos* were driven off their land during the implementation of the one reform measure that should have assured them an opportunity to improve their lives. In March 1980, the government announced a long overdue land reform, the first phase of which required expropriation of the largest estates. However, the military sent to carry out the land reform also moved against *campesino* organizations far away from the large estates. Thousands of *campesinos* fled to San Salvador to become the first politically displaced persons.[6]

Armed conflict increased and reached peak intensity during the major FMLN offensive in January 1981. Repression intensified as well. Human rights organizations reported 300 to 500 murders a week in the early months of 1981, the vast majority of which were committed by the armed forces and death squads.[7] The civilian population remained under pressure to collaborate with whichever side was dominant at the moment. While government forces killed by far the most people, the FMLN often executed *campesinos* who had been forcibly recruited or pressured into giving information to the armed forces.

Families abandoned combat areas, seeking safer ground. Salvadorans from urban and rural areas left the country in droves. From every part of the country and every social sector, they left their homes to find safety and a better life. As early as 1981, there were Salvadoran refugees throughout Central America. A half a million or more journeyed north during the 1980s, into Mexico and especially the United States. Some went to Europe and Canada. At least a half million persons who did not join the refugee flow became displaced persons within their own country. The majority were officially classified as persons displaced by war and were allowed to live in poorly attended official settlements. Some 120,000 others, who had been pursued and fired upon by the military, were essentially internal refugees, assisted by religious or other private groups.[8] As much as one fifth of the Salvadoran population has suffered some form of displacement.[9]

THE SALVADORAN REFUGEES IN HONDURAS

Profile of Flight

Poor Campesinos to Honduras — The refugees in Honduras represented only a small portion of the Salvadorans who left or were forced to leave. As noted, they were subsistence farmers from the land-poor areas of the North, mainly Chalatenango, Cabañas, and Morazán. The first refugees had begun to cross the border in 1979, but the majority arrived in Honduras between 1980 and 1982, fleeing battle zones and military sweeps. Small groups and families continued to cross the border until 1986, when their numbers sharply decreased.[10] After 1984, the major motive for flight was the intense military bombardment of rural areas where the guerrillas were active. In Morazán and San Vicente, the guerrillas were essentially in control by the early 1980s, but were unable to protect the *campesinos* from continual military bombardment.

Driven Out: Violence at the Border — Until early 1980, Salvadorans encountered no serious difficulties in crossing the Honduran border.[11] Once on the other side, they were taken in by the local population, often by families with whom they had forged ties prior to the 1969 war. As in El Salvador, they also received help from local churches.

The Catholic Church, through its relief agency Caritas, first called attention to the refugees. In 1980, Caritas asked for assistance from the U.S. based Catholic Relief Services so that the local churches could continue to assist the new arrivals. Refugees settled in the remote border area near the villages of La Virtud and La Guarita. At first their presence brought no response from Honduran authorities. However, the United Nations High Commissioner for Refugees (UNHCR) began to assist them in March 1980 once it was informed of their presence.

From March 1980 to 1983, crossing the border was a dangerous and deadly endeavor. The refugees were likely to consist of groups or families caught in the fighting between government and FMLN, rather than individual refugees. They were fleeing death threats and attacks against popular organizations.

On the Salvadoran side, the military sweeps through populated areas drove survivors away from their villages. Those who could headed toward the border. When they attempted to cross, however, they were sometimes fired upon by Honduran forces. The Honduran authorities told UNHCR and human rights groups that their fire was directed at armed guerrillas. Later, citing the alleged presence of combatants among the refugees, Honduran authorities permitted Salvadoran military and paramilitary operatives to enter the refugee settlements, where they kidnapped or killed several residents.[12]

Some of the first large refugee groups, predominantly made up of civilians, were escorted to the Honduran border by FMLN units. It is not clear whether these units remained for a period of time in Honduras. Nevertheless, Salvadoran and Honduran troops turned their fire on civilians of all ages. Their operations resulted in the deaths of thousands of refugees during 1980 and 1982.

Two well publicized incidents that took place within a year of each other reveal the depth of the problem. On May 14, 1980, the first large group of refugees, reportedly 800 to 900 people, fleeing ground and air fire, sought to cross the Sumpul River near Guarita, Honduras.[13] As they crossed, they were fired upon both by the Salvadoran and Honduran militaries. Survivors reported that 300 to 600 had been killed.[14] Salvadoran officials characterized the event as a confrontation between government and opposition forces.[15] Hondurans expressed their concern at the time that the cross-border flight might carry the war into Honduras.

On March 18, 1981, between 4,000 and 5,000 Salvadoran villagers from the Department of Cabañas were led to the border at the Lempa River by some FMLN units. The Salvadoran army pursued them by air, dropping grenades and mortars, and firing from helicopters as they struggled across the river. On the Honduran side, troops began to arrest those who managed to reach the shore. The attempt to prevent the refugees from arriving was thwarted by a group of foreign religious workers and local people who happened to be in the area; having witnessed the bloody events, they insisted on protecting the refugees. Their eyewitness accounts were widely published in the U.S. and European press. After three days, about 3,000 persons managed to cross into Honduras, near Los Hernández. Refugees subsequently reported that between 19 and 35 persons were killed during the crossing.[16]

The Establishment of Refugee Camps — These new arrivals, along with previous refugees who lived in La Guarita and Los Hernández, were brought together in a newly constructed camp at La Virtud. To the south of La Virtud, between 4,000 and 5,000 refugees from Morazán began to arrive in December 1980 in the border area near the Honduran town of Colomoncagua. By February 1981, they were sheltered in a formal camp outside of the town from which it took its name. By May, there were close to 8,000 refugees in Colomoncagua. At the end of 1981, it was estimated that about 30,000 Salvadoran refugees were in Honduras, with the UNHCR providing assistance for 20,000.

During the early months of 1981, most refugees sheltered in La Virtud and refugees in the town of La Guarita were moved to another camp, Mesa Grande. The number of refugees in Mesa Grande was initially about 7,000, but increased by about 2,500 between July and September 1982. The newcomers consisted of Salvadorans who had been living near the border for some time, but had not relocated with the refugees from La Virtud, as well as newly arrived refugees. In 1983, another 2,000 new refugees came to Mesa Grande from the region around Copapayo.[17]

In June 1983, 2,000 refugees crossed the border from San Vicente, where the Salvadoran government had initiated heavy bombing and a pacification program. Most were sheltered in the town of San Antonio, which soon thereafter became a separate camp. A few went to Colomoncagua. By mid-1983 refugees were in camps in four locations: Colomoncagua, San Antonio, Mesa Grande, and Buenos Aires.[18] The majority were women and children.

The refugees were denied the freedom of movement to leave the camp to work or make purchases. Their needs had to be furnished from outside. Honduran authorities militarized the camp perimeters, patrolled the surrounding areas, and, at frequent intervals, harassed refugees and relief agency personnel.

Salvadorans found outside the camps were often assumed to be FMLN guerrillas and might be shot or detained. However, the Honduran military was never able to close off the refugee camps fully. Honduran officials, moreover, maintain that more Salvadorans lived on Honduran territory outside of the camps than within.[19] While most Salvadorans outside camps had family ties to the local population, Honduran authorities insisted that FMLN guerrillas made frequent use of the area. Controversy abounds about the level of FMLN activity in and around the refugee camps. It can be safely concluded that the border remained quite porous.

The Organization of Refugee Relief

As noted, after January 1980, the refugees were assisted by local Catholic churches, supported by Caritas of Honduras which, in turn, sought international resources. Caritas and local church workers had participated in CEBs similar to those in El Salvador and felt a close rapport. It was Caritas that informed UNHCR of the Sumpul River massacre of May 1980. After Sumpul, UNHCR sought to maintain some presence in the area, with one or two protection officers almost always in residence. The High Commissioner, Mr. Poul Hartling, visited Honduras in May, and initiated a program to assist 1,000 refugees. At this time, UNHCR activities were coordinated from the regional headquarters in San José, Costa Rica. In July 1980, a UNHCR representative was established in Tegucigalpa.

Between March and July 1980, UNHCR negotiated over its assistance and protection role with the Honduran government. Honduras was not a signatory to the UN Convention or Protocol Relating to the Status of Refugees. However, UNHCR had worked closely with the Honduran government to assist the thousands of Nicaraguan refugees fleeing the Somoza dictatorship at the end of the 1970s. Despite its previous collaboration in assisting the Nicaraguan refugees, the Honduran government made it clear to UNHCR that it would only accept Salvadoran refugees with reluctance. Salvadoran refugees were finally allowed to remain in the country on humanitarian grounds, but the Honduran government insisted that UNHCR take full responsibility for assisting them.[20]

To implement its program, UNHCR appointed a Council of Agencies in July 1980, consisting of Caritas, the Evangelical Committee for Development and National Emergency (CEDEN), Médecins sans Frontières, World Vision of Honduras, the Mennonite Church, and the University of Honduras. Catholic Relief Service (CRS) also participated, at first channeling aid through Caritas and later sending its own personnel. In August, CEDEN was appointed as the Coordinating Agency.

CEDEN had been assisting the Salvadorans since March 1980. Its program was small in comparison to Caritas, which had been assisting the refugees from the beginning. Caritas, however, had poor relations with the Honduran government, which considered it to be leftist and accused its workers of collaborating with the Salvadoran guerrillas. CEDEN, representing the Evangelical churches, had a more conservative image. The agencies, as well as UNHCR, were pleased with the early leadership of CEDEN, whose director, Nohemy de Espinoza, took consistent positions strongly in favor of the refugees' protection. She was fired in January 1982, because, according to other relief workers, she had protected refugees sought by Honduran military officials.[21] Thereafter, other agencies tended to be more vocal than CEDEN in denouncing human rights violations. Later that year, UNHCR itself took on the coordinating role.

At first, the agencies divided their work by sector, with each responsible for specific areas, i.e. within La Virtud, Guarita, and Colomoncagua. Later, under UNHCR coordination, the agencies took responsibility for a specific type of work: Caritas of Santa Rosa de Copán was in charge of education, social services and the distribution of the World Food Program grains; CRS, workshops and training; the Mennonite Church of Honduras, construction and roads; CEDEN, water, agriculture, and animal husbandry; Médecins sans Frontières, health care. Médecins sans Frontières worked in the camps until 1988, when it was removed at the refugees' insistence. During the first two years, the medical school of the University of Honduras also contributed medical services, and CONCERN, a California based agency, ran special nutrition centers until 1984. The latter's contract was terminated on grounds that malnutrition had been virtually eliminated. Honduran authorities raised objections to both the University medical students and the volunteers from CONCERN as being too leftist and lacking political neutrality.

Virtually every able-bodied refugee worked and the children attended school. In this respect, refugee children were fortunate. Their counterparts in El Salvador were far less likely to have access to education. The adults, in effect, attended school as well. Many learned one skill, e.g., shoe making and, having mastered it, moved on to another. The refugees were determined to prepare themselves for a future life in El Salvador that would be different from their old lives as campesinos. They readily expressed their gratitude to the relief agencies and UNHCR for these programs.

In January 1981, the Honduran government established the National Committee for Refugees (CONARE), its members included the Ministers of Defense, Interior, and Foreign Relations. Retired Colonel Abraham García Turcios has headed CONARE throughout its existence. CONARE has been wholly or largely responsible for all refugee-related decisions, including negotiations with UNHCR, approvals of projects and personnel, repatriation agreements, and general oversight for all refugee camps in Honduras. While CONARE, through Colonel García Turcios, has been the focal point for refugee policies in Honduras, the military have had responsibility for controlling access to the camps. Visitors to the Salvadoran camps are required to obtain signed authorizations from both CONARE and the military.

REFUGEES, REGIONAL WARS, AND POLITICAL AGENDAS

El Salvador, Honduras, and the United States

El Salvador and Honduras: Making Peace to Make War — At the end of October 1980, thanks to U.S. mediation, Honduras and El Salvador signed a peace treaty that formally ended the state of war existing between the two countries since 1969. Disputed territory along the border remained unresolved.[22] Following the treaty, the U.S. enlisted Honduran assistance in operations against the Sandinista government in Nicaragua and against the FMLN in El Salvador. At U.S. insistence, Salvadoran troops were trained in Honduras until Honduran objections against having their traditional enemies trained on their soil finally prevailed. The treaty further facilitated collaboration between the two armed forces against the FMLN and sometimes the refugees in the border region. As described, the two forces had fired on fleeing refugees at the Sumpul River the previous May, without the benefit of a peace treaty.

Following the truce, human rights abuses against the refugees increased. These included frequent incursions by the Salvadoran military and ORDEN forces into the camps, with the acquiescence of Honduran troops, and with numerous kidnappings and deaths resulting.[23] Once the refugee camp at La Virtud was moved, combat stepped up at that portion of the border. Later, as the fighting in northern Salvador diminished, some commerce and intermingling of population returned along much of the border. A more tranquil border facilitated contacts between the refugees and relatives in El Salvador, but access to the camps remained difficult, especially in Colomoncagua and San Antonio.

The Role of the United States — The United States, having invested deeply in the wars in El Salvador and Nicaragua, established a major military presence in Honduras from which to direct the wars. More than a billion dollars in U.S. military and economic aid went to Honduras during the 1980s. With Honduras at the center of U.S. operations, its armed forces expanded, and the country's human rights situation deteriorated. During much of the decade, the U.S. maintained the Nicaraguan Contra armies in southern Honduras. In the early 1980s, as we have already noted, the U.S. promoted joint Salvadoran-Honduran military actions against the FMLN from Honduran bases close to the refugee camps.

No other embassy came close to matching U.S. involvement in Honduran refugee issues. U.S. officials paid particular attention to the Salvadoran refugees, regularly visited the camps, and actively participated in all major decisions affecting them. The refugee issue was considered a factor in the FMLN strategy. Therefore, policy makers in Honduras, El Salvador, and Washington paid close attention to the problems between the refugees and the host government.

Sharing the view of the Honduran and Salvadoran governments that the camps were at the service of the FMLN, the Embassy supported Honduran measures to maintain the tightest possible security in and around the camps. U.S. officials believed the solution to FMLN contacts was camp relocation. From 1980 to about the end of 1985, the U.S. exerted its considerable influence with the Honduran government and UNHCR to move the refugee camps far enough away from the border to prevent easy access to and from El Salvador. Subsequently, U.S. officials came to revise their perspectives, and looked more favorably on the prospects for repatriation.

The Refugees: Toward a Political Profile

Perceptions — The political involvement and affiliation of the refugees in the camps were the subject of sharp controversy from the moment they arrived. Characterizations of the refugees and particularly of the nature of their possible ties to the FMLN differed according to their source. Strongly expressed views on the subject seemed to have at least as much to do with observers' attitudes toward the major players in the regional conflict as with what was (or was not) happening in the camps.

Salvadoran, Honduran, and U.S. officials complained that FMLN operatives regularly went back and forth between El Salvador and the camps, that large quantities of food, clothing, boots, and medicine were being channelled from the camps into El Salvador for the guerrillas,[24] and that the refugee leadership answered directly to the FMLN.[25]

The refugees overwhelmingly saw themselves as victims of government rather than guerrilla forces, and believed that the Honduran armed forces and the United States were in league with their oppressors. They blamed the U.S. for supplying the weapons and aircraft with which the Salvadoran army attacked them. They experienced Honduran military hostility on a daily basis since their arrival. The refugees, and many of the relief agency personnel who largely shared their perceptions, categorically denied charges that serious quantities of food and medicine left the camps or that FMLN combatants entered camps. They countercharged that such stories were inventions motivated by hostility toward the refugees and were intended to force refugees to relocate or repatriate.

Refugee camps were not "thinly disguised guerrilla bases," as some Honduran and Salvadoran officials charged.[26] Most refugees identified with and supported the anti-government organizations in El Salvador, including the FMLN. Many refugees had family members in the FMLN forces or had been associated with organizations from which the FMLN had drawn members. This was one reason that they had been driven into Honduras. The majority of the refugees, who were women with young children, probably had not been politically active in El Salvador and had fled military sweeps and bombardment. For these refugees, the camp leadership provided political direction and, it was widely believed, defended their security.

Organization and Leadership — The refugees organized the various aspects of their lives and their representatives negotiated on their behalf with UNHCR and the relief agencies. The camp coordinators were comprised of representatives from each sub-camp. There were nine sub-camps within Colomoncagua and seven in Mesa Grande, which was physically separated into a smaller upper camp and a larger lower camp. San Antonio, much smaller than the other two, had just two sections but no sub-camps. In San Antonio and Colomoncagua, the coordinators were appointed or self-selected, rather than elected, and some served during the entire period. In Mesa Grande, the coordinators were named by an assembly of committees. The committees, responsible for camp activities — health, religion, education, workshops, and construction — were elected by families residing in groups of about 10 dwellings.

The camp leaders never revealed their political identities, or disclosed political differences among them. Rifts emerged in the later 1980s, but these may not have been present at the outset. At a minimum, one can conclude that the FMLN was in fairly close communication with the camp leaders and, at times, counted on their assistance for recruits or material. Camp leaders were also aware of and in contact with emerging grassroots, leftist political opposition movements that re-emerged in El Salvador during the later 1980s. The latter were to play a prominent role in the massive repatriation movements of the 1980s.

As one listens to and reads the testimonies of the refugees and relief workers, it becomes clear that the lives the refugees were obliged to lead in the camps formed or intensified their political commitments and their militance. The refugee experience profoundly affected the

Salvadorans who passed through it and forged genuine political unity among the majority.

Coming to Honduras from scattered villages and hamlets, refugees had to live in closed camps, isolated and permanently surrounded by the Honduran military. Unable to leave camps, much less to farm, life-long *campesinos* became artisans and mechanics who grew accustomed to "urban" living and work habits. Finding themselves in a difficult and extremely hostile setting, they mobilized and defended their interests with growing militance. They were hard working, tightly organized, and politically disciplined, which helped them survive and remain intact as a community. They were also a community closed off and under siege, whose leaders demanded and largely obtained absolute loyalty from the members. Over the years, many visitors praised the refugees' remarkable capacity for organization under harsh conditions, others described the camps as regimented and politically stifling. Not surprisingly, these opinions tended to vary with their sympathy, or lack thereof, for the refugees.

The Move to Mesa Grande, November 1981 to April 1982

Refugees and Relief Agencies Opposed to the Move — Refugees and many voluntary agency workers believe that Salvadoran and Honduran military forces had been enlisted by the United States military to undertake joint operations along the border, but were impeded from expanding these operations by the refugees' presence. Ultimately, Salvadoran, Honduran, and U.S. military officials decided that it was imperative to move the refugees. UNHCR, according to this argument, was forced by political pressure to advocate moving the refugees, and did so forcibly, without adequate preparation.

> *The UNHCR has been, at best, an equal in the command struggle with the government of the U.S. in Honduras. Their initial concerns about relocation faded, and at the end, U.S. officials came to Honduras to "kick the ass of UNHCR" and to get the refugees moved out quickly. It is important to remember that one-third of the UNHCR budget comes from the U.S. government.* (Rep. Ronald Dellums, December 1983).[27]

The agencies acknowledged that the refugees were not at all safe in their border locations, but most shared the refugees' contention that the threat posed by the Honduran military would not diminish if the refugees were moved. They expressed particular concern about the difficulties future refugees would face attempting to cross the border were the international presence to be removed.

The relief agencies opposed to relocation sought to call international attention to the frequent and serious human rights violations against refugees and local agency personnel. They encouraged missions by foreign dignitaries and sponsored private volunteers from North America and Europe whose purpose was, by their presence, to reinforce refugee protection. The American Friends Service Committee and the Canadian Inter-Church Committee formalized what was in fact an ongoing "International Observer Program," through which volunteers from the two countries would spend two weeks in Honduras "to help provide safety and bring back information."[28] The program was maintained until the mid-1980s. Many among the agency personnel and short term visitors criticized UNHCR for what they characterized as insufficient efforts to protect the refugees, and for failing to defend the refugees' interests.

UNHCR in Support of the Move to Mesa Grande — Almost from the outset, UNHCR officials promoted relocation and tried to convince the Honduran government to permit the refugees to move to a more secure place. UNHCR officials at the time maintained it was necessary to separate the refugees from the warring parties and to distance them from the security concerns of the border. Although they did not say so publicly, officials also believed that some of the refugees and probably a few of the voluntary agency personnel were in contact with FMLN combatants, thereby endangering the refugee population in general. Concurring with the agencies that neither the Salvadoran nor Honduran military forces made efforts to distinguish combatants from civilians, UNHCR concluded that it was not possible to assure adequate protection either for refugees or agency personnel near the border. Acknowledging the Honduran hostility to the Salvadoran refugees, UNHCR nevertheless believed that if the refugees were no longer inhabiting security zones, they would be seen to pose less of a threat and could be protected more easily.

The Honduran authorities at first were reluctant to implement the move, preferring to maintain the camps as isolated as possible from the Honduran population and under maximum military scrutiny. Honduran authorities frequently expressed their concern that the leftist Salvadorans would fuel ideological opposition among Hondurans. The arguments of U.S. officials in favor of the move proved decisive in persuading the Hondurans to agree.

UNHCR and the relief agencies lost out to military priorities on the issue of a reception center at the border. Instead of a border facility accessible to incoming refugees, UNHCR was permitted to send roving protection officers who would walk at regular intervals along the border to identify incoming refugees and assist them. This system generally worked, but UNHCR officers often were barred from the border during periods of combat — precisely the times when refugees were very likely to flee. Many refugees were obliged to hide near the border until help appeared, enduring days of hardship before reaching the UNHCR camps.

The Move to Mesa Grande — Military incursions into the refugee camp at La Virtud and the refugee settlements in La Guarita took place regularly. After repeated incidents that resulted in the deaths of several refugees and two Caritas workers, the UNHCR decided to expedite the move to the new camp at Mesa Grande. Mesa Grande is located in the province of Ocotepeque, near the town of San Marcos, about 40 kms from the border. The camp had been only minimally prepared for the refugees. The first arrivals lacked adequate shelter, water, and sanitation. In December 1981, relief workers insisted on a halt to refugee movements so that infrastructure could be put in place. Conditions remained difficult until after the entire relocation had been completed.[29]

Meanwhile, refugee relief workers reported that each time the buses came to a site to transport refugees to Mesa Grande, some slipped back into El Salvador. By January 1982, hundreds of refugees were openly refusing to board the buses. In response, UNHCR cut off supplies of food and medicine and warned the refugees that they would be in increasing danger.[30] Evidently, several thousand Salvadorans who had been living in border settlements avoided relocation either by returning to El Salvador or by finding refuge in Honduran villages. By April, just over 8,000 refugees were in Mesa Grande. The refugees angrily addressed the first of what would be many letters to the High Commissioner in Geneva complaining about the conditions, requesting resettlement in countries other than Honduras, and listing several hostile actions against them by the Salvadoran and Honduran military forces.[31]

Salvadoran and Honduran military actions against refugees and relief workers continued during or after the relocation. Indeed, the refugees brought to Mesa Grande presumably to improve their safety were still subject to military incursions and abuses, although less frequently than before.

Further Relocations and Other Contentious Issues

Evolving Positions on Refugee Relocation — Before the refugees were fully settled in Mesa Grande, discussions were underway about further relocations, from Colomoncagua and San Antonio and from Mesa Grande itself. No issue was more divisive.

U.S. officials were the strongest advocates of relocation until late 1985. The U.S. and Honduran discussions about relocation focussed largely on security concerns, because both governments continued to view the camps as supply stations and resting places for the guerrillas. They advocated moving the refugees to places where this could not happen. U.S. and Honduran officials, however, were not in total agreement. The latter wanted another closed, militarily controlled camp rather than open, agricultural settlements. The former urged a more flexible approach that would incorporate some of the improvements requested by UNHCR.

UNHCR continued to negotiate with the Honduran Refugee agency, CONARE, in favor of relocation until the mid-1980s, but insisted that the refugees be moved peacefully. UNHCR advocated giving refugees a large tract of land so that they could farm, establish economic relations with neighboring communities, and live more normal lives. UNHCR also wanted freedom of movement for the refugees. UNHCR's advocacy of this alternative to a closed camp was fully in keeping with its worldwide policy of locating refugees away from borders and seeking forms of local integration that permit the greatest possible self-sufficiency. UNHCR seeks such forms of local integration for financial as well as humanitarian reasons. So long as the refugees are unable to produce their basic food needs, assistance remains costly.

When CONARE announced that beginning in 1984 Colomoncagua refugees would be moved to a site in Olanchito, in the province of Yoro, the refugees organized themselves to oppose being moved and repeatedly promised to fight and die before agreeing to it.[32] They spoke of their investment in the existing camps, their workshops, and facilities, and recalled how traumatic the relocation to Mesa Grande had been. They argued that in view of the hostility of the Honduran public toward them, they would be at greater risk if they were dispersed in the Honduran countryside. Seeming to make virtue of necessity, they insisted that the closed camps that had supportive relief workers and protection staff enhanced their safety, in spite of the surrounding military units. Rejecting the UNHCR's vision of a "more normal life," they claimed that farming was inappropriate for a population predominantly composed of women and children.

The relief workers generally supported the refugees' stand against the move and helped mobilize international support among refugee advocacy and religious groups. The private agency workers vigorously rejected UNHCR's efforts to enlist their support for

promoting the relocation option among the refugees. The agency
workers accused UNHCR of succumbing to Honduran and U.S.
pressures on the issue.[33] They argued that their contracts with
UNHCR required them to implement refugee assistance projects, but
not to take UNHCR's side against the refugees' wishes.

In the Honduran press, meanwhile, UNHCR was attacked almost
daily and accused of running camps for subversives and guerrillas and
for bringing the war into Honduras. The press defended military
actions against refugees and repeatedly recommended that they be
repatriated rather than relocated inside the country.

Had UNHCR achieved its objective, the refugee population
would have been dispersed and perhaps become vulnerable to local
hostility. Almost certainly, it would have weakened the authority of the
refugee leadership and the political unity of the camps. The leaders not
only saw this, but also recognized that the parties promoting the move
considered their weakened leadership to be a desirable outcome.

The refugees were not relocated. In September 1984, after the
fall of Honduran strong man, General Gustavo Alvarez, the
government, responding to the growing nationalism in the country,
withdrew the relocation proposal for Olanchito, considering it to be
against national interests. Instead, the government requested UNHCR
to take "the necessary steps" with the Salvadoran government toward
repatriation. The Honduran Foreign Ministry raised the question of a
mass repatriation with the Salvadoran Foreign Ministry and received a
positive reply.[34] Honduran authorities continued to talk in terms of
relocation from the border camps to other closed camps, an alternative
unacceptable to UNHCR. UNHCR, as well, firmly opposed subsequent
suggestions that the refugees from Colomoncagua and San Antonio be
moved into an enlarged Mesa Grande.

At the end of 1985, the United States joined the retreat from
insistence on relocation. The shift followed an August 1985 armed
Honduran attack against the refugees in Colomoncagua that left three
dead and ten refugees in detention, and which the Embassy publicly
defended. Immediately afterwards, the State Department Bureau for
Refugee Programs sent its consultant, Robert Gersony, to the camps to
report on political conditions and assess the progress toward relocation.
The report, which was never released to the public, was widely reported
to have downplayed some of the claims of FMLN activities in the camp
and to have advised strongly against forcing the refugees to relocate.
The report also raised the issue of refugee protection inside the camp
and abuses by the refugee leadership.[35]

Although the refugees in all these camps continued to display banners proclaiming their unaltered opposition to relocation or repatriation, by 1986 relocation was no longer a serious possibility. Repatriation, however, was on everyone's mind.

UNHCR Under Fire: Diverging Demands and a Limited Mandate — U.S. authorities in Honduras and Washington often commented despairingly that UNHCR coddled the Salvadoran refugees and caved in to far too many of their demands. For example, when the refugees staged a hunger strike in June 1988 in opposition to proposed changes in the nutritional plan, UNHCR defended the changes but eventually relented. Soon afterwards, the refugees launched a campaign against Médecins sans Frontières (MSF) demanding that another agency take over health care.[36] Although UNHCR defended MSF and sought conciliation, MSF withdrew and the Honduran Ministry of Health assumed responsibility for the program.

Honduran and U.S. authorities believed that the refugee protests were politically motivated. Some contended that the protests were to assure that food and medicine would continue to be available to pass on to the FMLN. The U.S. and Honduran officials insisted that UNHCR had the responsibility to guarantee refugee compliance with the wishes of the host government.

Far from seeing the UNHCR as having caved in to refugee pressure, relief agency workers and international refugee advocates denounced it for seeking to deprive the refugees of essential needs (food, medicine, health care) and control over their own lives. During the mid-1980s, they accused UNHCR of imposing the Honduran government's wishes on the refugees instead of representing the refugees' interests to the government. Whenever the Honduran authorities entered the camps and harassed the refugees or relief workers or whenever a refugee or relief worker was detained or killed, UNHCR was held partly responsible.

Although UNHCR and relief workers worked together reasonably well, they remained distrustful of each other. UNHCR contended that what the agencies characterized as a policy of non-interference with the refugees' wishes was in fact resistance to UNHCR direction over the refugee program. UNHCR was particularly dismayed by sharp criticism from relief workers and refugees over agreements negotiated with the Honduran government that UNHCR believed advanced the refugees' security.[37] In the face of the agencies' refusal to defend or ally themselves with UNHCR decisions, UNHCR officials involved them less in the decision-making process, thereby reinforcing the existing mutual distrust. Refugees and refugee advocates repeatedly asked UNHCR to increase the number of protection officers in the camps. Repeatedly, Honduran military patrols detained refugees and relief workers, some of whom were killed. Soldiers frequently denied camp access to agency vehicles, including those of UNHCR, or denied entry to visitors. Refugees complained of hearing constant gunfire around the camp.

The proportion of protection officers to refugees in Honduras, ten officers per 14,000 refugees, was one of the highest among refugee programs. UNHCR protested military incursions. The High Commissioner sent letters denouncing the murders and interceded with authorities to secure the release of refugees and refugee workers. UNHCR trained military personnel in refugee law and human rights and generally sought to diffuse hostilities. But UNHCR's contention that it alone could not protect refugees, and that the responsibility for protection had to be borne ultimately by the Honduran government was neither understood nor accepted by its critics.

Protecting Refugees from Refugees — In 1987, UNHCR began to take new action against quite a different problem of refugee protection. UNHCR officials began to see camp leaders as so authoritarian that they posed a threat to refugees who challenged their policies or their personal leadership. The question of reprisals against refugees had been raised previously, especially by U.S. officials, but the charges were judged to be exaggerated. Besides, while the leadership clearly had the support of the majority of the refugees, challenging the former's authority could have had negative repercussions. Nevertheless, when more incidents of forced recruitment and punishment were brought to the attention of UNHCR officials by the refugees themselves, UNHCR undertook corrective measures.

First, protection officials began to sleep in the camps every night. (CONARE had ruled against international personnel in the camps, but relief workers had begun to do so after the August 1985 military assault on Colomoncagua.) Second, reversing past compliance with the refugee leaders' demand that they be the ones to deliver personal mail, UNHCR officials delivered it directly to the addressees. Third, as dissent in the camps became more open, probably to some extent due to the new policies, UNHCR obtained permission to move refugees threatened with reprisals to houses outside of the camps. Above all, UNHCR staff fought efforts by the camp leaders to interfere with or punish persons seeking to repatriate.

INDIVIDUAL REPATRIATIONS

Repatriation Procedures

In February 1985, after over 2,000 Salvadorans had already repatriated on their own, El Salvador put formal procedures in place for the reception of individual voluntary repatriates.[38] The first tripartite meeting of the Honduran and Salvadoran governments and UNHCR was held in April 1986 at the initiative of UNHCR.[39] About 3,000 refugees repatriated on an individual basis between 1985 and 1987, and a few hundred did so individually thereafter, once the massive repatriation was under way.

The procedures created by the Salvadoran government for handling the voluntary repatriations from Honduras and other Central American countries permitted two options. Refugees wishing to receive assistance from the government would agree to have their names submitted in advance. They could choose to be met by the government agency that assisted internally displaced persons, the Salvadoran National Commission for Assistance to the Displaced Population (CONADES), which would provide them with food and shelter in designated places.[40] Those choosing to enter without assistance would not be obliged to notify the authorities in advance and could be met by family members, civilian officials, or both. Theoretically, they were also eligible for government assistance, but Salvadoran officials made known that there would be none for persons who returned to zones of conflict. The government assured UNHCR that the returnees would be welcome, but recognized that they could not provide protection "beyond what was possible in a country at war."[41]

The overwhelming majority of refugees, most of whom repatriated from the Mesa Grande camp, chose to enter unassisted. Those repatriating individually prior to the establishment of the UNHCR office in El Salvador in March 1987 were escorted to the border by UNHCR officials and left to fend for themselves.

When the office opened in El Salvador, UNHCR began to put pressure on the government to shorten the repatriation process and make it less threatening. After March 1987, repatriates were met by officials from UNHCR. Between 1987 and 1989, refugees wishing to repatriate made their wishes known to the UNHCR officials in the Honduran camps and were informed of the day they could expect to leave. Prior to departure, they completed a form declaring that their repatriation was voluntary, the number of persons repatriating and their desired destination. The UNHCR officials then notified their counterparts in El Salvador and informed the Honduran immigration and military officials. The returnees from Mesa Grande traveled a short distance to the border at El Poy, where they passed through Honduran immigration. From Colomoncagua and San Antonio, which were located next to the border, repatriation took two days. Refugees traveled with a Honduran military officer and an immigration official, as well as a UNHCR official to the capital city of Tegucigalpa. The immigration officer continued on to the border at El Amatillo. (UNHCR paid the expenses of both Honduran officials).

In El Salvador, the refugees were met by a UNHCR protection officer who accompanied them during registration with Salvadoran immigration and military officials. Mesa Grande returnees were taken to the Fourth Brigade for questioning, which sometimes lasted for hours. From there, they went to the Governor's office in Chalatenango to receive a safe conduct pass, valid for an indefinite period of time. Those coming from Colomoncagua were originally taken from the crossing point at El Amatillo in La Unión to the Third Brigade.[42] By 1988, the military had eliminated the stop at the Brigade and repatriates were instructed to go directly to the Governor's office for a brief interview, after which they received safe conduct passes valid for one year. The procedure normally took less than a day.[43] UNHCR then accompanied the refugees to their chosen locations.

In 1987, 1,200 refugees repatriated, 300 more than the previous year. The easier procedures were clearly a factor in many cases.

Moving Against the Collective Will: Repatriation Motives

Despite the refugees' evident interest in and requests for repatriation, the camp leadership vigorously opposed individual repatriations. Virtually none occurred from Colomoncagua and San Antonio until 1987. In Mesa Grande, however, where the refugees were more heterogenous and contentious, a modest ongoing repatriation movement began taking place after 1984.

Refugees who finally left Colomoncagua and San Antonio were generally subjected to threats and serious reprisals. As a rule, the refugees from Mesa Grande who made known their wish to repatriate voluntarily were subject to serious harassment only if they had been politically active and were considered to be defecting. The Mesa Grande leadership made sure refugees took nothing beyond their few personal possessions, but tended to interfere little in the proceedings prior to departure. Since meals were prepared jointly and all tools belonged to the community, the refugees carried very little.

In 1987, individuals from Colomoncagua and San Antonio also began repatriating, although they had to sneak out of the camp, usually with nothing more than the clothes on their back. Only 27 refugees repatriated from Colomoncagua in 1987, but UNHCR officials considered even this number to be a breakthrough. Over 100 returned in 1988 and about 60 as of May 1989.[44] The increase seems to have been due in part to UNHCR resistance to the demand of Salvadoran refugee coordinators that they be notified about forthcoming repatriations. In mid-1988, UNHCR informed the coordinators that they would not receive the names of the persons due to repatriate until after they had left the camp. UNHCR continued to inform coordinators when a repatriation was being planned and how many persons were involved.

Motivations

Individual repatriations were motivated largely by the tension and hopelessness of life in Honduran camps. Many were eager to be reunited with loved ones and family members. "A farmer likes to work the land," said one, and "even if the war is still going on, it is better to take the risk to return to farming."[45]

One 45 year old man living outside of San Salvador declared that he "had lived too many years outside of the country," and that despite the war, he wanted to go home. He decided not to leave with the group in a mass repatriation so that he "would be more free," although he "felt a lot of pressure to go with the group." He also knew that he would receive "less help," because he was returning only with his family, but that he expected "to be fed by UNHCR."[46]

For a 26 year old woman interviewed in the La Libertad province living with her uncle, the "war was irrelevant. A person needs to be in her own country."[47]

A young man, also living in the La Libertad province, had first left the Mesa Grande camp as a scout charged by his fellow refugees with investigating the situation on the ground in El Salvador to report back to those still in the camp. He indicated that he had been reasonably happy in the camp and also back in El Salvador, despite the "high price of food." Even though he knew that life at home would be "difficult and expensive," he reasoned that the war was responsible for making life "hard."[48]

The decision to repatriate also reflected the refugees' awareness that life in many areas of El Salvador had become less violent by the mid-1980s. They were told that the Salvadoran authorities had made the re-entry process less onerous and threatening and that UNHCR would meet them. One man living in La Libertad said that despite the fact that the "war was still going on, there has been much talk about peace." He also had heard "a lot of conversation about Esquipulas II," which he interpreted as strengthening the possibility that "human rights would be respected."[49]

It appears that among the repatriates there were a significant number of families of young men who were seeking to avoid recruitment into the FMLN.[50] Others consisted of individuals not only tired of life in the camps, but also politically disillusioned with the camp leadership. During the period that the mass repatriations were being organized, many refugees whose actions or attitudes had placed them at odds with the community repatriated individually to locations other than the communities that were established by the returnees in El Salvador. Most returned to places near family members who could help them get started.

A number of families who returned from Colomoncagua and San Antonio went to San Salvador or San Miguel. One family that was originally from a small village along the Honduran border in Morazán and which left Colomoncagua in July 1988, was interviewed in Apopa (an hour's drive from San Salvador). The family members offered several reasons for repatriating after seven years in Colomoncagua: a) they grew tired of working without earning a wage; b) the children had learned skills and gotten an education, yet were unable to find jobs; c) the children constantly talked about going back to El Salvador; d) they had been accused of being "contras" by the coordinators in the camp for refusing to obey instructions and were fed up with the camp's coercive organization. (Their names were given to the coordinators only after they left the camp, in keeping with the new UNHCR policy.) After securing work as a street vendor in the city, the father, because of his association with Colomoncagua, had been detained for questioning by the authorities and was subsequently rearrested. (As of this writing his whereabouts remain unknown. His family finally resettled in Canada, having received further threats.)

A substantial number of repatriated refugees left El Salvador as soon as they had their papers in order and headed for the United States, Mexico, Belize, or elsewhere.[51] Since the late 1980s, UNHCR has become more active in its solicitations for third country asylum for returnees and displaced persons in need of protection. Canada and Australia both indicated their interest in facilitating transfers when the circumstances warranted. Few cases have been moved through this channel, however, as the procedure is slow, and it may typically require as long as eight months.[52] One young man, feeling pressured by both sides and eager to leave El Salvador as soon as possible, indicated that if going to a third country was not a viable option, he wanted "to return to Honduras."[53]

Assistance and Follow-Up

Soon after upgrading the office in San Salvador in 1987, the UNHCR sought an agency with which it could cooperate in providing services and material support for the refugees who were returning individually. UNHCR observed a polarization among virtually all private voluntary agencies. The small number of private organizations working with government programs for the displaced received substantial subsidies from the U.S. Agency for International Development (AID) and, for this reason, were perceived by other agencies to be tainted by the controversial U.S. policies toward El Salvador. On the other hand, many of the potential cooperating agencies supported opposition groups and were not perceived to be neutral. Unable to locate a suitable organization, the UNHCR created its own. The first attempt failed, reportedly because of poor personnel choices. The Salvadoran Association for Comprehensive Support (ASAI) was subsequently formed as an independent agency, yet wholly funded by UNHCR. ASAI vehicles bear the UNHCR emblem.

ASAI has a two-fold mandate. Documentation of all refugees is a priority. However, because of the commitment by other church and relief organizations to providing material and logistical support to those returning in the mass repatriations, ASAI decided to concentrate on facilitating the reintegration of individuals and families.

ASAI provides services and goods for the returnees' general well-being. It is authorized to secure either construction materials for those who need to build houses or tools needed to generate income, such as sewing machines and hand tools. ASAI has asked other non-government relief agencies to inform it whenever the latter provide additional supplies or equipment to returnees in the ASAI program.[54]

The UNHCR, with ASAI, seeks to monitor the whereabouts and security of the individuals who have repatriated. Threats of reprisals have come from both the army and the FMLN. The military often suspects that young men continue to associate with the guerrillas. The FMLN, on the other hand, believes that the former fighters who abandoned its ranks to seek refuge in the camps in Honduras may have defected to the government upon their return. When the army is suspected of capturing someone, the UNHCR appeals directly to the

authorities to exert pressure for the individual's release. When the
FMLN is suspected of a kidnapping, no such recourse is available. The
UNHCR decided against creating safe houses in El Salvador for those
fearing persecution from either side because such a facility might
become a target, thereby augmenting the danger to their inhabitants.

When returnees are threatened by either the guerrillas or the
army, ASAI works in conjunction with UNHCR to take an active role in
monitoring the returnees' movements as a safeguard against reprisal.
ASAI candidates for third country resettlement are given short-term
support to cover basic living expenses.

Monitoring the whereabouts of individual returnees is a
formidable challenge for both ASAI and UNHCR. The small ASAI
staff is able to follow up on a limited number of families. After their
initial contact with ASAI, most returnees fend for themselves, and face
the daily challenge of trying to scrape out an existence in a hostile
environment.

ASAI was not created to replace the material aid provided by the
government's CONADES program. In places where it is feasible, ASAI
strives to coordinate with existing government programs. ASAI can
only provide limited short-term assistance to cushion the impact of
return.

BACKGROUND TO THE MASS REPATRIATIONS

The Changing International and National Contexts

On August 6, 1987 the governments of Central America signed
the Esquipulas II agreement which underscored the need to develop
regional humanitarian solutions to the problem of refugees and
displaced persons. The refugees were well aware of developments in
the peace process among the Central American governments and tried
to schedule their collective repatriations to coincide with important
international meetings. In this way, they identified their movement with
efforts toward peace, and made it more embarrassing diplomatically for
the Salvadoran government to obstruct their return. The Salvadoran
government, as well, framed its agreements to accommodate the
returnees in the context of the ongoing peace process in Central
America.

The refugees also heard about changes in El Salvador that followed the election in 1984 of José Napoleón Duarte, a Christian Democrat, as President of the country. Gradually, the political process had begun to open. For the first time, the government met with FMLN representatives at a much publicized event in La Palma. Despite little substantive progress, domestic and international expectations for a negotiated settlement were heightened even though the war continued. The individual repatriations described above were early responses to these changes in perceptions.

The political opening permitted renewed efforts to organize labor, *campesino*, and student sectors, as well as a resurgence of activity among religious, human rights, and grassroots support groups. The Christian Democratic government permitted the Salvadoran churches a wider latitude to undertake humanitarian activities. The most important of these were efforts by several church institutions to meet the needs of displaced persons. Approximately 120,000 people, who were viewed with hostility by government authorities, depended wholly or in large part on church assistance.

Virtually from the beginning of the long conflict in El Salvador, churches played an active pastoral role by engaging in a ministry of solidarity and support for the victims of the war. Diaconia, an ecumenical committee of assistance, was created by Archbishop Oscar Romero for the express purpose of serving victims of the repression and the war. Resources were solicited and received from church sources in Europe, Canada, and the United States. The plight of the displaced and the refugees became the catalyst for bringing together, under the umbrella of Diaconia, Lutherans, Episcopalians, Baptists, the Social Secretariat of the Archdiocese of San Salvador, and two cooperatives.

Camps for the displaced in the early 1980s were run by a number of religious institutions. The Lutherans supported a community called Fe y Esperanza (Faith and Hope), the Episcopal Church operated La Florida, and the Baptists maintained an orphanage and a shelter.

Diaconia operated as a clearinghouse that enabled major donor organizations e.g., Christian Aid, Pan Para el Mundo, Novib, and OXFAM to coordinate their material and financial support efficiently. For example, Catholic Relief Services (CRS) became the channel for all food aid. CRS brought into the country all donations of basic food staples and powdered milk, which was subsequently distributed through Diaconia.

Repopulating: Bringing the Displaced Home

The large scale repatriations to El Salvador in the latter part of the 1980s would not have taken place had it not been for the repopulation process that brought internally displaced persons back to their regions of origin in areas of conflict and which provided them with political and material support. The same groups that provided the support structures for this process laid the groundwork for the subsequent mass repatriations from Honduras of refugees to these same regions.

After Duarte's election in the spring of 1984, the Archdiocese intensified its negotiations with the government. Both President Duarte and Archbishop Rivera y Damas encouraged the displaced to return to their places of origin, even though these zones were still considered to be areas of conflict. By the end of 1985, the displaced camps in and around San Salvador were closed with the assistance of the government. The one notable exception was the Calle Real facility, which the government created with the understanding that it would serve only as a temporary processing point for people returning to their communities. The original plan, as crafted by the churches, provided for the return of individuals or small groups of people.

The seeds that led to the first mass repatriation were probably planted by the Archdiocese of San Salvador. In September 1984, three months after the June 1 inauguration of President Duarte, the small town of Tenancingo was destroyed by the war. All the residents were forced to flee. Tenancingo was chosen as a pilot resettlement project by the Archdiocese.

Under the guidance of Archbishop Rivera y Damas, negotiations were undertaken with both sides in the conflict to establish a neutral zone that would be respected by the military and the guerrillas. Tenancingo was to be demilitarized. Both sides were urged to respect Tenancingo's neutrality by refraining from tactical or strategic use of the town. Combat, weapons, and troop movements through the town were prohibited. The Archdiocese wanted ironclad guarantees that the former residents who decided to return would not be harmed by the army or the guerrillas.

Through the intervention of the Archbishop, the negotiations with both sides were completed, funding was secured, and people returned home. The Church and the operational agencies it created were the prime movers of the Tenancingo project. The former residents only participated to the extent that they agreed to return home.

The Tenancingo project lent credibility to the idea of large numbers of people returning at the same time. The church organizers of Tenancingo mobilized international support and were able to open new political space by pressuring the Salvadoran government into accepting the concept of the massive repopulation of former communities.

Other displaced persons observed this process and were motivated to take matters into their own hands. Some months later, the Christian Committee for the Displaced of El Salvador (CRIPDES) and the National Coordinator for Repopulation (CNR) were founded. Although rooted in the church and Christian base communities, CRIPDES organizers had no formal church ties. Some of the CRIPDES organizers were grassroots Christians, while others clearly drew their inspiration from the political orientation of the FMLN. Sensing that a historic moment had arrived, these activists decided to take the initiative and create a formal organization dedicated exclusively to facilitating the return of the displaced. CRIPDES was formally launched at a public ceremony at the National Autonomous University, where it announced its goals and named a board of representatives of the displaced from seven Salvadoran departments.

Soon after its formation, CRIPDES launched an ambitious plan to resettle, *en masse*, the town of San José Las Flores in Chalatenango, which was in the midst of contested territory. The displaced had already learned the hard lesson that returning alone to zones of conflict could be hazardous. There had been a slow trickle of individuals back to their homes and the reports from those who experienced difficulty highlighted the concern for personal security.

The vulnerability of these individuals was forcefully demonstrated by the plight of a man who left Fe y Esperanza and returned home to the western slope of Guazapa. He was subsequently picked up and badly beaten by the First Brigade. Fortunately he survived and was eventually given passage to Mexico. Similar stories circulated widely among the displaced and convinced them that, for the sake of their own welfare and safety, they had to return to their places of origin in groups.

In preparation for the first repopulation effort, CRIPDES contacted international funding agencies, solidarity groups, religious organizations and local activists in search of support. High on the list of potential CRIPDES supporters were Diaconia and the churches.

Archbishop Rivera y Damas, other high church officials, and Diaconia played leading roles in encouraging people to return to their places of origin in order to relieve the harsh conditions in the camps of the displaced in and around San Salvador. However, Diaconia incurred the wrath of the extreme right which accused the former of collaborating with the FMLN by encouraging the displaced to return to contested areas or areas nominally under the control of the FMLN. Arch-conservatives launched a blistering attack on Diaconia and vilified its leaders both in the print and electronic media. The military was also a source of condemnation. As the opposition to Diaconia grew, CRIPDES sought a grant from its director, Octavio Cruz. However, because it was under fire from the right wing and some military sectors, Diaconia felt it had to refuse to cooperate with CRIPDES.

CRIPDES also requested assistance from the International Committee of the Red Cross (ICRC), CRS, and other agencies. However, they also feared that the repopulation movement was too confrontational and too closely identified with the political objectives of the FMLN, so most international funding agencies joined Diaconia in adopting a wait-and-see attitude.

CRIPDES decided to press ahead with the resettlement of San José Las Flores, which occurred in June 1986. It raised its own money and led the first massive grassroots repopulation of a community.

CRIPDES made an issue of mass repopulations. It created conditions that set in motion an unstoppable process. Other agencies, including the Archdiocese, soon felt obliged to help facilitate the return of the displaced to the zones of conflict. When it became apparent that the repopulation of San José Las Flores was inevitable, Archbishop Rivera intervened directly with the military, and urged it not to intrude or obstruct the movement of people back to their places of origin. On the day of the departure to San José Las Flores, the *repoblados*, as the returning internally displaced were known, gathered for a mass in the Cathedral, from where they boarded buses provided by CRIPDES. They were accompanied by several international volunteers from organizations in solidarity with CRIPDES (e.g. the SHARE Foundation). They were stopped *en route* to San José Las Flores by the military at the Colimar Bridge, but were finally allowed to continue.

The idea of going home captivated the communities of the internally displaced. Tired from years of living as virtual prisoners in confined spaces under constant harassment and military watch and with few opportunities either for decent work or education for their children, the displaced were eager to return home to reconstruct their lives.

In July, there was a second repopulation movement of displaced persons who returned to San Antonio and El Varillo. This time, the role of Diaconia began to change. The campaign against Diaconia had produced an international backlash that convinced the Christian Democratic government that it was in its best interest to intercede on behalf of Diaconia. With Archbishop Rivera y Damas' unwavering insistence, the campaign of intimidation against Diaconia subsided and Diaconia was legally recognized. Other organizations began to operate with a higher public profile, including Lutheran World Federation, CRS, the Mennonites, American Friends Service Committee (AFSC), OXFAM, and the Jesuit Refugee Services.

During the repopulation movement of San Antonio and El Varillo, Diaconia's member institutions established an effective *modus operandi* that became a model for subsequent repatriations, as well as repopulation movements. For example, with financial support from the Lutheran World Federation, FEDECOPADES became involved in providing support for reactivating agricultural production. The ICRC played a key role by agreeing to help install a major water system and latrines in San Antonio and El Varillo. The ICRC assistance gave the repopulation movement a stamp of international respectability.

These repopulation efforts began to attract considerable international attention. Expressions of support came from Europe and the United States. CRIPDES mobilized considerable international solidarity primarily through religious networks. Just before the movement back to San Antonio and El Varillo, a group organized by the Washington, D.C.-based SHARE Foundation arrived in El Salvador to accompany the community back to their homes. The military reacted with increasing distress to this group of 23 foreign religious persons who came for the express purpose of accompanying people into the zones of conflict in Chalatenango. During the procession back to San Antonio and El Varillo, the international contingent was separated from the group led by CRIPDES, held for 24 hours by the Treasury Police, and expelled from the country.

Following this action, the Salvadoran legislature passed a law requiring all foreigners to have visas to enter El Salvador. The new regulations were designed specifically to prevent access to the country by international solidarity volunteers including those interested in working with the movement of people returning to their homes in the war zones.

News of these successful repopulation movements reached the refugees in Mesa Grande and convinced them that their safety too depended on returning in large numbers. In concert with their CRIPDES allies, the refugees in Mesa Grande began to make plans for a collective return. CRIPDES created the "National Coordinator for

Repopulation" (CNR) in June 1986, precisely to help facilitate the return of refugees from Honduras. CNR was quickly able to establish affinities with the Mesa Grande refugees on the basis of shared goals and mutual agreement on methodology and tactics. International solidarity was considered to be a key component by CRIPDES/CNR and the refugees themselves. "Going Home," an offshoot of the SHARE Foundation, responded to their appeals for international support by organizing delegations to "accompany" the refugees.

The Refugees Opt to Repatriate

Just before the Esquipulas II meeting, the U.N. High Commissioner for Refugees, Jean Pierre Hocke, visited the Mesa Grande camp. According to former residents of the camp, he suggested that the refugees faced three options: a) integration in the country of asylum; b) return to El Salvador under a total amnesty; or c) third country asylum.[55]

For most, these options were either unavailable or unacceptable. In an assembly convened by the coordinators of the camp, substantial numbers opted for what was now seen as a fourth option, namely a collective return. The mass repatriation movements were conceived as an alternative to individual repatriations.

The refugees complained of what they characterized as nearly a decade of confinement. They conceded that they had learned important skills in the refugee camps, but saw no future for themselves or their children in Honduras. They were *campesinos* who, as refugees, had learned to do other things as well. Their children, unlike most of them, were being educated, but knew nothing about how to cultivate or what it was like to live without being dependent on others for food and necessities.

Nevertheless, as already described, the refugee leadership regularly pronounced its opposition to returning to El Salvador denouncing returnees for giving into pressures and abandoning the community. Despite their feelings of hopelessness, their bitterness over their experiences with the Honduran military, their dissatisfaction with the support from UNHCR, they insisted they would not allow themselves to be forced to return until peace was restored in El Salvador. The leaders warned that former refugees would be at risk in El Salvador.

*The main goal of the Honduran and Salvadoran governments
was for us (the refugees) to repatriate individually to El
Salvador so that they might do whatever they wanted with us or
our comrades. . . . We have a list of 8 people killed and thirty
imprisoned, comrades who had repatriated individually.*

By contrast, the mass repatriations were considered a positive
step in which the repatriates could take control of their own lives and
confront their enemies as an organized force:

*The community saw that those who repatriated individually
were tortured, jailed, and massacred in El Salvador; and
seeing the situation in the (refugee) camp, it then took the
initiative on its own to organize to repatriate to El
Salvador....Groups were organized in order to have a larger
force of witnesses and defenders for those comrades who could
have been captured, beaten, jailed. [This was organized] with
the humanitarian help of international agencies in the
resettlement areas, so that there would be observers.*

*With international help we can rebuild our houses and
reconstruct new lives.*[56]

Unlike the individual returnees who sought to return discreetly
without calling attention to themselves, the refugees participating in the
mass repatriations intended to test the political space in El Salvador.
The large-scale returns were undertaken with the intention of creating
new communities in El Salvador, along similar lines to those of the
formerly displaced persons, which would reflect their determination to
preserve the political and social unity they had built in the camps.

THE MASS REPATRIATIONS

By late 1989 there had been four mass repatriations from Mesa
Grande, ranging in size from 800 to over 4,000 people. Nearly 8,000
Salvadorans from Mesa Grande had returned to areas of conflict. To
the surprise of most observers (and very likely to the refugees
themselves) the coordinators from Colomoncagua announced in May
1989 that they were ready to repatriate, and that all the refugees from
that camp (population 8,300) would return together to "build peace."[57]

San Antonio (population 1,090) made a similar pronouncement a few months later.

The refugees sought to determine their own destination, chart their own course, and handle the politics and the logistics of their returns. In their view, the agencies would be helpful only to the extent that they buttressed and reinforced the decisions that they, the refugees themselves, would make. CRIPDES embraced this agenda wholeheartedly. Its role was to organize the Salvadoran side of the repatriation effort and promote the refugees' demands at home.

The CRIPDES/CNR network responded to the concerns of the Mesa Grande refugees, but had little contact with the Colomoncagua camp. The latter was more remote and isolated, as well as still militantly opposed to the repatriations at the time of the Mesa Grande mass return. Moreover, Diaconia and the Social Secretariat of the Archdiocese had few links with the Colomoncagua refugees, in part because the episcopal jurisdiction of the Archbishop was limited to the capital.

As of this writing, repatriations have reduced the size of the Mesa Grande refugee population to about 2,200 persons, and they are expected to repatriate in the near future. Virtually all the refugees from Colomoncagua and San Antonio repatriated early in 1990.

The First Mass Repatriation

In the early morning of October 10, 1987, the first vehicles in a long convoy of 150 buses, 127 trucks, and several automobiles crossed the Honduran border. Two and a half days later the 4,300 Honduran refugees from the Mesa Grande camp completed their journeys to the five Salvadoran communities that they indicated were their places of origin. At the time of the repatriation, Mesa Grande held about 11,000 refugees.

It was the first mass repatriation of its kind from the Salvadoran refugee camps in Honduras, or anywhere else in Central America, and the prototype of several similar ones in 1988 and 1989. The first mass repatriation was a prototype not only in organizational and logistical terms, but also in establishing a pattern of confrontations about disagreements between the refugees and the Salvadoran government. The politics underlying the conflicts over the conditions of repatriation challenged the traditional UNHCR role as a humanitarian and apolitical mediator.

This first and largest refugee convoy from the Mesa Grande camp took the repatriates to the provinces of Chalatenango, Cuscatlán, and Cabañas, which most of them had left between 1980 and 1982. These provinces, close to a decade later, were still considered zones of conflict, areas contested between the Salvadoran military and the forces of the FMLN. When the refugees had first announced their intention to return *en masse* to these areas, the Salvadoran government, citing the conflict, resisted.

The refugees insisted on their right to return to their places of origin, conflict or no conflict. In the negotiations prior to the first repatriation of October 1987, the UNHCR supported the refugees' position. The government insisted with equal adamance that refugees should instead return to areas under government control. The UNHCR decided not to participate further in the repatriation because of the inability of the two sides to reach an agreement on this fundamental point and on other issues.

On October 8, the day prior to the scheduled departure, the refugees declared their intention to walk home if necessary. The possibility of a violent confrontation at the border was looming. The High Commissioner for Refugees sent the President of El Salvador an urgent plea that he take steps to permit a peaceful return. President Duarte interceded and averted what might well have been an embarrassing and explosive situation. Salvadoran officials returned to the camp late on October 9, to resume negotiations, which ended well past midnight. An agreement was reached permitting the refugees to return to their places of origin. At dawn the convoy was underway.

Other unresolved points had to be dealt with along the way. The refugees rejected the government's attempts at the border to issue documentation that would have required them to answer lengthy questionnaires. The government rejected the refugees' attempt to stop one branch of the convoy to attend a public mass in the San Salvador Cathedral. The issue of the mass, judged by UNHCR as well as the Salvadoran government to be of a political nature, required long discussions involving the Salvadoran Church.

The churches and support groups accompanied the repatriations and were given primary responsibility for subsequent assistance to the returnees. A tripartite meeting held on October 14 and 15, 1987 confirmed UNHCR access to the returnees and its responsibility to oversee their reception, integration, and documentation.[58] UNHCR, it was agreed, would seek funding for assistance, but the Archbishop of San Salvador would coordinate the actual assistance and reintegration projects for a period of about three years.[59]

In the first repatriation, CRIPDES played only a secondary role, helping to identify the five sites chosen as destinations by the refugees: Las Vueltas, Guajila, Copapayo, Santa Marta, and Teosinte. However, both CRIPDES and the refugees emerged from the experience determined to augment their roles. CRIPDES realized that Diaconia's support was indispensable in providing long-term aid to the repatriated communities, and it quickly set about establishing a deeper and more systematic working relationship with it. The returnees also expressed interest in soliciting the material support and political protection afforded by the churches and their links to the international community. The churches recognized as well that effective work with the returnees required close cooperation with CRIPDES/CNR.

Diaconia and its member agencies reciprocated in light of CRIPDES' firm entrenchment in these recently resettled communities. CRIPDES assumed major responsibility for a number of essential functions, including: 1) organizing the resettlements; 2) denouncing human rights violations; and 3) providing a physical place in San Salvador for the repatriated to stay when they went there for administrative or medical reasons. The repatriated communities thus came to view CRIPDES/CNR as their main ally. CRIPDES raised its own budget, with funds from international donors, churches, and international solidarity groups.

The Organization of the Mass Repatriations

The refugees initiated the mass repatriations and took charge of their own organization and preparation. Agency workers and UNHCR generally knew when plans were under way because of preparations in the camp, but were not formally notified until considerable agreement had been reached among the refugees themselves. At the point of formal notification, the refugees selected a coordinator for the repatriation and announced their proposed date and desired conditions in letters to UNHCR and to the Salvadoran and Honduran governments. Typically, these communications asked for the right to go to their places of origin, to be accompanied and assisted by religious and international agencies on the journey and afterwards, to be free from interference from the military during or after the journey, to be free from recruitment attempts by any group, and, in general, to be able to live their lives in peace. The refugee leadership held several meetings in the different sections of the camp, at which the camp inhabitants were informed of the repatriation plans and given an opportunity to voice their opinions.[60]

After receiving announcements of the refugees' intentions, UNHCR undertook informal discussions with the Honduran and especially the Salvadoran government. Honduran authorities were willing to cooperate fully with any plans for departure so long as they were carried out in "an orderly fashion" and the refugees did not stray from the direct route of the convoy.[61] The negotiations with the Salvadoran government also involved communication with the U.S. Embassy, which took a strong interest in the preparations. Finally, when the basis for agreement had been established, a special tripartite meeting was held, during which the two governments and UNHCR finalized the points of the proposed repatriation. The Salvadoran authorities visited the camp prior to each repatriation to inform the refugees of the plans and to hear their objections and alternative proposals.

In the fourth repatriation from Mesa Grande — and in the Colomoncagua and San Antonio repatriations — Salvadoran immigration officials documented the refugees in the camps. Where, when, and how the refugees would be documented remained a thorny issue in all the repatriations.

The refugees, for their part, involved the whole community in preparations for the departure. The coordinator of the repatriation took the names of those wishing to leave, together with details of the number of family members and place of destination. Meanwhile, workers in the various workshops constructed or assembled items needed for the trip, such as crates and boxes, construction materials, and food for the journey. The refugees who were leaving dismantled their houses, and some of the workshops as well. One of the divisive decisions among the refugees themselves was how much of the common property would be removed and how much left behind.

Like the first repatriation, the second, third, and fourth were initiated without full accord on all points. However, as tensions mounted during the hours or days that departures were delayed, everyone was anxious to set the process in motion, even if that meant leaving some details to be sorted out *en route*.

Immediately prior to departure, UNHCR required each adult refugee to sign a voluntary repatriation form. To the extent possible, these documents were signed in private. In addition to its protective role during the repatriation, UNHCR had full responsibility for the organization and preparation of the convoy; i.e., contracting trucks and buses, hiring drivers, and working out logistics with the governments and agencies. UNHCR officials accompanied the refugees the entire distance to the various communities. The agencies working in the camps took responsibility for the tasks that corresponded to their normal work with the refugees; e.g., CRS was in charge of the workshops and supervised the construction of material needed for the trip; MSF and subsequently CEDEN traveled with the convoy to provide medical attention. To support the efforts of its Honduran and Salvadoran staff, UNHCR called on staff members from other regional branch offices and its Geneva Headquarters. Additionally, the ICRC and other private agencies sent vehicles and staff to accompany the convoys.

Independently, the refugees from Mesa Grande were accompanied, at their request, by private individuals who characterized their mission as providing protection. On the Salvadoran side, the refugees were met by representatives of the Salvadoran churches and support groups. The roles of these groups will be discussed below.

The Armed Forces of the two countries were present on their respective sides of the border. Their general disposition was to remain on the sidelines and not to interfere. When problems arose that required negotiations, the civilian authorities handled the discussions. However, on a number of occasions when tensions were especially high, the soldiers let it be known that they were prepared to act.

The four Mesa Grande repatriations were all confrontational. Prior to each tripartite meeting, the Salvadoran government attempted to impose conditions the refugees were bound to reject, such as demanding that only small groups return and that they go elsewhere in the country instead of to their places of origin. The refugees sought to obtain conditions that they maintained were essential to their safety, but which the Salvadoran government either was unwilling or reluctant to concede. In each case, the departure of the convoys, the border crossing, and the transit through El Salvador were delayed or halted for hours as refugees, support groups, UNHCR, Salvadoran church groups, and government officials engaged in verbal battle over sundry points of contention. Often disagreements broke out over points that were previously believed to have been resolved to everyone's satisfaction.

Viewing the repatriations together, it seems clear that the confrontations had less to do with the specific points of disagreement than with the process of deciding. The collective repatriations were intended to demonstrate that the refugees could control their own lives; thus, they challenged the terms of repatriation they considered to be imposed rather than initiated by themselves. To this end, each mass repatriation, to a greater or lesser extent, rejected decisions adopted jointly by the governments and UNHCR, regardless of whether these decisions were in the long-term interests of the refugees.

In insisting on points which they knew would be rejected, the refugees also wished to demonstrate to the Salvadoran government the extent of their international support. This derived from their assumption that their protection and well-being in El Salvador would come from international support and domestic solidarity, outside of any government structures. Therefore, from the moment of their departure, they mounted as much support as possible to reinforce their defiance.

Issues of Contention During the Repatriations

In each of the repatriations, UNHCR found itself on the defensive, as refugees and their supporters refused to hold to the agreements UNHCR had reached with the Salvadoran government during tripartite meetings. The refugees, with the backing of private individuals from North American and European support groups, insisted that UNHCR should defend all the demands the refugees made, in fulfillment of its role to protect and assist them. UNHCR maintained that its mandate to protect the refugees did not, and should not, extend to support for their political objectives or actions. UNHCR usually negotiated on behalf of the refugees' demands and generally attempted to mediate between the government and refugee supporters. However, UNHCR supported the government's position with respect to contested actions that it considered political rather than humanitarian. As the UNHCR had briefly done in the course of negotiations during the first repatriation in 1987, it threatened on several occasions when agreements could not be reached to withdraw from the repatriation activity altogether.

In the midst of the particularly divisive and bitter confrontations that accompanied the second repatriation in August 1988, the High Commissioner sent the various parties an appeal making clear the conditions under which UNHCR would participate in that repatriation and subsequent ones. The document laid out four conditions: that the repatriations be voluntary; that they be carried out in a "strictly humanitarian and apolitical spirit;" that UNHCR's protection role be respected by all; and UNHCR and the two governments be in agreement on the arrangements for the repatriation and UNHCR participation. The High Commissioner went on to appeal for support to UNHCR in its humanitarian undertaking. The document, especially the last point, formalized and hardened the UNHCR approach. Mass repatriations would not be initiated until agreement had been reached on all major points by UNHCR and the two governments. (See Annex.)

We have already mentioned a number of the areas over which disagreements typically occurred. In the following pages we will

elaborate on eight confrontational issues that appeared in at least one
of the repatriations from Mesa Grande and which involved some or all
of the participants; the refugees, UNHCR, private international and
local agencies, churches, and military and civilian authorities.

   The Destinations of the Refugees — Prior to the first repatriation,
the government, especially the military, had tried to prevent the
refugees from returning to the provinces of Chalatenango and Cabañas
where they had chosen to settle. Reluctantly, the government and some
of the military officials accepted that subsequent Mesa Grande
repatriations also would return to these provinces. The refugees in fact
originally came from these areas, but did not necessarily return to the
actual communities from which they had originated. When the refugees
from Colomoncagua and San Antonio announced their repatriation, the
government again sought to convince them to settle on land that it
controlled, instead of going to their chosen sites that were under FMLN
control. In the case of the refugees from Colomoncagua, the refugees
established that they owned a large portion of the land in the
Meanguera area to which they proposed to return. The groups
supporting the San Antonio refugees purchased land in Gualcho to
satisfy the government that the refugees' return would not cause land
tenure conflicts.

   Salvadoran officials argued that if the refugees returned to zones
of conflict, it would be impossible to protect them. Hence, the
government could not fulfill its obligations under the Tripartite
agreements to assure the safety and dignity of those who repatriated.
The refugees argued that they were not returning with any expectation
of protection from the government; they needed their own community
because it would afford them better protection.

   The Size of the Repatriations — Following the first repatriation in
which 4,300 refugees returned in an exhausting and complex operation,
the Salvadoran government attempted to impose a limit of 500 per
convoy for the second repatriation. The refugees utterly rejected this
alternative and insisted on their right to travel together. UNHCR was
sympathetic to the plan of limiting the numbers because it made the
organization easier and a bit less expensive. UNHCR, however, did not
seriously object to the refugees' desires. Having lost the point during
the negotiations for the second repatriation, the Salvadoran government
did not insist again; however, its officials representing the newly-elected
ARENA government of Alfredo Cristiani, vainly attempted to
resuscitate the notion.

International Accompaniment — The issue of who could accompany the repatriating refugees has been perhaps one of the most contentious. Because the refugees attached great importance to the international support they received in the camps, they wanted to augment that support to the greatest extent possible in El Salvador. What they sought and largely obtained were individuals they trusted to accompany them during the repatriation, represent their positions, and act as buffers between themselves and officials of Honduras and El Salvador and UNHCR.

Diaconia, representing the Protestant churches of El Salvador, and the Archdiocese organized international accompaniment by religious groups and mobilized international support for the repatriations.

> *National churches and international religious bodies are in agreement to support the call from our refugee brothers, with one sole purpose, within the context of our Christian commitment, to these people who have suffered the cruelty of an unjust and inhumane war....It is also important to realize that in the case of El Salvador, this repatriation process has unique characteristics and cannot be compared with processes in other countries. In this case, our people left due to the war and have decided to return and repopulate their places of origin within the framework of a deepening of the conflict.*[62]

The international accompaniment during the second repatriation in August 1988 ultimately proved embarrassing to the Salvadoran churches.

Diaconia disseminated periodical circulars to churches and related groups inside and outside El Salvador, and described repatriation plans and the various points of view on issues being debated. One circular, a few days before the departure of the second repatriation, remarked that UNHCR might not be successful in its negotiations with the Salvadoran government in favor of the refugee requests. Therefore, it called for international backing for these requests. The circular went on to suggest:

> *It would be useful if international agencies could express their concern for the security of the returnees to their respective governments, asking them to communicate their concern to the government of El Salvador through their embassies. Moreover we suggest that the agencies also express their concern to the UNHCR in Geneva.*[63]

UNHCR, rather jealous of its role as the agency in charge of the negotiations, did not believe any call for support from international churches was needed. Moreover, by the time the publication was sent, the Salvadoran government had agreed in principle to the major refugee demands.

The U.S.-based group, "Going Home," sent a delegation to Honduras to accompany the refugees, citing the refugees' request that had been transmitted through the churches.[64] Additionally, prior to and during the repatriation, the individuals responded to Going Home's call with hundreds of telegrams and phone calls protesting what they claimed was UNHCR's abandonment of its protection mandate and lack of support for the refugees.[65]

The delegation from Going Home that went to Mesa Grande did not consider its role as one of observers, but rather as proponents of what the refugees wanted.[66] When the refugees asked the members of the delegation to remain on the buses during the border crossing, they readily complied, in violation of the agreement UNHCR had reached with the Salvadoran government regarding international accompaniment.

That agreement stipulated that the international delegation accompanying the refugees from Honduras was to leave the buses at the border. On the other side of the border representatives of the Salvadoran churches would meet the convoy and accompany them to the various destinations. As with the first repatriation, the Archdiocese was to have given the names of those meeting the convoy in advance to the authorities.

The convoy was delayed by a standoff that lasted nearly two days at the border. The international group insisted that its members would leave only in response to a request from the refugees, which did not happen. The scene became increasingly tense. Animals began dying in the heat; elderly people were growing weak; and both the Honduran and Salvadoran military forces moved from the periphery to the center of the action. Finally, the Salvadoran church representatives, who had tried to distance themselves from the confrontation, ordered the group to leave the bus. They did so.

Having invited international accompaniment, the Church found itself implicated in charges from government and press that this foreign presence had politicized the repatriation.[67] The Church, in turn, defended the humanitarian spirit underlying the response to its call for international delegations. Church spokesmen blamed what had happened on a lack of adequate communication and coordination, which left the U.S. delegates in doubt about whether to obey the refugees or local churches.[68]

The Salvadoran Ministry of Foreign Relations issued a formal statement condemning the interference of foreign subversive elements in the repatriation:

> *In light of the political manipulation by subversive groups, interested in continuing to undermine the foundation of the democratic process, and of their zeal to create the international impression of non-compliance with the principles of international humanitarian law by national authorities, [the government of El Salvador] condemns and regrets that the return of the refugees has been obstructed and utilized for negative purposes, having nothing to do with humanitarian considerations.*[69]

In a number of articles, the press repeated similar charges.

During the third repatriation, on November 5, 1988, a similar delegation from Going Home again refused to leave the buses at the border, but the church representatives waiting on the Salvador side wasted no time in telling them to leave. The fourth repatriation gave rise to another prolonged standoff and a telephone assault against UNHCR. But the issue on that occasion was documentation rather than accompaniment. The newly installed ARENA government permitted the members of the delegation with proper visas for El Salvador to cross the border with the convoy.

Reception of Family, Friends, and Support Groups — Attempts to keep accompaniment of the convoy to a minimum held up even less well on the Salvadoran side than on the Honduran side during the second and third repatriations. Church groups charged with assisting the refugees sent trucks of food and medicine to the settlements during the repatriation. Having been prevented frequently from supplying the settlements following the first repatriation, the church groups apparently thought they could take advantage of the visibility of the second repatriation to do so. Instead, the military blocked their trucks at the Colima bridge. At the same time, buses with members from various support organizations, including CRIPDES-CNR and some private voluntary agencies that planned to meet the convoy, also found themselves blocked at the Colima bridge. The situation was as tense at Colima as it was on the border. In all, some 25 buses and 15 to 20 trucks were blocked by soldiers.[70]

The refugees returning with the third repatriation also encountered their relatives and support organizations. This time the churches did not plan supply shipments to coincide with the arrival, rather they delivered supplies before and after the refugees arrived. However, buses with about 1,000 people from CRN and CRIPDES assembled outside of Aguilares.

The Salvadorans at Aguilares expressed the wish to welcome their relatives who were repatriating by having all the buses travel together, mixing the groups among the buses. UNHCR refused to break the convoy and told the Salvadorans they could only take responsibility for a convoy of repatriating Salvadoran refugees. The refugees refused to continue unless their relatives and supporters were allowed to travel with them. UNHCR representatives responded that if the convoys were merged, UNHCR would have to withdraw. That being the case, the refugees answered, they would walk home to Santa Marta. The church representatives agreed to accompany the returnees, whatever their decision, but counselled them that only UNHCR could maintain the convoy and protect them. Several hours later, both refugees and support groups agreed to a UNHCR suggested compromise. The 30 or so buses of the support groups traveled behind the refugee convoy, with one UN vehicle in the very rear to assure that the enlarged convoy was not broken. This arrangement held for the fourth repatriation as well.

The refugees' arrival, typically, was preceded by considerable press coverage, both in the form of articles and paid announcements by the various groups, supporting the demands that refugees were making on the government. Likewise, the Salvadoran government at times published its own announcements of welcome, assuring its compliance with international commitments to assist the refugees, who are "to be incorporated into the democracy and work of the country."[71]

Documenting the Refugees — The great majority of refugees who returned from Mesa Grande to El Salvador lacked the documents they needed to move freely, work, send their children to school, or engage in other activities as citizens of the country.[72] As of mid-summer 1991, documentation remains to be completed.

The documentation process has had two phases: First, Salvadoran officials gave some refugees leaving Honduran camps safe conduct passes with their photographs, a form of temporary documentation which would permit them to move within the country and to engage in most activities permitted to Salvadorans. However, to regain full rights as citizens, such as buying and selling property and voting, the refugees need a personal identity card. To obtain this, they must formally establish their time and place of birth, a step that is far from easy in El Salvador.

The returnees from the first repatriation could not be documented prior to their departure, because their departure had been in doubt until the last minute. At the border, they were delayed while Salvadoran immigration officials questioned them in ways they regarded as intrusive, but gave them no documents. Once in El Salvador, the process of obtaining the needed identification cards was extremely slow. One of the principal demands of subsequent mass repatriations was to accelerate the process of permanent documentation, once refugees returned to their communities in El Salvador.

The refugees of the second and third repatriations rejected the government's attempt to provide temporary documentation pending the receipt of their identification cards. Instead, they contended that the government should accept the refugees' own registry identifying the repatriates. Formal documentation by the government would take place in their Salvadoran communities.

When the refugee coordinators of the fourth repatriation acquiesced to the new ARENA government's insistence that the refugees be documented by the government prior to departure, it seemed that a conciliatory arrangement might be possible. Events proved otherwise.

Early in October 1989, several refugees refused to postpone their departure to await the arrival of the documentation team from El Salvador. The repatriation leaders said they would follow the pattern of the preceding mass repatriations and obtain documentation in El Salvador. The Salvadoran government would not agree. Negotiations dragged on for days. Meanwhile, several carloads of Salvadorans from CRIPDES and CNR arrived in San Marcos, where the local UNHCR office is located. The refugees had specifically requested that CNR represent them and mediate their demands, along with several international observers similar to those present in the previous repatriations.[73]

On October 17, 1989, approximately 200 refugees announced their intention to walk home without documentation and left the camp. They walked as far as San Marcos, where they remained and were housed in a local Protestant church. UNHCR greeted the possibility that the refugees might walk home by restating the position it had established in August 1988; i.e. there would be no UNHCR participation in a repatriation to which the governments had not agreed, except to provide protection, limited accompaniment, and emergency medical care.[74]

The refugees in San Marcos, backed by the various support groups, confronted Salvadoran authorities and UNHCR, demanding that UNHCR begin the repatriation. In the meantime, UNHCR persisted in its negotiations with Salvadoran authorities over where and how documentation might ultimately take place. Agreement seemed close on October 18, when the refugees in the camp agreed to be documented there and the Salvadoran government seemed to accept a Honduran government proposal to document the group that had left the camp in San Marcos. However, the Salvadorans quickly reverted to their previous insistence that all refugees be documented in the camp.[75]

Documentation finally began in Mesa Grande, but the situation remained very tense. The refugees and supporters in San Marcos began a hunger strike; Honduran military officials became visibly impatient with the presence of the refugees in San Marcos; and the Salvadoran and international support groups showered international contacts with rumors that UNHCR's refusal to bring the refugees home had brought about an epidemic of dengue fever, leaving the refugees near death.[76]

Finally, the Salvadoran government agreed to document the refugees in San Marcos, as well as those in the camp. They did this work slowly. The convoy did not move until the morning of October 25, 1989.

Transfer of Property From the Camps to El Salvador — With each new repatriation, the refugees had to determine which part of the common property should go and which should stay. The accepted rule was that the portion of common property to be taken (animals, supplies, tools, and machinery) should correspond to the proportion of the community leaving. Those staying should not have to do without. Therefore, in the second repatriation, UNHCR objected to the removal of one of the two tractors in the camp and, at the last minute, the only water pump. A serious dispute developed among the refugees over the possession of the camp's only remaining tractor in the fourth repatriation.

The refugees repatriating in the first and largest group took very little with them in the way of machinery or tools. Those departing subsequently took as much as they could. Until the last Mesa Grande mass repatriation, there was no major protest when important pieces of machinery were loaded onto the trucks. The refugee leaders knew that they soon would be repatriating themselves, and would need the equipment in the Salvadoran communities.

The loss of expensive equipment was an important issue for UNHCR and voluntary agencies because they would have to replace it for the remaining refugees. They tried to monitor the packing, but could not prevent the refugees from taking most of what they wished.

Installation Grant — The refugees persuaded UNHCR to furnish full adult installation grants for everyone 12 years of age, rather than 14 and over as had previously been the case. The repatriation grants amounted to $50 for adults and $25 for children.

Mass in the Cathedral — In each of the first three repatriations, the refugees demanded that the branch of the convoy passing through the capital city be permitted to attend mass in the Cathedral. As already noted, UNHCR was not sympathetic to this prospect, viewing it as a political show rather than a religious need.

The departure of the third repatriation was delayed by several hours due to the inability to reach agreement on this point, and it remained unresolved when the convoy finally left. Refugee representatives, UNHCR, the Salvadoran Vice-Ministry of the Interior, and church representatives debated the issue subsequently in El Poy at the border. The discussion was cast in terms of the refugees' desire for religious worship which the government claimed it would facilitate outside of the capital city. The real issue in everyone's mind, however, was the political significance of a mass in the Cathedral for the refugees. The spokesman for the Church assured the refugees that the Cathedral would remain open to them, but talked to them about the need to proceed home to take up their new lives. The convoy left the border the next morning, passing through San Salvador without stopping.

The Repatriations from Colomoncagua and San Antonio

Soon after the Colomoncagua refugees announced their intended collective repatriation in May 1989, the San Antonio refugees followed suit. In both cases, the leadership declared that everyone would move and re-establish their communities in the same regions in El Salvador from which they had fled. Those from Colomoncagua returned to Meanguera in Morazán where they founded the new settlement called Ciudad Segundo Montes.[77] From San Antonio the repatriates returned to Nuevo Gualcho in Usulután. They emphasized that they did not intend to revert to simply being *campesinos*. They hoped instead to use the skills they had acquired as artisans and skilled workers in the closed refugee camps.

Like the refugees of Mesa Grande, the refugees from Colomoncagua and San Antonio counted on the assistance and collaboration of grassroots organizations in El Salvador, which were largely funded by religious organizations both within and outside the country. However, the Colomoncagua and San Antonio refugees did not request direct assistance from the Archdiocese, Diaconia, or CRIPDES/CNR. In contrast to the Mesa Grande refugees, refugees from these two camps and their Salvadoran supporters readily entered into negotiations with Salvadoran authorities. They obtained their essential demands: return to their chosen locations by the shortest route across the border, international assistance, the support of their chosen agencies, and prior documentation.

The repatriation of about 7,000 refugees from Colomoncagua and 1,000 from San Antonio took place virtually without incident between January and March 1990. However, on November 18 and December 9, prior to the major exodus, some 1,300 refugees returned spontaneously from Colomoncagua in the midst of a major FMLN offensive.

UNHCR officials accepted the Salvadoran government's postponement of the repatriation due to the fighting during the November 1989 offensive on the grounds that: first, it had previously stated that it would not undertake a formal repatriation unless all parties agreed; second, in the view of UNHCR, conditions for a "secure and dignified" return did not exist due to the ongoing offensive; and third, the government's position and the war situation made it impossible for UNHCR to organize assistance or accompany the returnees to their destination in Morazán.[78]

The refugees did not accept the postponement of the repatriation. In various communications, the refugees emphasized their desire to return to El Salvador after nine years in exile.[79] Far from being daunted by the conflict, they noted that with the military occupied in other parts of the country, they would be able to return with relative safety to Morazán. If they waited, they feared the government might suspend repatriations altogether.

Honduran authorities made no attempt to restrain the refugees' movements. To the contrary, during the December 9 exodus, Honduran authorities accompanied the refugees and assisted with logistics from the camp to the border. The Salvadoran government responded with anger to the spontaneous return of the refugees. The press and government branded them as guerrillas and accused the FMLN of bringing them back to join the insurrection.

The refugees returned in an organized fashion, and thanked their Honduran hosts on their way. They were accompanied from the camps to the border by international observers from the United States, and, during the second movement, observers from Italy and Germany as well.[80] Some members of the press also accompanied the November 18 group to the border. Salvadoran immigration officials who left the camp with the refugees on November 18 attempted to check their documentation at the border, but the refugees did not stop. On the Salvadoran side of the border they were met by about 50 persons representing the support groups that had been organizing their return in El Salvador. A short time later, the FMLN's Radio Venceremos announced that the refugees had returned safely to Morazán.[81]

UNHCR officials debated what to do, but ultimately decided to accompany the repatriating refugees as far as the Honduran border, without actually participating in the convoy. Subsequently, they explained this decision by citing their responsibility to protect the refugees so long as they were in Honduras under the UNHCR mandate. The refugees and many who supported their wish to return criticized UNHCR for agreeing to suspend the planned repatriation and for refusing to provide logistical assistance to the returning refugees. UNHCR, they argued, had a responsibility to assist refugees to repatriate voluntarily and should not suspend its own repatriation preparations at the dictates of governments.

NEW COMMUNITIES IN EL SALVADOR

The refugees presented the mass repatriations as a method to end their exile in Honduras, maintain their community and its commitment to political struggle, and enjoy greater protection and assistance than those who struck out on their own. The refugees used the mass repatriations to insert themselves as a community into pre-existing structures of grassroots support in El Salvador. International support groups and governments pledged assistance and oversight.

The Salvadoran government, for its part, has formally accepted the links between international assistance and humanitarian policies. In its submission to the First Follow-up meeting of the International Conference on Central American Refugees (CIREFCA) in June 1990, the government committed itself to "reincorporating the displaced, refugee, and returnee populations into the economic and social development process of the country," promising to seek "not only the material means but also the political measures and attitudes which can potentially involve the affected groups in their own development."[82] The government asked for international assistance to this end, welcoming funds to be channelled through nongovernmental and international agencies. In response, most international donors pledged continued support for displaced persons and returnees through such agencies.

The Organization of Assistance

Documentation, a Continuing Obstacle to Integration — For the many returnees, who still lack regular personal identification, life is particularly difficult and dangerous. Salvadorans are required to carry documents and present them upon command. Soldiers who encounter persons without documents, especially in zones of conflict, generally assume them to be members of the guerrilla. One elderly refugee reportedly was killed under just such circumstances as he was gathering corn husks for tamales.[83]

Some of the resettled community leaders persist in believing that UNHCR bears the responsibility for securing their identification cards. UNHCR, on the other hand, maintains that while it is prepared to help with the procedures required to obtain the requisite papers as a matter of priority, in the final analysis the government of El Salvador is obligated to provide each person with documentation.

The returnees who did not obtain safe-conduct passes often carry papers provided to them by the Catholic Church as they crossed the border. The human rights office of El Salvador's Archdiocese, *Tutela Legal*, gave each returnee a piece of paper with a photo and the seal of the organization. Although it imparts no officially recognized status nor is it a legal document, the Tutela Legal paper has been so widely used that it has had a kind of *de facto* legitimacy bestowed upon it. The government is unhappy about its use, in part because it considers this identification to be an usurpation by the Church of an essential government function. The ARENA government has criticized the slow delivery of documents by its predecessors, and now appears to be moving more expeditiously in providing official documents.

The documentation process has been complicated and tedious, despite the efforts of UNHCR and its operational agency, ASAI, to assist. In the zones of conflict, many municipal buildings have been burned or bombed, destroying birth and marriage records in the process. In such cases, ASAI conducts a census of residents, and with that information goes to the corresponding Central Electoral Council where microfilms are often preserved. These records are then taken to the respective city halls, and when the mayor is present and cooperative, the process can be moved along rather swiftly. Unfortunately, in many of the municipalities the mayors live elsewhere, fearing reprisals from the FMLN, which believes it "governs" the town.

An additional complication involves the requirement that an official of the Ministry of the Interior be physically present when the documents are distributed. Although the FMLN is generally cooperative and allows Interior officials to move unhampered into the zones of conflict, there appears to be some ambivalence about documenting residents of zones they consider within their jurisdiction. At least one case of guerrilla harassment of Interior officials has been reported.

Of the 6,000 refugees who had repatriated in the mass repatriations until May 1989, 3,023 documents had been secured and 1,270 had been completely registered with the issue of identification cards. The collective repatriations of the end of 1989 and 1990 increased the number of repatriated refugees in need of documentation by more than a thousand new cases.

Another issue is the status of the 4,000 children born in Honduras. As a rule, newborns were registered with Salvadoran consulates in Honduras. In many cases, however, the only document these children carry is one that was provided by UNHCR, attesting to their parentage.

Roads — Roads are another issue of contention. Despite repeated attempts by UNHCR to disembarrass them of the notion, the returnees believe that the UNHCR is, or at least should be, responsible for the construction and maintenance of the roads to the resettlement areas. The returnees complain loudly about the poor condition of the roads. According to UNHCR, the Salvadoran government's Ministry of Public Works, under its contract with the UN agency, is charged with this obligation. Government road building crews are reluctant to travel to remote areas of conflict and government bureaucrats are reluctant to assign heavy equipment to these zones.

Assistance: Refugees From Mesa Grande - The churches working with Diaconia have remained the essential channel for all material support to the repatriated communities from Mesa Grande. Diaconia has established a rather clear-cut division of labor: Diaconia itself is limited to coordination and fund-raising and is not involved in the design of projects. Program implementation rests with the member agencies. The Lutheran Church secures all the building materials for reconstruction and provides technical assistance, although the residents assume responsibility for the actual construction. Distribution of food is handled by the Social Secretariat of the Catholic Church. The Foundation to Promote Cooperatives (FUNDPROCOOP) and the Federation of Farming Cooperatives of El Salvador (FEDECOOPADES) concentrate on helping farmers resume agricultural production by securing such inputs as seeds and fertilizer. For those returning to Chalatenango, the department's Catholic Church has created its own social service structure and is concentrating on health promotion. The Lutheran church focuses on the health care needs of those in other departments (Cabañas and Cuscatlán).

        CRIPDES remains important. The churches are sensitive to questions of paternalism and intervention and believe that their responsibility is to support the process as defined by the returnees and their CRIPDES allies. By working with the CRIPDES/CNR, the churches feel they encourage the empowerment of the refugees themselves, thus breaking the legacy of dependency.

        Because Diaconia is not operational, CRIPDES works at the local level with the staff of the churches to sort out priorities and establish goals. A permanent dialogue between CRIPDES/CNR and the churches has permitted the articulation of a common strategy and approach. By stressing their role as facilitators, while nevertheless orchestrating the supply of essential commodities to the resettlement areas, the churches hope to encourage the community style of organization which had prospered in the Honduran refugee camps. The churches and supportive international agencies believe that, despite their flaws, these egalitarian "new societies" are a new example of Christian ideals.

        The interaction of CRIPDES with UNHCR has been less frequent, primarily because CRIPDES essentially views UNHCR as compromised by its relationship to the government and the military. Driven by their antagonism toward the military and the Salvadoran government, CRIPDES/CNR have acted on the premise that by making things difficult for the UNHCR, they also were making things difficult for the government. As described by an international volunteer, the UNHCR was more accessible and visible than the Salvadoran Government. Hence, it became a convenient target for complaints from the returnees and, therefore, a scapegoat for the government.

        There have been quarrels at the local level between the churches and CRIPDES. The churches wished to retain some oversight over the distribution of material support, in part because they felt that their bargaining strength with the government was more secure. CRIPDES realized that the churches enjoyed greater credibility with the government and the international community, which brought enhanced leverage. Notwithstanding the pragmatic rationale for giving the churches a more pronounced role, CRIPDES resented the limitations that its own more outspoken, militant profile brought on. The churches argued that their operational involvement was in the best interest of the repatriates.

The repatriates likewise have had an ambivalent attitude toward the churches. The leaders argued that they did not need a buffer. While they acknowledged their great appreciation for the churches and their support, they maintained that they were in fact part of the church. The repatriated insisted that they had the right to live in dignity and security without having an intermediary.

The repatriated communities have urged that the supervisory functions and policy guidance provided by church organization be reduced. Yet when difficulties arise, these communities quickly seek the protection that the formal church structures, particularly of the Catholic Church, and the UNHCR can offer.

The churches have served as a communications clearinghouse, proving crucial help in advocacy, mediation, communication, and conflict resolution. On several occasions, the churches and agencies have mediated between UNHCR or Salvadoran authorities and the repatriated, paving the way for accommodations acceptable to the military and the Salvadoran government. For example, a caravan of repatriates returning to the small rural village of Teosinte insisted on military authorization to follow a road from Chalatenango that they had been accustomed to taking before their exile. They refused to take the word of the military that the road was impassable. After a heated debate, a small scouting party made up of international agency volunteers was sent to investigate; it returned confirming the military's assessment of the road.

Assistance: Refugees From Colomoncagua and San Antonio — In planning their repatriations, the refugees named the agencies in El Salvador that would arrange for their reintegration. These were, the Foundation for Salvadoran Workers' Empowerment and Solidarity for Colomoncagua, the Community Development Endowment for Morazán, the Salvadoran Association for Integral Development for San Antonio, and the Committee for Repatriation of San Antonio.

During the planning phase, these agencies established what were described as productive working relations both with UNHCR and government officials. Subsequently, during the November 1989 offensive, when some of the leaders of these agencies appeared to be associated with the FMLN, the government sought to replace them. They were later reinstated, after a brief period during which the refugees were assisted by the same church agencies that had assisted the Mesa Grande refugees.

To a large extent, the refugees from Colomoncagua have reproduced their camp organization in Morazán in a community they named Segundo Montes City, after one of the Jesuits murdered by the military in November 1989. The refugees from San Antonio, also maintaining their camp community, are in the Province of Usulután in the community of Nuevo Gualcho.

Protection in the New Settlements

The military's perception that repopulated areas are the kitchens, laundries, and hotels for the FMLN provides the rationale for unrelenting distrust. Both residents and visitors are required to secure safe-conduct passes from the authorities before travelling to these communities. Residents bitterly complain that they are often detained and interrogated before being able to proceed home. In one instance, four people returning to northern Chalatenango were removed physically from a UNHCR vehicle over the strenuous objections of the UN official.

UNHCR visits the communities daily, covering as much ground as it can with its small staff. At times, however, even UNHCR vehicles are denied access to certain areas where local military command posts claim there is conflict. Protection officers respond to complaints by the families of returnees and agency workers in the settlements by bringing cases of detention and harassment to the attention of local and national military and government officials. During regular meetings with the government and military, UNHCR has sought to modify specific practices, as well as overall attitudes, and particularly to assure continued access for the delivery of assistance.

Nevertheless, protection problems exist throughout the areas to which the refugees have returned. Residents complain bitterly about what they characterize as a campaign of systematic harassment by the military. The most frequent incidents tend to occur where there is still conflict. The Salvadoran Air Force continues to bomb adjacent fields, often destroying the crops. Occasionally an errant bomb falls close enough to populated areas to injure or kill someone. Communities such as Teosinte and Santa Marta are located near FMLN camps and are frequently visited by rebel soldiers, who are cordially received. This proximity and cordiality inspires military retaliation, which takes various forms. According to agencies working with those who have returned to Santa Marta, the military at one point embarked on a propaganda campaign among neighboring communities to discredit the resettlement. Santa Marta residents responded by offering the health services available at its clinics to all the surrounding villages.

The communitarian character of the repatriates' communities is viewed as socialist (and hence unacceptable) to the authorities. Some of the individuals working with the returnees believe that the military fears that the potential success of these communities would offer an example that other poor villages in rural El Salvador might emulate.

The Future of the Repatriated Refugees in El Salvador

After as long as three years in El Salvador, the returnees remain extremely dependent on international assistance. The question still unanswered for all the new settlements is the dilemma over what to do with skilled artisans in a rural setting. Material inputs are required to keep the cottage industries of shoes, clothes, spare parts, and simple machinery in operation. Moreover, the available land is often not sufficient to produce enough food for the community. There are two realistic explanations for the continued dependence of the settlements on direct assistance. The first relates to the organization and implementation of projects in the communities; the second is rooted in the conflict and mutual distrust between the returnees and Salvadoran authorities.

Development plans in these new settlements have been hampered by organizational challenges, competition for scarce resources, and ineffective supervision and management. Funding agencies sometimes have timetables for project design and implementation that fail to coincide with the rhythm of work in the communities. One agency complained that the rush to commence new projects (prompted by the demands of funding agencies) prematurely interrupted efforts to complete existing projects. Projects on the way to completion were sometimes short-circuited as managerial expertise and labor were diverted to new assignments.

Coordination between funders and implementing church agencies is often complicated by the returnees' commitment to maintain communitarian ideals and their strict adherence to the principle that

they are the masters of their own destiny. During one memorable
episode, the Salvadoran military arrived with much fanfare at Los
Ranchos de Guajila with food supplies. The military, over the
objections of the community leaders, insisted on distributing the food to
each person individually. The next day, after the military departed,
virtually all the families opted to place their portion in the
community-run warehouse.

The Salvadoran military, fearing that food and medical supplies
delivered by church agencies might be diverted to the FMLN,
periodically halt the delivery of these supplies, preventing passage into
the conflictive zones, and disrupting life in the settlements.

Agricultural production has suffered due to fear of military
incursions. On some occasions, the army reportedly has taken or
destroyed crops just prior to harvest, leaving the returnees with little or
nothing. Hence, the repatriated refugees are reluctant to invest any
funds in improving the land on the supposition that they could be left
not only without food for themselves, but also in debt.[85]

Although the new settlements are likely to remain economically
dependent at least until the conflict can be brought to a close, they
continue to exude a kind of missionary zeal. The pedagogical features
of their experience are eagerly transmitted to all who will listen,
including international visitors, and neighboring villages. Bonded by
the experience in the camps, each settlement takes a lively interest and
concern in the welfare of all the others. Soccer games, anniversaries,
and other community events routinely draw people together from other
repopulated areas, creating an unusual base of mutual support.

The adversity encountered in the camps in Honduras has made
the refugees more willing to subordinate certain individual rights for the
defense of the community; the same ethic has guided their conduct in
rebuilding their communities in El Salvador. Community coordinators
believe that unity is a prerequisite for survival. "Urbanized" in the
camps, they continue to marshall their organizational and technical
skills to respond to the challenges of maintenance and survival in a war
zone. Although in a technical sense, these Salvadorans have
repatriated, they see themselves as communities set apart from the
larger society, not yet integrated into it.

CONCLUSION

Deciding to Repatriate Prior to Peace

Nearly 30,000 Salvadorans have voluntarily returned to their country since 1984, according to Salvadoran government figures, the majority from Honduras.[85] More than half the total, about 16,000, returned in group repatriations from refugee camps in Honduras. Most of the remaining returnees came back individually from these same camps or from other countries in Central America; i.e., Costa Rica, Guatemala, Nicaragua. By 1990, nearly the entire population of Salvadoran refugees had left Honduras.

The Salvadorans did not return to conditions of peace, much less to significant changes in the political-military control of the country. During the government of José Napoleón Duarte, civilian deaths declined and greater tolerance developed for organized opposition activities, which the succeeding Cristiani government by and large has upheld.[86] Nevertheless, armed conflict has continued until the present (Summer 1991). It is most intense precisely in the areas to which the majority of the refugees — those who repatriated collectively — chose to return.

The refugees who repatriated individually generally returned for the usual reasons that refugees decide to end their exiles, even when conditions at home have not greatly improved: because of the hopelessness of their situation as refugees, particularly for those confined to closed camps and because they missed their families and wished to raise children in their own country. A small number of Salvadorans repatriated to distance themselves from the political influence of the refugee community leadership. An undetermined but substantial number of those who returned to El Salvador from other parts of Central America left again soon thereafter to seek better lives elsewhere as undocumented workers. UNHCR has sought resettlement for those refugees whose security is at risk and might be subject to political threats in El Salvador. The individual returnees who remain have received relatively little assistance and are difficult to monitor and protect. They live their lives as best they can.

After years of resisting repatriation and sometimes punishing persons who decided to repatriate, the leaders of the refugee communities spearheaded a massive return. The mass repatriations that brought the majority of the refugees from Honduras back to El Salvador had little to do directly with the refugees' individual desires to go home, however strong those desires may have been. The refugees who returned collectively from Honduras in the mass repatriations probably had the same personal reasons for returning as did others. But, unlike the others, their intention was not to live inconspicuous lives, adjusting as best they could to the difficulties of the regime. Rather, they went home because they believed that the moment had come when, as organized communities in El Salvador, they could contribute to the political struggle against the government and military. They had never ceased to support this struggle when they were in the remote, military controlled refugee camps in Honduras.

Although most of the refugees had been neither politically committed nor accustomed to collective activity when they first entered the camps, they invariably supported the objectives of the FMLN because of what they had suffered at the hands of the Salvadoran authorities. The majority readily accepted strong leadership and adapted to the discipline and organization demanded of them by this leadership. Such leaders seemed all the more essential in view of the hostility they experienced from the Honduran government and military. The camp experience, in effect, molded a group of *campesinos*, accustomed to being victims without the means to fight back, into a community more than willing to subordinate individual interests to the interest of what they saw to be their collective security.

Like their counterparts in Pakistan, Ethiopia, on the Thai-Cambodian border and much closer to home, on the Atlantic coast of Honduras, the Salvadoran refugees did not consider that their exile or refugee status separated them from the struggle in which their compatriots were engaged. Such communities have been described as "refugee warriors."[87] However, unlike refugee militants in other settings, the Salvadorans could not bear arms and were confined to their camps. They were supporters of the struggle. There was, to be sure, ongoing refugee contact with FMLN, which benefitted from some material assistance from the refugees as well as some new recruits.

The refugees felt they were under siege in Honduras, their country of refuge, just as they had been in El Salvador. In response, they did not soften their militancy or attempt to comply with the wishes of their hosts. Rather, they organized themselves and, with the help of sympathetic relief workers, mobilized international solidarity on their behalf. Unquestionably, the refugees considered their ability to defy the objectives of the Honduran and U.S. authorities — and frequently the UNHCR as well — to be blows against the Salvadoran government.

Refugee workers and observers were uniformly struck by the refugees' apparent unity. There were, however, dissidents and defectors among the refugees whose numbers grew as the years passed, and hopes for change diminished. There were also many who passively accepted the discipline imposed on them, but opted to leave camps when given the opportunity. The refugee leadership dealt harshly with the dissidents, defectors, and sometimes even with those who simply wished to withdraw from the collective. Defection, particularly when the individual in question had formerly been an active participant in camp political life, was viewed as treason.

Humanitarian Assistance in a Political Context

The Salvadoran refugees were ideal subjects for projects and programs that sought to promoted skills training, self-help, and refugee participation. This particularly impressed the relief agency staffs, who willingly endured the hardships of life in the isolated remote camps in order to contribute to the refugees' well-being. These relief workers found the Salvadorans to be excellent workers as well as articulate about their experiences and beliefs, and ready to take advantage of whatever opportunities were offered them. Many of the camp workers were from North American or European agencies. Few had previously worked with refugees or had any prior knowledge of UNHCR operations. Some came to Salvadoran camps with strong sympathies for the Salvadoran left; others had little or no previous knowledge of Central America realities, but were impressed by the refugees' strength in the face of suffering. The refugees cited the agency staff as their most important and, perhaps, only trusted allies in Honduras. Notably, Médecins sans Frontières, the only agency that sought to impose its own *modus operandi* over the refugees wishes was subjected to such a barrage of hostility and protest that it withdrew from the program in Honduras.

All the relief workers described their work as humanitarian and apolitical. In response to criticism that their reliable defense of the refugees' demands constituted political bias, the agency personnel contended that their task was to support the refugees, not to dissuade them from what they had decided was in their own best interest. The relief workers valued the trust the refugees held for them and wished to preserve it by avoiding interference in the management of their affairs. The also saw themselves as the refugees' only allies. One religious worker in the camp described how she attempted to convince the refugee leaders to be less harsh with defectors who wished to leave by reminding them that they too were struggling for human rights and freedom to speak. But, she noted, she did not defend particular individuals against the community because, in doing so, she would lose the trust of the community.[88]

Since the agencies were under contract to UNHCR, UNHCR felt that agencies also bore some responsibility to assist UNHCR efforts. UNHCR staff complained that the attitudes of some relief workers were undermining essential UNHCR efforts to reach understandings acceptable to both refugees and the governments. UNHCR officials prided themselves on having averted confrontations and having ameliorated abuses thanks to good working relationships with government officials. UNHCR had ample experience working in settings where host governments were hostile to refugees in their territories and where the wars they sought to escape followed them to the camps. Unlike the relief agency personnel, UNHCR officials considered the Salvador program in a comparative context and, in particular, in the context of other programs in the region.

The UNHCR approach remained relatively consistent despite frequent personnel changes in its field offices. It sought from the Honduran government the same privileges for Salvadorans which had been conceded to the Nicaraguans; i.e., freedom of movement and more space in which to cultivate. It rejected refugee demands for conditions unavailable to other refugees — and beyond the budget. It protested the mistreatment of refugees and relief workers to Honduran authorities. However, in response to criticism that it should expand its protection staff and role, UNHCR officials contended that their ability to protect the refugees depended less on the number of staff than on the commitment of the Honduran government. The staff was, however, expanded to cope with the continuing problems.

In speaking the language of its mandate, i.e. the search for durable solutions (voluntary repatriation, local integration, or resettlement), UNHCR alternately aroused the ire of the Honduran government and the refugees. Until the decision to organize the mass repatriations was made, voluntary repatriation was anathema to the refugee leadership. Attempts to obtain greater freedom of movement were rejected by the Honduran authorities. Attempts at relocations that implied increased self-sufficiency and integration were vigorously opposed by the refugees and finally abandoned by the government. Eventually, the option of repatriation assumed increasing importance.

Other involved actors (e.g., the U.S. Embassy, voluntary agencies, and international observers) periodically criticized the management of the refugee program: too few sanctions against refugee politics, not enough protection, greater or lesser consultation with the Honduran government, and so on.

The Repatriations

When the refugees repatriated individually, they depended on UNHCR to make preparatory arrangements to conduct them through the frightening, sometimes onerous, bureaucratic steps on both sides of the border, and to bring them home. In the mass repatriations, however, the refugee leadership tried to diminish this dependence. The refugees wished to demonstrate to the Salvadoran government, through their collective repatriations to the zones of conflict and guerrilla control, the extent of their political will and organizational strength. The refugees from Mesa Grande, Colomoncagua, and San Antonio established their own timetables, destinations, and routes as well as the agencies that would accompany and receive them. UNHCR and the Salvadoran government then negotiated during the tripartite meetings on the basis of what the refugees demanded, with no assurance whatsoever that the latter would actually accept the compromises they reached. The difference between the Mesa Grande refugees, as opposed to the others, was their intention to turn the repatriation process, and not just the fact of repatriating, into a political confrontation.

The Salvadoran mass repatriations posed a unique and unprecedented challenge to UNHCR and the Salvadoran government. Many refugee groups in the past have bypassed UNHCR and government repatriation plans by simply proceeding home on their own. The Salvadorans, on the contrary, embraced the benefits that came along with an organized repatriation: logistical support, food maintenance along the way, and protection, but they appropriated the decision-making authority for themselves. They did so, moreover, with the backing of Salvadoran political activists and international supporters.

The participants in the mass repatriations returned as a group to the zones of conflict from which they had come and, once in El Salvador, re-established the small collective living patterns they had created as refugees. They had become "urbanized" during almost a decade in exile and did not wish to live as before. More importantly, as an organized community, they could maintain political unity, deal more effectively with the military, and represent their needs to the various international and domestic agencies that assisted and sought to protect them. They remain dependent on their agencies to this day, unable to achieve economic self-sufficiency as the war continues to be waged around them.

REFERENCES

[1]Philip Berryman, in **The Religious Roots of Rebellion: Christians in Central American Revolutions** (New York: Orbis Books, 1984), 95, accepts the 10,000 estimate made by Thomas Anderson, **Matanza, El Salvador's Communist Revolt of 1932** (Lincoln: University of Nebraska Press, 1971), based on the size of the armed forces engaged in the killing, and representing a retaliation of 100 to one, the military killing 100 alleged rebels for each person killed during the insurgency.

[2]For a brief time, outright war was averted, when in October 1979 a progressive military Junta seized power in El Salvador. For a few hopeful months the new leadership, supported by a number of centrist and leftist civilian political figures, undertook what seemed to be a reformist path. By December the progressives in the Junta had clearly lost out to the military hardliners. The civilians, most notably Guillermo Ungo of the Social Democrats, Rubén Zamora of the Christian Democrats, and Roman Mayorga, the rector of the Central American University, left the government to become leaders of the opposition. Education minister Salvador Samayoa joined one of the armed groups that later merged with other founding members in the FMLN.

[3]For accounts of the early development of the armed Salvadoran right, see Michael McClintock, **The American Connection: Volume I, State Terror and Popular Resistance in El Salvador** (London: Zed Books, 1985); Robert Armstrong and Janet Shenk, **El Salvador, The Face of Revolution** (Boston: South End Press, 1982); Martin Diskin and Kenneth E. Sharpe, "El Salvador," **Confronting Revolution**, eds., Morris Blachman, William LeoGrande, and Kenneth Sharpe (New York: Pantheon Books, 1986). See also reports of Amnesty International, Americas Watch, the Lawyers Committee for Human Rights and other human rights groups.

[4]Berryman, **Religious Roots of Rebellion**, 100-109; see also Tommie Sue Montgomery, "Liberation and Revolution, Christianity as a Subversive Activity in Central America" in **Trouble in our Backyard** Martin Diskin, ed. (New York: Pantheon Books, 1983), pp. 75-100.

[5]"La cuestión de las masas," **Estudios Centroamericanos** (July 1987), 423. Although the article is unsigned, it was almost certainly written by Ignacio Ellacuría, S.J., then Rector of the Universidad Centroamericana José Simeón Cañas, who was among the six Jesuits murdered at the university by the Salvadoran military in November 1989.

[6]Berryman, **Religious Roots of Rebellion**, 149.

[7]See Americas Watch, **Report on Human Rights in El Salvador** (January 26, 1982), 43-48; 280-289. The number of civilian deaths ranged between 5,000 and 6,000 during the following years. There continued to be extremely high numbers of individual killings until 1984 when they declined largely due to pressures from U.S. authorities concerning death squad activities. Although the death squad murders declined, the military continued to target civilian populations with military sweeps and aerial bombing.

[8]Lawyers Committee for Human Rights and Americas Watch, **El Salvador's Other Victims: The War on the Displaced**, New York, (April 1984), 30.

[9]See the discussions on displaced persons in the publication of the Lawyers' Committee and Americas Watch, **El Salvador's Other Victims**, and Elizabeth Ferris, **The Central American Refugees** (New York, Praeger, 1987), 22-25.

[10]According to UNHCR figures, over a thousand refugees entered in 1985, some 430 came in 1986 and only 47 in 1987.

[11]Except where otherwise stated, the material in this section has been drawn from the accounts of Pax Christi International, "Salvadoran Refugees: Honduras" (findings based on a July 1981 mission) Human Rights Reports No. 1. Belgium, 1981; Diane Kuntz, **Politics, Refugees and Health: An Assessment of the Nutrition Program of the Salvadoran Refugee Camp at La Virtud, Honduras**, unpublished MA/MPH thesis, University of California, Los Angeles, 1983; Inter-American Council on Refugees, "Salvadoran Refugees In Honduras, November 1981-February 1982," Washington DC, 1982; and an interview with Father Jesús Orellana of Caritas by Ricardo Stein, January 9, 1989.

[12]Interview by author with UNHCR official, March 1990. See also the annual reports of Amnesty International, Americas Watch.

[13]A refugee from Mesa Grande, Gladis Guardardo, cites this figure in Renato Camarda, **Forced to Move: Salvadoran Refugees in Honduras**, (San Francisco: Solidarity Publications, 1985).

[14]Berryman, **Religious Roots of Rebellion**, cites 300 deaths, apparently based on later newspaper accounts; Guardardo says 600. Father Earl Gallagher, a Capuchin priest, was the first to visit the scene and interview the survivors. His report appeared almost a year later in the **Sunday Times**, London, February 22, 1981, and was reprinted in a number of publications thereafter, e.g., in Philip Wheaton, **The Iron Triangle: The Honduran Connection**,(Washington DC: EPICA, 1981).

[15]Amnesty International, **Amnesty International Report**, 1983, p. 133.

[16]This account was drawn primarily from Diane Kuntz, **Politics, Refugees and Health**, 46-49, and Pax Christi, "Salvadoran Refugees", 32-33.

[17]Interview with Sarah Shannon by Ricardo Stein, E. Hayek, December 13, 1989.

[18]Buenos Aires, located in the village itself of Colomoncagua, consisted of a few hundred persons, from a single village in El Salvador, who fled a guerrilla attack. Thus, they represented the victims of the other side of the Salvadoran civil war and their characteristics were quite distinct from those in the other three camps. Their experiences did not form part of this study.

[19]Interviews with Colonel Abraham García Turcios, Coordinator of the Honduran National Commission for Refugees, CONARE, August 8, 1989 and Leo Valladares Lanza, Consultant to the Honduran government interviewed by Patricia Weiss Fagen.

[20]Interview by author with then-Head of the Regional Office of UNHCR in San José, Costa Rica, March, 1990.

[21]See Camarda, **Forced to Move**, 85. Interview with relief worker from Caritas, December, 1988 by author. The relief workers complained that World Vision, one of the initial agencies involved in assisting the refugees—and like CEDEN supported by Evangelical churches—had passed lists of alleged subversives to the military authorities, and therefore was responsible for several kidnappings and deaths. World Vision itself investigated the charges. The investigation team rejected charges of collaboration between World Vision and the military (or U.S. authorities), but criticized the World Vision operation on grounds of leadership, relations with other agencies, and management. **A Report on the Refugee Relief Program of World Vision in Honduras**, World Vision International, 1981.

[22]The territory consisted of areas called pockets (bolsones). These pockets occupied about 400 kms along the border, and were said to serve as places to which the FMLN could retreat in relative safety.

[23]The Salvadoran military and paramilitary forces entered with the apparent permission of the Honduran forces. Honduran soldiers often arrested and otherwise harassed refugees. These incidents are described by a number of human rights reports, citing voluntary agency personnel. A chronology of the events is found, for example, in World Vision, "Report."

[24]Diane Kuntz, **Politics, Refugees and Health**, 113-114, cites a letter from U.S. Ambassador Jack Binns to CEDEN (July 3, 1981) in which the relief organizations are accused of involvement in passing food to the guerrillas. In a portion of the letter reprinted in Kuntz, the Ambassador notes that "effective control over the distribution of food (is) practically impossible, especially in the area of La Virtud."

[25]The head of CONARE, Col. García Turcios, described the camps as the "rear guard of the FMLN, where one finds indoctrinations, executions, and kidnapping." Interview conducted by Ricardo Stein, December 15, 1986.

Honduran authorities cited intelligence sources in their reports to the U.S. Embassy personnel who by and large believed them, but disagreed as to whether some of the allegations might be exaggerated. To establish the extent of contact between the refugees and FMLN and other issues related to the refugees, the State Department hired a consultant, Robert Gersony. He prepared several classified reports between 1983 and 1987. According to interviews with U.S. and Honduran officials, the Honduran authorities frequently captured Salvadorans outside of the camps who admitted to being guerrillas and who were carrying clothing, boots, and medicine known to have come from the camps.

[26]The statement of a Salvadoran officer quoted in **Newsweek** Magazine, November 30, 1981, cited in Lawyers Committee, **Honduras: A Crisis on the Border, A Report on Salvadoran Refugees in Honduras**, (January 1985), 19. Other similar quotations from Honduran and Salvadoran military officers appear in Kuntz, **Politics, Refugees and Health**, 112-113.

[27]This quote is from Congressman Dellums' Introduction to Camarda, **Forced to Move**, 4.

[28]Arthur Schmidt "Report on a Visit to Refugee Camps in Honduras," (American Friends Service Committee, Philadelphia, June 1982), 4.

[29]Kuntz, **Politics, Refugees and Health**, 126-127; Schmidt, **Visit to Refugee Camps**, 6-14.

[30]Ibid., 128. UNHCR "Fact Sheets" estimate a case load of 20,000 Salvadorans in November 1981 and a total of just under 15,000 in September 1982. Kuntz cites an estimate of 7,000 Salvadorans who returned to El Salvador instead of going to Mesa Grande. Camarda, **Forced to Move**, also gives accounts of refugee resistance to the move. UNHCR also cut food and medicine to the Nicaraguan Miskito refugees along the Atlantic coast, in order to oblige them to move from Mocorrón to outlying settlements.

[31]The Canadian Inter-Church Committee distributed translations of two of the letters, (March 23 and September 1, 1982) and referred to another written on June 4. "Report and Recommendations to the United Nations High Commissioner for Refugees regarding the Protection of Refugees and the Coordination of Material Assistance by the UNHCR in Honduras" (September 1982). The refugees regularly sent letters to the UNHCR in Geneva relating their grievances.

[32]This choice was criticized as too close to a major military installation.

[33]The polarization over relocation is described, largely from the voluntary agency point of view, in the Lawyers' Committee report, **Honduras**, Chapter V.34.

[34]UNHCR "Fact Sheet," No. 12, January 1985; Ferris, Central American Refugees, 104.

[35]See footnote 25.

[36]At issue were questions about the general quality and policies of health care, complaints about lack of sympathy by MSF staff. Another delicate issue was the degree to which refugee health promoters as opposed to MSF doctors might control the distribution of medicines. MSF did not usually identify itself with the other agencies' position to defend the refugees.

[37]In a "Memorandum of Understanding Between the Government of Honduras and the UNHCR Governing the Treatment of Refugees" of June 2, 1987, UNHCR secured what it considered a Honduran commitment to humanitarian principles of refugee protection. The Memo, which also included a recognition of Honduras' right to have permanent access to the camps and to place Honduran nationals in the camps, was vigorously criticized by refugee advocates.

[38]UNHCR officials went to El Salvador from February 19 to 22, 1985 to discuss issues related to voluntary repatriation with Salvadoran authorities and to report on the agreements to the Honduran government.

[39]Subsequent tripartite meetings took place on: April 9, 1986; July 1, 1986; August 27-28, 1987; October 14-15, 1987; December 10-11, 1987; February 27, 1988; October 25, 1988; October 3, 1989; and December 20, 1989.

[40]There were about 500,000 internally displaced in El Salvador during the mid 1980s. As will be discussed below, CONADES did not assist those internally displaced persons who were considered to be sympathetic to the FMLN. These people, numbering approximately 200,000, were assisted primarily by the Catholic and Protestant churches, and were subject to frequent and serious government harassment.

[41]UNHCR, "Notes on a Mission to El Salvador and Honduras, February 19-23, 1985."

[42]Although the camps were located only a few miles from the border, the repatriating refugees spent more than a full day traveling first to Tegucigalpa and then to the border. This was done in order to avoid crossing the border into FMLN controlled regions.

[43]Earlier, prior to the UNHCR presence, refugees sometimes had to spend up to a week in the military barracks, without benefit of any UNHCR presence.

[44]Twenty persons had repatriated from San Antonio during the first five months of 1989.

[45]Interview by author in La Libertad, August 14, 1989.

[46]Ibid.

[47]Ibid.

[48]Ibid.

[49]Ibid.

[50]FMLN entries into the camps to recruit were difficult to confirm. However, refugees have reported strong pressures being exerted on them for recruitment.

[51]There are no formal counts of the number of refugees leaving the camps in Honduras, returning, then seeking asylum or refuge in other countries. The information is largely anecdotal and the existence of a pattern to this effect inferred. For example, several asylum lawyers and the UNHCR legal advisor confirm that many asylum applications are from former UNHCR refugees in Honduras. Refugees and refugee workers reported that considerable mail came to the camps from the United States, Mexico, and Belize. U.S. researcher, Michael Stone, found a number of former refugees from Honduras in a survey he conducted among Salvadoran refugees in Belize.

[52]Australia let it be known that in emergency cases, people could be relocated within a week.

[53]Interview by author in San Salvador, August 16, 1989.

[54]Following the International Conference on Central American Refugees, CIREFCA, in Guatemala, ASAI and other supporting agencies began to plan and implement programs oriented toward the longer-term development requirements of the repatriated population.

[55]Interview conducted by author Weiss Fagen in Teosinte, August 12, 1989.

[56]Interview conducted by Ricardo Stein with a group of refugees in Mesa Grande, January 6, 1989.

[57]The message was sent to the international meeting of governments in Guatemala, CIREFCA, held at the initiative of the governments of Central America, under the auspices of the United Nations, and organized by UNHCR.

[58]The Fourth Meeting of the Tripartite Commission on Voluntary Repatriation, attended by officials of El Salvador, Honduras and the UNHCR.

[59]Funding for assistance to the refugees who returned through the mass repatriations came largely from the European Economic Community, but also from a variety of private and religious international groups.

[60]Only in the case of the fourth repatriation, when the leadership of Mesa Grande had been seriously undermined (largely because of a growing movement of refugees wishing neither to remain or to repatriate, but rather to **resettle**) were the UNHCR and other refugee workers made aware of a lack of consensus.

[61]Interview with Colonel Abraham García Turcios, director of the Honduran National Commission for Refugees (CONARE) August 8, 1989 with author. During the fourth repatriation, the refugees did not depart in an orderly fashion from Mesa Grande, and a confrontation ensued with Honduran authorities.

[62]Coordinación Ecuménica para las Iglesias y Agencias Internacionales de Cooperación, "Informe de las iglesias locales sobre el proceso de repatriación-repoblación del campamento de Mesa Grande, Honduras." San Salvador, September 22, 1988, p.5.

[63]Diaconia, **Circular** No. 6/88, August 9, 1988, Item No. 10.

[64]Going Home is tied to another agency, SHARE, (as noted in the discussion on internally displaced persons) that for years has organized delegations to El Salvador to observe and support displaced persons and their return to their communities. Its activities related to the repatriations from Honduras are organized under the Interfaith Office on Accompaniment.

[65]In conversations with some of the individuals who took part in the activities, one of the authors learned that they were never informed of the nature of the agreements made or the fact that the refugees' demands had largely been met.

[66]One author discussed the objectives of the delegations with the leaders of Going Home and the Interfaith Office on Accompaniment, as well as other delegates to the third repatriation.

[67]UNHCR also blamed the delegation for politicizing the repatriation, but thanked the churches for having mediated the situation.

[68]Coordinación Ecuménica, **Informe**, September 22, 1988, p. 6.

[69]Head Office for Culture and Communications, Ministry of Foreign Relations, August 14, 1988.

[70]Still another confrontation took place in Tejutla, as some of the refugees insisted that UNHCR alter the planned route.

[71]In **Prensa Gráfica**, October 7, 1989.

[72]According to the Documentation Team in the Salvadoran Ministry of Information, 99.5 percent of the refugee population was undocumented. (Interview by Ricardo Stein, November 25, 1988.) The nationality of their Honduran-born children was confirmed thanks to a previous agreement under which the Salvadoran government accepted the UNHCR verification of the births in the camp and allowed them to be registered in the Salvadoran consulate in Nuevo Ocotepeque, where Mesa Grande is located.

[73]Plataforma Reivindicativa de los Refugiados de Mesa Grande Honduras, August 8, 1989.

[74]UNHCR Cable, October 17, 1989.

[75]In an effort to preserve the initial agreement, the High Commissioner wrote to President Alfredo Cristiani on October 19th, 1989 urging his influence in the direction of flexibility on the documentation issue.

[76]Three refugees died during the standoff, but their deaths occurred in the camp, and of causes entirely unrelated to the events.

[77]The settlement is named after one of the Salvadoran Jesuits murdered in November 1989. Fr. Montes had worked with the refugees and had written extensively about them. See, for example, Segundo Montes Mozo, S.J., and Juan José García Vásquez, **Salvadoran Migration to the United States: An Exploratory Study** (Washington, D.C.: Hemispheric Migration Project, CIPRA, Georgetown University, 1988).

[78]Interviews by author with UNHCR officials, November 20, 1989. The refugees said they intended to go to Meanguera in Morazán, the originally planned destination of the Colomoncagua repatriation.

[79]Circulated in Spanish and English, dated November 21 and 25, and December 4 and 9, 1989.

[80]The U.S. observers were sent by a group that had long been particularly interested in Colomoncagua and San Antonio, called Voices on the Border.

[81]This overview of events is based on first-hand accounts of persons who accompanied the repatriation and from UNHCR communications. The military strafed the place where the refugees were located on November 29, wounding three of them.

[82]Summary of the Official Document of the Republic of El Salvador, presented at the first meeting of the International Follow-Up Committee of the International Conference on Central American Refugees (CIREFCA), New York, June 27-28, 1990. The first meeting was held in Guatemala from May 29-31, 1989.

[83]Interview by author with Fr. Segundo Montes, November 4, 1989, Washington, D.C.

[84]Interview by author with Father Segundo Montes, November 4, 1989.

[85]Summary of the Official Document of the Republic of El Salvador presented at the First International Meeting of the Follow-up Committee, CIREFCA, New York, June 27 and 28, 1990, p. 1.

[86]The period during and following the November 1989 FMLN offensive, however, was characterized by harsh repression against civilian groups. Agencies working with returnees and displaced persons were hit especially hard.

[87]Aristide Zolberg, Astri Suhrke and Sergio Aguayo, **Escape from Violence: Conflict in the Developing World** (New York: Oxford University Press, 1989), 275-282. Zolberg, et al. define refugee warriors as: "Highly conscious refugee communities with a political leadership structure and armed sections engaged in warfare for a political objective." Although without "armed sections," the Salvadoran refugees did consider themselves engaged in the same struggle as their compatriots still in El Salvador.

[88]Interview by author in Mesa Grande, August 1989.

ANNEX

APPEAL FROM THE UNITED NATIONS
HIGH COMMISSIONER FOR REFUGEES,

Mr. Jean-Pierre Hocke

1. In accordance with its mandate to seek durable solutions to refugee problems, UNHCR regularly initiates or is called upon to facilitate movements of voluntary repatriation. UNHCR can facilitate such movements provided the following requirements are met:

a) All governments concerned, namely the country of origin and the country of asylum, must agree with the modalities of the repatriation and of UNHCR participation;

b) The operation should be carried out in accordance with the UNHCR Mandate and in strictly humanitarian and apolitical spirit;

c) The UNHCR protection mandate should be respected by all concerned.

2. The fulfillment of the above conditions has allowed, in the last years, UNHCR to repatriate a significant number of Central American refugees, including Salvadorans in Honduras, to their respective countries of origin. Worthy of particular mention in the successful operation of voluntary repatriation in October 1987 involving some 4,500 refugees from Mesa Grande to their areas of origin in El Salvador.

3. Recently, a group of around 1,400 refugees from Mesa Grande expressed their wish to repatriate to their villages of origin in one single movement. The Salvadoran Government authorized the return and, further to UNHCR demarches gave a positive reply to the mentioned modalities. The Honduran Government was also in agreement with the operation.

4. Consequently, UNHCR has prepared an action plan in co-ordination with competent authorities covering all logistical aspects of the movement and has strengthened its presence in the area in order to ensure smooth implementation. The Salvadoran authorities offered facilities to undertake migratory arrangements in the camp. The movement was due to take place within the same day and started on 13 August as requested by refugees.

5. UNHCR regrets to inform that a number of incidents are taking place leading to believe that there is a serious risk of deviation from what should be a strictly humanitarian operation of helping refugees to return from a lengthy asylum.

6. In this connection the High Commissioner wishes to address the present appeal to all those who could have an influence on this operation to cooperate with his office in order to fully respect the peaceful and apolitical nature of the voluntary repatriation of refugees. Should these conditions not be respected, the situation could take new and unforeseen dimensions preventing UNHCR from carrying out satisfactorily this operation in compliance with its Mandate. This appeal expressed UNHCR's willingness to protect and assist the refugees who could otherwise be made victims of an unfortunate turn of events.

Geneva, August 14th, 1988.

CHAPTER V

REFUGEE REPATRIATION IN CENTRAL AMERICA
Lessons from Three Case Studies

by Adolfo Aguilar Zinser

INTRODUCTION

Over the last two decades, Central America has seen massive numbers of its people flee to other countries within the region and beyond. Various economic, social, and political factors have contributed to this migratory phenomenon. The population movements in the region have taken various forms, ranging from well planned individual migration for economic reasons to the precipitous exodus of large communities fleeing persecution or areas of generalized violence. As the region as a whole begins to pull out of a long period characterized by widespread violence and upheaval and begins to enter what appears to be a time of concerted efforts to end political and social unrest, several crucial research topics have emerged whose examination may provide some insight into the region's future. Among the most important is the extent to which relative peace and stability will compel those Central Americans who left their homes during the last decade to return to their countries and places of origin, as well as the form such repatriations may take.

International organizations working on behalf of Central American refugees must direct their efforts and resources in ways that will make a positive contribution to the stable and dignified resettlement of displaced populations. For those refugees who do not wish to repatriate, serious consideration should be given to permanent assimilation in countries of asylum or even relocation to third countries. The most desirable scenario, however, is the return of international refugees and the internally displaced to their places of origin, thereby enabling them to resume their normal lives with dignity.

A viable peace in Central America must, therefore, include mechanisms to ensure that those people who were forced to leave their homes as refugees have the option to return with adequate guarantees for their personal security, social needs, and economic opportunities.

These research papers provide an understanding of the influences behind the repatriation process in Central America. Our study covers the following repatriation cases: Guatemalans from Mexico, Salvadorans from Honduras, and Nicaraguans from Honduras and Costa Rica. The researchers suggest useful recommendations for international and nongovernmental organizations. This paper attempts to draw from the three case studies the most relevant general issues emerging from the phenomenon of the return of Central American refugees to their respective countries. It is hoped that our studies will serve those working on behalf of Central American refugees to determine the most useful role they might play in planning and preparing for an eventual, voluntary and safe repatriation.

THE NATURE AND EXTENT OF
CENTRAL AMERICAN MIGRATION

Central American population movements have become so enormous and widespread that one must exercise caution in trying to draw any general conclusions from the three case studies analyzed here. Since the 1970s at least, two structural factors—population growth and economic stagnation—have contributed to the Central American propensity to migrate. During the 1980s, additional factors relating to revolutionary insurgency and the breakdown of political order in the three countries under consideration also provoked the periodic, precipitous exodus of numerous rural and semi-urban communities directly or indirectly affected by political violence and war. In addition, hundreds of thousands of urban dwellers chose to migrate to other countries, particularly to the north, rather than face intolerable conditions in their own countries.

Between 1950 and 1985, the Central American population increased at a steady rate of 3.1 percent a year, almost tripling from 9.1 million to 26.4 million. This population explosion was made possible in part by the region's impressive economic expansion. The six republics — Guatemala, El Salvador, Honduras, Nicaragua, Costa Rica and Panama — experienced a high aggregate economic growth rate of 5.3 percent in the three decades since 1950, which contributed in every case except Costa Rica to the reinforcement of an enduring and highly repressive political order. Costa Rica is the only non-militaristic and truly representative democracy in the region. High birth rates and an elevated growth in GNP based on high international prices for the region's export crops and on the profitable Central American Common Market, led to the emergence of a sizeable urban middle class. Economic growth, however, aggravated social disparity rather than eliminating it, especially in El Salvador, Nicaragua, and Guatemala.

At a time when the economically active segment of the Central American population doubled from 2.08 million in 1970 to 4.16 million in 1985, the global economic decline brought down the prices of Central American cash crops, causing a regional recession and a sharp decline in investments. Unemployment rates increased to 30 percent. According to accepted estimates, by the mid-1980s, when the region's refugee problems peaked, almost 65 percent of the Central American population was "either extremely poor or unable to satisfy all of its basic needs."*

Highly inequitable land distribution meant that most of the rural population was unable to withstand the devastating impact of this economic crisis. (Seventy-two percent of the land in Central America is concentrated in holdings of over 35 hectares that represent only six percent of individual farms in the region.) The combination of social and economic factors alone would have led to widespread migration even without the political violence. The destinations of migrants has varied greatly. Domestically, people have migrated from rural to urban areas; within the region, from densely populated and depressed areas to more prosperous regions in neighboring countries; and, outside the region, migration from Guatemala, El Salvador, Nicaragua, and Honduras has reached Mexico and the United States.

Refugees and Economic Migrants

To a great extent, international migration has taken place outside of legal channels. In addition, because widespread economic migration began before the large-scale migration of refugees fleeing war, the receiving countries, both within and outside the region, tended not to recognize people fleeing violence and persecution as refugees. Rather, receiving countries would treat most Central American migrants as undocumented workers. For instance, when the first large numbers of Guatemalans fled for their lives to Mexico, the Mexican authorities refused to grant them asylum, despite all the available evidence identifying them as genuine refugees.

The tendency to portray refugees as undocumented workers has prevailed over the years, not just in Mexico, but in the region as a whole and in the United States. This tendency has generated a great deal of confusion over who is purely an economic migrant and who legitimately deserves the protection and assistance reserved for refugees. Guatemalans and Salvadorans have been particularly affected by this confusion. The problem has been compounded by the fact that, when the violence intensified, many more people fled their country alone or in small family groups, either mixed in with economic refugees or deliberately posing as economic, rather than political, refugees. It is highly likely, therefore, that thousands of undocumented Central Americans living in other countries are genuine refugees.

These three studies make clear, however, that in Central America and Mexico, refugee status is enjoyed almost exclusively by people who settled in camps. The distinction between recognized and unrecognized refugees not only depends on individuals' legal migratory status, it also depends on the kind of settlement in which they live, the situations they encounter in exile, and the conditions under which they eventually return home.

Although the three case studies in this volume suggest that the number of unofficial refugees may be substantially higher than the number of official ones, the subject of study in all three papers was limited to official refugees. This limitation was forced on us by the virtual impossibility, given existing resources, of clearly identifying unofficial refugees and of monitoring their movements.

The authors of these case studies also acknowledge that most of what we know about the experiences of official Guatemalan, Salvadoran, and Nicaraguan refugees is of only limited use in understanding the situation of unofficial refugees. All three case studies indicate that, for the most part, formal refugee status situates individuals and their families in a particular group dynamic not commonly experienced by nonrecognized refugees. In the refugee camps, an individual's fate is to a great extent decided on the basis of group criteria and collective decision-making. Conversely, unofficial refugees are often obliged to keep constantly on the move and to respond to circumstances individually. They tend to live in anonymity, to move around alone, to blend in discreetly with the local population, and to maintain their family and individual identity rather than their national or ethnic identity. Anonymity is crucial to the survival of unofficial refugees, whether in exile or after returning home. Shunning refugee status may simply be an effective means of ensuring individual protection when there is no available alternative to legal alien status in the host country. For the majority of unofficial refugees, anonymity is simply a means of survival, given the very precarious and uncertain conditions experienced by undocumented aliens.

Although there is no hard evidence to support the theory, Ortega, Aguilar Zinser, and Fagen and Eldridge suggest that unofficial refugees are often far more vulnerable than official refugees, despite the unofficial refugees' ability to protect themselves. This is true not only in exile, but also upon their return. Furthermore, the three studies suggest that the number of unofficial refugees who repatriate spontaneously may be greater than the number of official refugees who repatriate. For many, however, these unassisted and undocumented repatriations may be just another step in the ongoing diaspora. These repatriations may owe more to the tenuous status of the people in exile than to improvements in conditions in their homeland. Because refugees who repatriate unofficially lack access to the support systems that other returning exiles enjoy, they may eventually become a weakened sector of society whose impoverished state may influence other refugees and displaced groups not to repatriate.

One strong recommendation that emerges from these studies, therefore, is that closer attention needs to be focussed on those groups of refugees excluded from our research. Future international research must be focussed on unrecognized refugees and spontaneous repatriation. The obvious magnitude of the problem would more than justify the effort and may convince international organizations of the need to establish mechanisms to attend to the needs of such refugees.

BASIC PROFILES OF THE REFUGEE COMMUNITIES COVERED BY THESE CASE STUDIES

We may consider the refugees studied in this volume under five separate categories: (1) Indigenous Nicaraguans in Honduras, (2) Mestizo Nicaraguans in Honduras, (3) Mestizo Nicaraguans in Costa Rica, (4) Guatemalans in Mexico, and (5) Salvadorans in Honduras.

1. Between 1981 and 1986, 14,000 indigenous people from the Atlantic coast of Nicaragua entered Honduras, where they settled under the protection of the UNHCR. This number represents approximately half the estimated 30,000 Nicaraguan indigenous people, who, at one point, lived in exile in the Mosquitia region of Honduras. Those not living in UNHCR-supervised camps were assisted by, and mingled with, Honduran Miskitos. The group of indigenous refugees in our study on Nicaragua included Miskitos, most of whom belong to the Moravian Church, and Sumus. They settled in some seven camps, the overwhelming majority in three: Patuca, Mocorón, and Río Mocorón. A combination of factors forced them into exile: The Sandinista government of Nicaragua, after overthrowing the dictatorship of Anastasio Somoza in 1979, attempted to take control of their communal way of life; the indigenous communities were disrupted by the U.S.-sponsored, anti-Sandinista war in their native lands; and the Sandinista government imposed resettlement policies to force them to evacuate the war zones. A formal repatriation process began in 1986, following a series of agreements between indigenous representatives and Sandinista officials. As of 1987, more than 14,000 Nicaraguan indigenous people, out of a total of 30,000, repatriated with the assistance of the UNHCR. By 1989, there were only 9,000 indigenous refugees registered by UNHCR in Honduras. All but a handful that remained with relatives returned to Nicaragua after the change in government in 1990 (See chapter 2).

2. As of 1982, approximately 14,000 Nicaraguan Mestizo *campesinos* went into exile in Honduras where they were assisted by the Red Cross and the UNHCR in refugee camps located in the Department of El Paraíso. They were part of a larger group of *campesinos*, primarily from the northern Nicaraguan departments of Nueva Segovia, Jinotega, Estelí and Madriz, who left their country because of the counter-revolutionary war. A variety of factors caused them to migrate: some were direct victims of the armed conflict; some were disaffected *campesinos* who wanted to enlist with the Contras; others simply went to Honduras searching for relatives kidnapped or recruited by the Contras and, once there, were unable or unwilling to return to Nicaragua. There were also a number of individuals whose unsuccessful attempts to migrate north to Mexico or the United States eventually compelled them to enter the refugee camps. The three camps administered by the UNHCR and the Red Cross in El Paraíso, i.e., Jacaleapa, Teupacenti, and Las Vegas, were controlled by the Nicaraguan resistance, or Contras. From 1983, when the UNHCR established a formal repatriation process, until 1989, almost 1,500 Nicaraguan *campesinos* returned voluntarily to their country. Typically, they were recent arrivals to the camps and refugees without counter-revolutionary ties. Repatriation among this group picked up

only after the Tela Agreement set down plans for the dismantling of the Contras in mid-1989 (See chapter 2).

3. As many as 200,000 Mestizo *campesinos* fled from Nicaragua to Costa Rica in several different waves. However, only about 30,000 were officially recognized by the Costa Rican authorities. Those who began arriving in 1982 were groups of *campesinos* from the Department of Río San Juan bordering Costa Rica in southeastern Nicaragua. They were either directly affected by the military conflict between the Sandinista regime and the Contras, or members of communities opposed to the government-imposed relocation away from war zones. Later, as the war intensified, refugees from the Departments of Chontales and Nueva Guinea joined the first group. After 1984, many more Nicaraguans, particularly young people fleeing compulsory conscription, went to Costa Rica from the Pacific coast, especially from the large urban centers of Granada, Masaya, Managua, Rivas, Carazo, León and Chinandega. Only 30 percent of these Nicaraguan refugees settled in refugee camps; the rest took up residence in urban centers. In 1990, 4,800 Nicaraguans had returned home voluntarily, many of them assisted by the UNHCR (See chapter 2).

4. Between 1981 and 1985, 46,000 Guatemalan refugees entered the southern Mexican state of Chiapas that borders on Guatemala. Local peasant communities helped the refugees settle in camps run by the Catholic Church, the Mexican government, and the United Nations High Commissioner for Refugees (UNHCR). These refugees were the victims of counter-insurgency campaigns launched by the Guatemalan government in the Departments of Quiché, Alta Verapaz, Huehuetenango, San Marcos and El Petén. The overwhelming majority are *campesinos*, most belonging to the many branches of Maya-Quiché Indians; few are Ladinos. Between 1984 and 1985, the Mexican authorities relocated some of them to refugee camps in Campeche and Quintana Roo in the Yucatán Peninsula. At least half, however, refused to relocate and still live in Chiapas. By the end of 1989, approximately 5,000 had returned to their country and were registered as repatriates. Of these, fewer than 2,000 repatriated spontaneously before 1987; the rest went back under the official Tripartite Agreement established in 1987 by the Mexican Commission for Refugee Assistance (COMAR), the Special Guatemalan Commission to Assist Repatriates (CEAR), and the UNHCR (See chapter 3).

5. By 1986, there were just over 21,000 *campesinos* from El Salvador living in exile in Honduras. The majority arrived between 1980 and 1982; after several relocations they were ultimately confined to the refugee camps of Colomoncagua, San Antonio, Mesa Grande, and Buenos Aires. Salvadoran refugees in Honduras represent only a small

portion of the Salvadorans uprooted by civil war who have either left El
Salvador or been displaced within their own country. These refugees
came from rural war zones, mostly in the departments of Morazán and
Cabañas. They were either caught in the cross fire or directly targeted
by the Salvadoran armed forces in order to deprive the guerrillas of
their social base. In the beginning, Salvadoran refugees in Honduras
were assisted by the local Catholic Church and Caritas-Honduras, an
affiliate of the international Catholic relief agency of the same name.
Later, the UNHCR began to assist the refugees; since 1982, the
UNHCR has been responsible for coordinating all the private and
public relief in the refugee camps. The Honduran military controlled
the refugee camps, surrounding them at all times and severely
restricting movement into and out of them. Nonetheless, Salvadoran
refugees in Honduras have maintained close political ties with the
revolutionary organizations fighting in their country and the decision of
whether to return to El Salvador or remain in Honduras has been
strongly influenced by these relationships. Spontaneous repatriation by
individual refugees began almost immediately, so that by 1985, 2,000
had already returned to El Salvador on their own. In 1986, the
Honduran and Salvadoran governments and UNHCR established a
formal repatriation process. A limited but steady number of individual
refugees, particularly from the Mesa Grande camp, took advantage of
official repatriation procedures in order to return. Although the first,
smaller repatriations generally took place against the wishes of the
refugee leadership controlling the camps, the largest, most
controversial mass repatriations, which began in 1987, were organized
by the same camp leadership. By 1989, nearly 8,000 Salvadorans had
returned to their country in at least four large convoys to establish their
own communities in areas of conflict. The mass repatriations continued
in 1990, with the return of 8,000 refugees from the remaining camps at
Colomoncagua and San Antonio (See chapter 4).

Characteristics of the Central American Refugee Problem

Each of these groups has undergone different experiences, that
reflect a number of unique features: the intrinsic characteristics of the
refugee community itself; conditions in the country of origin; the
attitudes of the host government; the extent of the role of armed groups
in the lives of the refugees; and the behavior of international
organizations, nongovernmental organizations, the Church, and third
governments. Given the peculiar way in which all these factors have
combined in each case to mold attitudes and circumstances, the
refugees' experiences differ sharply. Despite their differences,
however, they are all linked to an overall Central American
phenomenon. The following points formulated on the basis of the three

case studies represent the most significant similarities among the refugee groups:

1. In Central America, the phenomenon of collective exodus and settlement in camps is characteristic of rural communities. Whether we are discussing Salvadoran *campesinos*, Nicaraguan Mestizos or Miskitos, or Maya-Quiché Indians from Guatemala, the overwhelming majority of refugees found in camps throughout the region come from rural communities. Few urban refugees are to be found in these camps. The camps themselves were often a response to mass flight.

2. The refugees' behavior is largely determined by the level of cohesion in their particular refugee community. There are two types of collective bonds: one is based on ethnicity, culture, language and religion; the other bond is forged by shared ideology or identification with a specific political cause or movement. In the case of the more segregated indigenous groups, culture, ethnicity and political affinities are often intertwined.

3. The organization and leadership of the refugee groups usually reflects practices and power structures typical of the original community. In the cases of both the indigenous peoples and the *campesinos*, however, conditions imposed by life in exile may seriously affect the traditional power structure within the community, the decision-making process, and the identity and authority of its leadership. There is a clear distinction between the collective forms of government characteristic of the indigenous groups and those adopted by Mestizos and other *campesinos*. Even so, the refugee experience of both indigenous peoples and Mestizos strengthens the role of collective discussion and facilitates an assembly or caucus process of decision-making. Clear representation has been of crucial importance to refugee communities due to the connection between the refugee phenomenon and the internal conflict in the country of origin as well as the intense and frequently contentious relationship between refugees and local communities, host governments, and relief organizations. Thus, the frequent need for representation outside the community often results in the expansion and centralization of the leaders' powers.

4. Attitudes toward repatriation are strongly influenced by the level of identification and cohesion within a given refugee community and by the political orientation of its leadership. Conversely, an individual's decision to leave the camp and repatriate is usually a result of that person's poor integration into the community, often because of ethnic, religious, or ideological differences, power struggles within and between groups, or an unwillingness to submit to camp rules.

PATTERNS OF REPATRIATION

Three patterns of Central American repatriation have been identified. The first pattern involves unassisted, spontaneous repatriation outside of formal channels. This was the prevailing pattern of repatriation until official mechanisms were established by the UNHCR, the host government, and the government of the home country. The second pattern is voluntary repatriation assisted by the UNHCR. Even though large numbers of refugees do not repatriate collectively under this procedure, it is the method most frequently used. The third pattern is collective repatriation. In the two cases of Salvadoran *campesinos* and the Nicaraguan indigenous people of the Atlantic Coast who dwelled in Honduran refugee camps, the majority of the camp populations participated in the mass repatriations. Among the Salvadoran refugees, the decision to repatriate *en masse* was made by the refugees, their leadership, and their supporting political organizations against the advice of international organizations and the will of the Salvadoran government. In the second case, the repatriations resulted from political agreements that the Sandinista government and the exiled communities first began to reach in 1985.

The decision to repatriate is based largely on collective attitudes. The case studies show that camp life and its political structure are among the most influential factors in the decision of the individual. Collective attitudes toward repatriation are thus a distinctive characteristic of Central American refugee camps. The fact that most refugee camps have endorsed collective repatriation does not mean that collective repatriation is the prevailing pattern, regardless of whether the endorsement was reached by a truly democratic decision-making process or through the imposition of camp leadership. In fact, the cases of the mass Salvadoran repatriations and the collective return of the Miskitos and Sumus are the exception, not the rule.

Collective returns take place under certain conditions: when a majority of the refugees have already decided to return and choose to do so collectively in order to minimize risks and optimize material support (as in the case of the mass Salvadoran repatriations) or when a collective understanding is reached with the authorities in the home country (as was the case of the Nicaraguan indigenous people).

However, actual experience also shows that the collective decision regarding repatriation may very well be, at least in the short and medium term, a decision *not* to repatriate. This was clearly the case with the Nicaraguan *campesinos* living in the Honduran refugee camps controlled by the Contras, and with the Guatemalans in Mexico.

The Contras were fiercely opposed to the repatriation of Nicaraguan refugees who served as their social base in Honduras. Their opposition was clearly displayed by the intransigent demands they attached to collective return, hindering a process that many refugees might otherwise have undertaken.

In Mexico, the majority of Guatemalan refugees also opposed collective repatriation and first insisted that a number of security and material conditions be met by the Guatemalan authorities. However, unlike the Nicaraguan Mestizos in Honduras, the Guatemalan camp leadership has tended to discourage, rather than forbid, voluntary repatriation. Still, the existence at least declaratory policies in favor of collective repatriation paradoxically provides an incentive for individual, voluntary repatriation outside of formal channels and without institutionalized assistance. Some refugees from these camps repatriate spontaneously to avoid any unpleasant retaliation (as was the case with the Nicaraguan Mestizos in Honduras) or to avoid openly defying the community (as has happened with Guatemalans in Mexico).

FACTORS INFLUENCING ATTITUDES
TOWARD REPATRIATION

In each case communities arrived at collective decisions by different processes and were motivated by different factors. It is clear from all the case studies that outside political organizations linked to the political struggle in the country of origin exerted varying degrees of influence on the attitudes of camp refugees toward repatriation.

For example, in the Nicaraguan Mestizo refugee camps in Honduras, the Contras played a decisive role in preventing refugees from returning home. Regardless of the conditions in Nicaragua or the preferences of individual refugees, the Contras viewed repatriation as contrary to its military and political interests. Similarly, the influence of the exiled, Nicaraguan indigenous leadership was decisive in the collective decision to repatriate. The leadership did not exercise its authority in quite the same dictatorial fashion as the *Contras*, however. Following a formal agreement with the Sandinista government in 1986, the Miskito and Sumo leadership promoted collective repatriation. Since then, virtually all the indigenous communities have returned collectively.

Salvadoran refugees in Honduran camps were also greatly influenced by political organizations directly or indirectly linked to the armed resistance of the Farabundo Martí National Liberation Front (FMLN) in their own country. The Salvadoran camp leadership also tended to impose its views in an authoritarian manner; however, it had to take account of the opinions and needs of the camp residents themselves. The mass repatriations, described in telling detail by Fagen and Eldridge, in fact resulted from a combination of circumstances, including the refugees' determination to run the risk of returning to El Salvador rather than remain in isolation in Honduras.

Guatemalan refugees in Mexico have also been influenced by the revolutionary organizations fighting in their country; however, this influence has not been nearly as powerful as in the other cases. The most compelling factor shaping the attitude of the majority is the shared perception that conditions in Guatemala remain too perilous for the refugees to return. The Guatemalan refugees agree that repatriation must be collective, a decision reinforced by their leadership. This decision is consistent with the political interests of the revolutionary organizations which want to rebuild their social base in Guatemala and take advantage of the refugees' cohesion, acquired during their exile in Mexico. However, the decision of the Guatemalan indigenous peoples to repatriate collectively cannot be traced back to the influence of revolutionary organizations.

The role of nongovernmental and international organizations in the repatriation process is politically conflictive and socially sensitive. The refugees' decision to repatriate collectively poses serious material and political difficulties for nongovernmental and international organizations. The collective repatriation issue often becomes highly politicized due to the camp leadership's vehement defense of its actions, whether against outside opinion or internal dissent. The governments involved, and particularly the government of origin, often equate collective repatriation with subversive activity on the part of revolutionary organizations.

Given the nature of their activities and the availability of their resources, organizations working with refugees tend to favor repatriation of individuals or small groups. This is inevitably a source of tension between the organizations and the refugee leadership. However, once the refugees have decided to carry out collective repatriation, the best course of action for such organizations is to work as closely as possible with the refugees and their representatives in order to facilitate the process.

In addition to counting on the support of the UNHCR, refugees who wish to repatriate collectively expect international and nongovernmental organizations to defend their actions and to participate actively in the repatriation process. Such participation provides the refugees with visibility, protection, and material assistance during the repatriation and resettlement process. However, the case of the Salvadoran refugees makes clear that organizations may actually contribute to conflict and confusion, particularly if they send inexperienced personnel to intervene in an overtly political fashion at the time of collective repatriation. Experience has shown that, in these circumstances, nongovernmental organizations may make a useful contribution by maintaining a visible, yet discreet, presence. It is vital that the various organizations confer with each other in order to define ground rules and coordinate activities.

When it comes to collective repatriation along the lines of the Salvadoran case, the UNHCR tends to be torn between its role as a humanitarian agency and its diplomatic and official constraints. In these circumstances, UNHCR representatives tend to link their participation in, and support of, the repatriation process to the fulfillment of various conditions which are a combination of agency procedures, refugee demands, and government requirements and restrictions. Once again, however, the Salvadoran experience suggests that once collective repatriation has begun, the UNHCR is not really in a position to withdraw or to restrict its role, and must follow through with the process, adopting a conciliatory stance and simply adapting to circumstances. Therefore, the UNHCR and nongovernmental organizations should be prepared to work out a prior understanding by which the UNHCR, acknowledging its limitations, assumes the leading role during the repatriation process, while other organizations take subordinate roles.

We have already seen that in all the cases under study, political organizations attempted to influence or determine the course of decisions made in the camps. However, we should also bear in mind a number of other factors that come into play:

1. *The quality of communications channels between refugees and their homeland* — The differences in communication among refugee communities are very pronounced. Radio broadcasts, newspapers, and, in some cases, televised news, have enabled refugees to stay informed of events in their country. Often, however, the remote locations of the camps and widespread illiteracy among the refugees have limited the role of the print media as a vehicle of information. However, radio played such a critical role that at times there was a virtual airwave war in order to influence the various refugee communities. The Nicaraguan

government tried to persuade the refugees to return home by using its official radio station to publicize its peace achievements and to describe the opportunities refugees would find on their return. The Contra radio broadcasts painted a very different picture. The Guatemalan government's broadcasts attempted to persuade individual refugees in Mexico to return; they also tried to cause confusion in the camps by painting a false picture of the country's political stability and security conditions.

Due to the low credibility of the media, and the absence of alternative information channels, the most influential and reliable sources of information available to the refugees on their homeland have been direct communications with their home communities, family and friends, and with people who have already returned. Conditions in exile are generally unfavorable to the initiation or maintenance of such channels of communication. Furthermore, conventional communication methods such as the mail and the telephone are either inaccessible to refugee communities or considered unreliable. However, because refugees are strongly motivated to keep in touch with those back home, many do all they can to keep such contacts alive, sometimes at great personal risk.

For example, Guatemalan refugees in Mexico in particular have been able to create and maintain ties with Guatemala for several reasons: (a) The refugees are not totally isolated, even though movement in and out of the camps is strictly controlled; (b) The length and the accessibility of the border makes strict surveillance by the Mexican and Guatemalan authorities virtually impossible; and (c) The ethnic refugees' cultural and linguistic skills allow them to use informal, often semi-clandestine, ancient forms of communication to keep informed of events at home. As discussed in the case study, Guatemalan indigenous peoples have managed to travel undetected across the border to carry news and personal messages back and forth. Thus, these refugees are generally well informed of events in their country and of how repatriates are treated there.

The Nicaraguan indigenous peoples living in exile on the Atlantic coast of Honduras engaged in a similar strategy. In general, communications and personal contact between Nicaraguan refugees and their families were relatively easy to maintain, which was a factor in the success of their repatriation from Honduras. However, internal and external camp controls may have been major obstacles to the refugees' personal communication with people back home, as was the experience of Nicaraguan Mestizo refugees living in Honduran camps. In his case study, Marvin Ortega refers to the strong opposition of the Nicaraguan Contras, which maintained political control of the camps and maintained contact between refugees in Honduras and people in Nicaragua. Salvadorans in Honduran camps were also prevented from communicating with the outside. Unlike the Nicaraguan case, however, such controls were imposed by the Honduran military authorities, who kept the camps virtually under siege.

Direct personal information about conditions in their homeland has proved to be a crucial factor in influencing the refugees' determination to return, even against the collective will of the majority. In fact, data collected in all three case studies suggest that individual voluntary repatriation is partly influenced by the refugees' perception of their particular opportunities for resettlement in their country of origin. To some extent, these perceptions are based on direct contact with family and friends. Therefore, one way in which international and nongovernmental organizations could better assist refugees in their decision to repatriate would be to create or improve communication channels between refugees and their home communities. Such organizations can lobby against tight military controls, speed up or offer alternative mail service (as was done by CEAR, COMAR, and the UNHCR for Guatemalan refugees), promote fact-finding visits for the refugees in their home communities, and, in general, discuss life outside the camps with the refugees. In some cases, these efforts may result in increased individual repatriation. While such efforts may well incur the hostility of a camp leadership that favors collective repatriation over individual return, the creation of such opportunities may also help improve some of the inflexible political overtones of collective decision-making.

2. *Individual Motivation* — Many factors shape both the individual decision to repatriate and collective perceptions about repatriation. Such factors include boredom in the camps, anxiety about the future, fear of losing cultural and ethnic identity, a desire to raise children in places of origin, family emergencies, apprehension about land, and a yearning for family reunification.

3. *Treatment of Refugees by Host Country Authorities and Other Organizations* — Different governments behave differently toward refugees in their territory. The most important factor influencing a refugee's reception in a given country is the host government's perception of the conflict that gave rise to the initial migration of refugees from a specific country.

The authorities of the receiving country may have made prior commitments to the militant forces involved in a specific conflict, as was the case with the Honduran government and the Nicaraguan Contras. Another government may profess political sympathy or antipathy for

certain causes, as displayed by Costa Rican hostility toward the
Sandinistas, or the lukewarm attitude of the Mexican authorities toward
the Guatemalan guerrillas. Refugees tend to be treated in accordance
with such commitments or sympathies. This may even result in a
government's contradictory attitudes toward different refugee groups
arriving in the same country. For example, the Honduran government,
which was clearly aligned with the U.S. counterrevolutionary strategy in
Central America, welcomed Nicaraguans who were hostile to the
Sandinistas. This stance contrasted sharply with the animosity the
Honduran government displayed toward the Salvadorans it viewed as
sympathetic to the FMLN.

However, the refugee phenomenon also tends to modify
substantially the way in which a host government behaves toward allies
or foes among the warring factions of the conflicts. The arrival of
refugees may dampen or reverse sympathies between the receiving
country and a given political force in the country of expulsion. This was
true of the Mexican government which, before the arrival of
Guatemalan refugees, did not attempt to mask its sympathies toward
Central American revolutionaries. After the Guatemalan refugees had
entered Mexico and settled in camps in Chiapas, the Mexican
authorities did all they could to distance themselves from the
Guatemalan revolutionaries, not wishing to be accused by the
Guatemalan army of supporting armed insurrection.

In any event, in the absence of an overriding commitment to the
refugees or a concrete benefit to be derived from the refugees' presence
in the host government's territory, its first priority is to repatriate them.
This attitude has been clearly exhibited by the harsh treatment meted
out to Salvadoran refugees (who have been victims of forced
deportations and armed attacks) in Honduras and to Guatemalan
refugees in Mexico. Additionally, governments attempt to conceal their
urge to repatriate refugees by limiting the assistance offered them,
isolating them from the rest of the population, relocating them to
hostile areas, and even encouraging anti-refugee sentiment. This has
been the case, to some extent, in all three countries studied.

The relationship between the host government, the UNHCR,
other UN bodies, and nongovernmental organizations is always
ambivalent and often conflictive. The national security concerns of the
governments and their desire to see refugees repatriated or resettled in
a third country both have an impact on the relationship. Two patterns
may be observed in this regard: on the one hand, the host government's
inability to define a coherent and sustainable refugee policy, the lack of
a competent bureaucracy, and the scarcity of economic resources to
assist the refugees together create the need for more active role for the

UNHCR. The presence of the UNHCR and other nongovernmental organizations greatly alleviates the financial burden of refugee assistance, which is always one of the host government's major concerns.

On the other hand, the presence of the UNHCR and, in general, of nongovernmental organizations that defend the rights of refugees, is perceived as an interference. Governments tend to perceive international organizations as too indulgent toward the refugees and too insensitive to the host government's national interests. A host government's defensive attitude toward the UNHCR results in the restriction of UNHCR activities, which is often in conflict with the UNHCR mandate to provide assistance.

The host government shows the same type of ambivalence toward national and international nongovernmental organizations, particularly religious ones. Sometimes the Catholic Church has been more prominent in its work on behalf of refugees than governments or international organizations; it has been crucial to refugees in all three countries, particularly in the repatriation process.

4. *Conditions in Exile* — The most important factor to be considered by any refugee contemplating repatriation is the political and economic situation in the country of origin. Nevertheless, experience has shown that conditions in exile have an overriding influence on the decision to repatriate. Refugees are particularly sensitive both to the overall political treatment they receive in the host country and its economic situation. Political hostility, particularly of the sort exhibited by military or police control of refugee settlements, may encourage a wave of repatriations. For instance, the mass returns of Salvadorans to their country may not be fully comprehended without a knowledge of the Honduran refugee camps and the refugees' uneasiness and despondency over their isolation. Likewise, when the Mexican government in 1984 forcibly relocated camps from the border state of Chiapas to the states of Campeche and Quintana Roo, many Guatemalans chose to return to Guatemala rather than face the hazards of relocation. In both cases, conditions in the refugees' homeland were unfavorable to repatriation. Less adverse conditions in the country of asylum may still prompt repatriation; such was the case of Nicaraguans in Costa Rica who returned home in response to the anti-refugee sentiment generated by the media in that country.

Refugee communities display remarkable endurance in the face of harsh economic conditions. In general, the experiences described in the three case studies reveal that, in exchange for security, refugees are willing to sacrifice all their worldly goods and endure a marked deterioration in their living conditions. In time, however, economic deprivation leads to frustration and despair, and, ultimately, departure from the camps and even repatriation.

These case studies document the different economic conditions in the region's various refugee camps; such conditions run the gamut from poverty levels below previous standards to living conditions superior to those left behind. Nevertheless, the refugee camps are totally dependent on outside assistance for their survival.

There are no self-sufficient refugee camps in Central America or Mexico, if self-sufficiency is defined as the refugees' ability to survive economically without the financial support of government agencies, the UNHCR, or nongovernmental organizations. In all three case studies, dependency is identified as a serious factor affecting the refugees' situation and behavior. Sooner or later, it is the frustration with the persistence of the dependent situation that provides a strong incentive for refugees to abandon camp life, either to seek employment elsewhere or to return home. Dependency may range from situations in which refugees live in camps in almost total economic passivity to those in which communities supplement outside assistance with farming or local salaried activities.

One of the greatest challenges faced by refugee agencies in the region is to transcend economic dependency and create conditions for self-reliance. Aside from financial constraints and administrative obstacles, host government policies are usually the most serious hurdles to camp self-sufficiency. In general, the three receiving countries of Honduras, Costa Rica, and Mexico have tried to ward off the arrival of more refugees by discouraging any economic improvements in the camps that might conceivably attract newcomers. Host governments have also separated the refugees from the local populations and made sure that economic conditions in the refugee camps are not perceptibly better than those elsewhere in the area. Governments fear that self-sufficiency leading to improvements in the refugees' lives may provide a dangerous vehicle for their unwanted integration.

Despite these obstacles, however, assistance agencies have insisted that they be allowed to finance projects geared toward self-sufficiency and training in specific skills. Although self-sufficiency has never been fully attained, economic conditions in some camps have improved, and refugees have learned new skills. However, the acquisition of skills in an environment in which they cannot be used becomes a further incentive for refugees to leave the camps and repatriate.

The self-sufficiency of refugee communities must continue to be a high priority for funding agencies. This type of economic improvement does not necessarily have to lead to the definitive integration of the refugees into the host country; rather, it should provide an incentive for the refugees to return home and prosper economically. Furthermore, self-sufficiency training may be the most effective and constructive way for nongovernmental organizations and international organizations to support collective repatriation.

5. *The establishment of formal repatriation mechanisms* — Refugees are generally loath to establish contacts and negotiate with the government of their home country, which they consider responsible for their misfortune. In the beginning, in fact, refugee communities insisted that, before they would return home, the existing power structure in their country would have to be replaced in order for their safety to be guaranteed. Nonetheless, all the repatriation cases covered in these studies, including the mass repatriations of Salvadoran *campesinos* and Nicaraguan indigenous people from Honduras, took place despite the survival of their respective regimes (or, in the case of Nicaragua, before the Sandinistas left power).

Initially, all repatriations were voluntary and spontaneous; they took place without official recognition or assistance. More recently, however, all repatriations, including those from the Nicaraguan refugee camps controlled by the Contras in Honduras, took place following international negotiations to facilitate the refugees' return.

The impetus for these repatriations has not always come from the refugees. In many cases, the host governments have been anxious for the refugees to repatriate in order to divest themselves of the economic, social, political, and even military problems associated with the presence of refugees in their territory. The UNHCR also has a vested interest in seeing that refugees return when their physical security and minimal material well-being may be guaranteed. Some of these negotiations have been carried out directly between the refugees and their leaders and the government of their country, as was the case with the Miskitos and the Sandinistas who began to hold talks in 1985. Other negotiations have included the indirect participation of the refugees, as was the case with the Salvadoran government and the refugees repatriating *en masse*; other repatriations were not really endorsed by the refugees themselves, but were implicitly or explicitly accepted, as was the case with the negotiations of the Guatemalan government for the return of refugees in Mexico.

The negotiations for the safe return of refugees had their
political origins in the Contadora peace talks and the Esquipulas peace
agreements. On the basis of these multilateral discussions and
understandings, tripartite voluntary repatriation agreements were
reached in 1986 and 1987: the former between the UNHCR and the
governments of El Salvador and Honduras, and the latter between the
UNHCR and the governments of Mexico and Guatemala. Although the
governments of Honduras and Costa Rica did not formalize procedures
for the repatriation of Nicaraguans with the Sandinista regime, the
UNHCR was able to establish a repatriation program with some
support from these governments. However, tripartite agreements and
UNHCR repatriation programs have not elicited a decisive repatriation
process. Commitments made by refugee-generating governments to
international organizations have not been trusted or perceived as
sufficiently attractive by the refugees. Nevertheless, repatriation
agreements have provided the crucial breakthrough for the creation of
the mechanisms, institutions, and conditions necessary for the
repatriation process. Because of such multilateral understandings,
long-standing impediments to UNHCR operations in countries of origin
have been removed. Currently, the UNHCR can extend its protection
and assistance with few impediments to returning refugees in
Guatemala, El Salvador, and Nicaragua. The presence of the UNHCR
in those countries has also improved operating conditions for other
nongovernmental organizations. Moreover, formal repatriation
programs have focussed international scrutiny on governments
ill-disposed to returning refugees, and these programs have also
encouraged the formation within those governments of non-military
agencies responsible for assisting refugees upon their return. This has
meant that civilian authorities are able to play a greater role in a
process usually handled by the military. In addition, formal repatriation
procedures have enabled those involved to develop expertise in
guaranteeing better security and in the administration of economic
assistance. Finally, these programs have helped camp refugees resume
contacts with the authorities in their country, develop bargaining skills,
and acquire a better understanding of both the hazards and
opportunities afforded by repatriation.

Although refugees are not always comfortable with the tripartite
agreements, nongovernmental and international organizations should
support such agreements with as many resources as possible in order to
influence their operation and to help assure their adequate
advancement. The framework created by these agreements could help
nongovernmental organizations expand their presence in countries of
origin and directly assist refugees upon their return.

LESSONS FROM THE REPATRIATION PROCESS

It is clear that the first priority of most refugees is to repatriate and return to their places of origin. This priority has been demonstrated by the refugees of rural origin who constitute the overwhelming majority of the Central American refugee camp population. The refugees' desire to return to their home communities is associated with family ties, cultural attachments, recovery of land, and, in the case of indigenous peoples, the rebuilding of their ethnic communities. A sizeable number of repatriates have been able to return to their places of origin or a nearby vicinity. There are also many, however, who have settled elsewhere, including *campesinos* who have repatriated to cities rather than return to cultivate the land. A variety of adverse conditions force refugees to settle in areas other than their places of origin. The greatest obstacle in certain regions is war and its accompanying hazards. Even in places where military hostilities have ceased, the resulting devastation may make resettlement very difficult. In some cases, family members who stayed behind were themselves displaced to other parts of the country; when refugees return, they rejoin their relatives in new areas, usually urban ones. Typically, many refugees wish to resettle in cities. This is particularly true of those who acquired new skills in the refugee camps.

The three case studies show that the repatriation process is an exploratory one for many refugees, such as the Guatemalans returning from Mexico and the Nicaraguan Mestizos returning from Honduras. The exploratory process may include a survey of security conditions in their places of origin, inspection of their land, investigation of the possibility of repossessing it, and a search for employment and economic opportunities.

Refugee reception policies in the country of origin may determine or influence the destination of the repatriates. In some cases, government authorities have created special development assistance programs in order to resettle repatriates in specific locations. To some extent, this was the method used by the Sandinista government to resettle many of the Nicaraguan Mestizo refugees who returned from Honduras. Another resettlement approach has been to designate model villages and development poles where refugees and displaced persons are taken in order to receive assistance and live under direct military control. Compulsory settlement in model villages has been just one of the many repressive conditions that the Guatemalan army has imposed on returning refugees, especially prior to 1987. This explains, in part, why many of the Guatemalans who returned from Mexico before 1987 did so spontaneously in an attempt to avoid military

control. In any event, the existence of model villages has been the chief
obstacle to the repatriation of Guatemalan refugees. Under the
Tripartite Repatriation Agreement, this unacceptable practice was
formally removed and, under pressure from international organizations,
practically discontinued.

Many refugees are understandably suspicious of settlement
policies dictated by governments. At the same time, however, the
tendency of many refugee camps to demand collective repatriation
involves complex resettlement arrangements. Unless specific
arrangements are made, such as in the extraordinary circumstances of
the Salvadoran mass repatriations, returning refugees will have to
accept some government involvement in their resettlement.
International nongovernmental organizations should help establish
resettlement arrangements acceptable to both refugees and
governments. This should not be done, however, by withdrawing, or
severely limiting, the assistance available to individual repatriates.
Individual repatriations continue to be the prevailing pattern. In any
event, a guiding principle for all nongovernmental organizations
providing assistance to repatriates should be to extend assistance
benefits to the larger communities where repatriates live.

Security is certainly the most important concern of the repatriate.
Indeed, repression and persecution are the greatest threats faced by
refugees on their return. Security conditions vary from country to
country. In Nicaragua, for example, the likelihood of repatriates being
targeted for government violence is not as great as in El Salvador or
Guatemala. In the three case studies, however, repatriates are typically
singled out by their government and the general public as being direct
or indirect supporters of militant factions, thus jeopardizing their
safety. Unless repatriates disguise the fact that they are former
refugees, their presence in the community may be very noticeable. As a
result, there may be conflict between repatriates and the rest of the
community. This has occurred in Guatemala, where the appearance of
refugees in certain communities has given rise to the possibility that the
army may accuse the repatriate's neighbors, friends, or relatives of
being guerrilla collaborators. In Guatemala, a substantial number of
refugees have suffered abuse at the hands of people who have taken
advantage of their vulnerability to usurp their land and expel them from
their communities. Refugees often take risks and accommodate
themselves to situations with little or no institutional protection. They
often choose anonymity, even if this means renouncing repatriation
assistance.

In general, the involvement of nongovernmental and international organizations in the repatriation process is the best guarantee available for promoting an overall respect for human rights in countries of origin. Paradoxically, the repatriates' conspicuousness may protect them, particularly when the presence of nongovernmental and international organizations acts as a deterrent to otherwise repressive governments that are sensitive to international opinion. The three case studies show that, while the repatriates' security is tenuous, they do not experience a greater level of human rights violations than the rest of the population. Furthermore, as has occurred in indigenous Nicaraguan communities, the return of refugees has contributed to improved conditions of peace and human rights in some localities. Such improvements have also transpired in El Salvador and, to a lesser extent, Guatemala.

After security, economic problems are the most serious problems faced by refugees on their return. In virtually all cases, the refugee exodus occurred alongside devastating economic loss, including the total destruction of homes and possessions, and the loss of crops, animals, and tools. Many *campesinos* lost their land, and many of them must decide whether and how to recover it from trespassers, reluctant relatives, or new cooperative members. Sometimes the land is unsuitable for cultivation either because it is located in a war zone or because it has become overgrown with vegetation. Their losses convince refugees that their government and society in general owe them a debt. They often view their situation as unique and worthy of special attention. They do not always realize that the people who stayed behind are often even worse off than themselves and deserve the same kind of support. These misunderstandings lead to conflict, particularly when the refugees have acquired international status and access to resources not extended to the internal victims of war. Nongovernmental and international organizations must help refugees understand that, although they are morally entitled to receive reparation for their losses, many of those who stayed behind have suffered comparable losses as a result of the civil strife.

The quality of life in exile is the most influential factor in determining the means by which repatriates rebuild their lives in their country of origin. Refugee camps are not the best place to prepare refugees for economic self-sufficiency. Poor health conditions, passivity, reliance on outside assistance, and camp tensions sometimes devastate work habits. Conversely, there is ample indication that refugees who improve their education, develop new skills, and participate in productive programs in the camps may, with limited assistance, actually improve their standard of living upon return.

Directing assistance toward repatriates is generally unavoidable, given the way international organizations operate. Aside from emergency assistance upon arrival, however, repatriation assistance should be directed to the improvement of living conditions, infrastructure, and the development opportunities of the larger communities to which refugees belong. This is the fairest and most efficient way of using scare resources; it is also the best way to reintegrate exiles into their country and demonstrate that repatriation may actually be a blessing rather than a curse.

SUMMARY OF RECOMMENDATIONS

Central America is still far from achieving peace, political stability, functioning democracy, respect for human rights, and economic recovery. Certain countries are moving in those directions, whereas others are still far from achieving these goals. Nevertheless, the refugee migrations which began in 1980 have greatly subsided. The slow process of repatriation, involving both individual returns and mass repatriations, has begun. Unless further outbreaks of generalized violence create new waves of refugees, certain established patterns may be expected to prevail. On the one hand, migrants will always leave the prevailing political and economic situation in their countries in order to seek employment and better living conditions elsewhere, mainly in Mexico and the United States. On the other hand, refugees will continue to face the same three options: return to their own country, establish themselves in the country of exile, or relocate to third countries. It is clear from the three case studies that the refugee situation has come full circle; the current situation is not acceptable to the refugees, the host governments, or assistance agencies. The refugees must either rebuild their lives in their country of origin or must be integrated into their country of exile to live a productive, independent existence. The current *status quo* serves no one's interest. Therefore, international and nongovernmental organizations must work with the relevant governments to assist in the transition by providing the refugees with options, rather than imposing obligations on them. The provision of options is the greatest challenge faced today by organizations working with refugees in Central America.

Our three case studies have interpreted the current phenomena and offered useful ideas and recommendations. They also provide suggestions on ways to make transition and repatriation an opportunity to improve the lives of refugees and contribute to peace, democracy, and development in the region.

Moreover, the three case studies show that the host governments of Honduras, Mexico, and Costa Rica are often under considerable pressure to provide assistance and to guarantee protection to refugees who have already been identified. These pressures have proved effective in restraining official hostility against refugees. However, such pressures have also had the adverse effect of prompting these governments to grant refugee status only to individuals whose circumstances make such recognition unavoidable. For various political reasons, these governments would prefer not to acknowledge the presence of many refugees in their country whose burden would be alleviated substantially if they became officially registered and assisted by the UNHCR. Such exclusions are further aggravated by external and internal pressures on these governments to adopt a generous and coherent refugee policy for Central Americans who have not been officially recognized as refugees, but who could prove that they merit such recognition.

To some extent, the UNHCR is directly responsible for this situation. In Mexico, Honduras, and elsewhere in Central America, the UNHCR has concentrated its efforts on refugees in camps. Although the UNHCR also extends its support and protection to several thousand individuals and families living outside the camps, particularly in Mexico City, Tegucigalpa and San José, it has made no serious effort to widen the pool of its beneficiaries to the many more who should be entitled to such protection. This oversight is a result of both the UNHCR's limited resources and its desire to accommodate host governments opposed to recognizing more refugees in their territory. Salvadorans in Mexico, Honduras, Nicaragua, and Costa Rica, Guatemalans in Mexico, and Nicaraguans in Costa Rica should all be targeted for such legalization efforts.

The refugee situations in Honduras and Mexico, in particular necessitate urgent action. The studies by Fagen and Eldridge and Ortega show that Salvadoran and Nicaraguan repatriation from Honduras is moving along at a steady speed. If this process depletes Honduras' official refugee population, the government may eventually toughen its stance against undocumented workers, forcing returns which may disrupt the organized repatriation process. The Guatemalan case study points out that the Mexican government, for the first time, recently dealt with the status of refugees in its laws. However, this legislation only benefits those refugees who have already been recognized under international law. The Mexican government should take the measures necessary to regularize the status of the thousands of undocumented Salvadoran and Guatemalan refugees within its borders. Furthermore, the UNHCR and other nongovernmental organizations should make efforts to pressure the Mexican government to take this action.

It is essential that governments legalize the status of thousands of Central Americans who are today classified as undocumented workers. The purpose of such an effort would not necessarily be to assure them permanent residency, but rather to help them return home with adequate support and assistance. This legalization process may, in fact, prove decisive in helping Central America resettle its huge refugee population and in encouraging other governments, nongovernmental organizations, and the UNHCR to channel the necessary resources into undertaking this task systematically. Therefore, in the spirit of Contadora and Esquipulas, the Mexican government and the six Central American governments are urged to enact national amnesty laws to regularize the status of all undocumented Central Americans residing in their respective countries. Such amnesty laws should include measures to modify the status of those individuals who are already legal residents but who are entitled to refugee treatment and wish to change their status. The passage of such amnesty laws would comprise a major contribution to the Central American peace process.

REFERENCE

*Edelberto Torres-Rivas, **Report on the Condition of Central American Refugees and Migrants,** (Washington, D.C.: Hemispheric Migration Project, Center for Immigration Policy and Refugee Assistance, Georgetown University, 1985),4.

BIBLIOGRAPHY

Aguayo, Sergio and Patricia Weiss Fagen. 1988. *Central Americans in the United States and Mexico, Unilateral, Bilateral, and Regional Perspectives*. Washington, D.C.: Hemispheric Migration Project, Center for Immigration Policy and Refugee Assistance, Georgetown University.

Aguilar Zinser, Adolfo. 1983. *Mexico and the Guatemalan Crisis. The Future of Central America: Policy Choices for the U.S. and Mexico*. Edited by Richard R. Fagen and Olga Pellicer. Stanford: Stanford University Press.

Americas Watch Committee. 1989. *Persecuting Human Rights Monitors: The CERJ in Guatemala*. New York and Washington, D.C.: Americas Watch.

_____. 1984. *Guatemala: A Nation of Prisoners*. New York and Washington, D.C.: Americas Watch.

_____. 1983. *Creating a Desolation and Calling it Peace*. Supplement to the Report on Human Rights in Guatemala. New York: Americas Watch.

_____. 1982. *Human Rights in Guatemala: No Neutrals Allowed*. New York: Americas Watch.

_____. 1982. *Report on Human Rights in El Salvador*. New York.

Amnesty International. 1983. *Amnesty International Report*. London.

_____. 1982. Guatemala: *Massive Extrajudicial Executions in Rural Areas Under the Government of General Efraín Ríos Montt*. London.

Anderson, Thomas. 1971. *Matanza, El Salvador's Communist Revolt of 1932*. Lincoln, Nebraska: University of Nebraska Press.

Araya Pochet, Carlos. 1979. *El enclave minero en Centroamérica 1880-1945*. Un estudio de los casos de Honduras, Nicaragua, y Costa Rica. San José, Costa Rica: Ciencias Sociales.

Ardila, Martha Lucía. 1985. Un Nuevo Flujo Migratorio Internacional: Los Refugiados Guatemaltecos en el Estado de Chiapas, México. Ph. D. Dissertation, Universidad Nacional Autónoma de México, Facultad de Ciencias Políticas y Sociales, México.

Armstrong, Robert and Janet Shenk. 1982. *El Salvador: The Face of Revolution*. Boston: South End Press.

Beckman, Anita, Barbara Lindell, and Karin Soderstrom. n.d. Y El Día Siguiente Seguimos Caminando: La Situación de los Refugiados Guatemaltecos en el Sur de México. Mimeo.

Berryman, Philip. 1984. *The Religious Roots of Rebellion: Christians in Central American Revolution*. New York: Orbis Books.

Bourgois, Phillip and Jorge Grünberg. 1980. *La Mosquitia y la revolución: Informe de investigación rural en la Costa Atlántica Norte*. Managua, Nicaragua: CIERA.

Camarda, Renato. 1985. *Forced to Move: Salvadoran Refugees in Honduras*. San Francisco: Solidarity Publications.

Centroamérica en Gráficas. 1990. San José, Costa Rica: Instituto Interamericano de Cooperación para la Agricultura (IICA) and Facultad Latinoamericana de Ciencias Sociales (FLACSO).

Centro de Documentación de Honduras. 1987. La Contra en Honduras. *Cronologías CEDOH*, No. 7. Tegucigalpa, Honduras.

_____. 1986. Los Refugiados en Honduras. *Cronologías CEDOH*, No. 6. Tegucigalpa, Honduras.

Centro de Documentación de la Unidad Revolucionaria Nacional Guatemalteca. 1990. *Cuatro Años de Gobierno Democristiano*. Guatemala.

Centro de Investigaciones y Documentación de la Costa Atlántica (CIDCA). 1987. Una Lengua Rama, para los Rama; La Naturaleza de la lengua Miskita y las principales dificultades para aprenderla; El Sumu; El inglés nicaragüense; Cuentos y narrativa costeña. *Wani* 6. Editorial Vanguardia. Managua, Nicaragua.

_____. 1986. Los Afro-Nicaragüenses y la revolución; La lengua Rama sobrevive; Proyectos pilotos de Autonomía. *Wani* 4. Impresión COMPANIC. Managua, Nicaragua.

_____. 1985. La Autonomía para la Costa: Bilingüismo y Educación Bilingüe; Las Elecciones. *Wani* 2-3. Impresión COMPANIC. Managua, Nicaragua.

_____. 1985. *Miskita Bila Aisanka Gramática Miskita*. Managua, Nicaragua: Primera Edición CIDCA.

Christian Coordinator of Aid to Guatemalan Refugees. 1985. *Boletín* (May-July):5-10.

Colectivo de Análisis de Iglesias en Centroamérica, Centro de Estudios Ecuménicos. 1989. *La Iglesia en Centroamérica. Guatemala, El Salvador, Honduras, y Nicaragua: Información y Análisis*. México, D.F.

Comisión Nacional de Autonomía. 1986. *Memorias de un sueño: Autonomía de la Costa Atlántica. Cerca de la vigilia*. Managua, Nicaragua: Edición Centinela.

Comisiones Permanentes de Representantes Refugiados Guatemaltecos en México. 1988-89. *Nuevo Día* 1-8. Campamento La Gloria, Municipio de la Trinitaria, Chiapas, México.

Comité Cristiano de Solidaridad, Diócesis de San Cristóbal. 1989.

Solidarios. San Cristóbal de Las Casas, Chiapas, México.

Conzemius, E. 1984. *Estudio Etnográfico sobre los indios Miskitus y Sumus, de Honduras y Nicaragua*. San José, Costa Rica.

Coordinación Ecuménica para las Iglesias y Agencias Internacionales de Cooperación. 1988. *Informe de las iglesias locales sobre el proceso de repatriación-repoblación de refugiados del campamento Mesa Grande, Honduras*. San Salvador.

Coordinadora de Ayuda a Refugiados Guatemaltecos, Secretaría General. *Boletín Informativo*. Mexico.

Diaconia. 1988. *Circular* (San Salvador).

Diagnóstico sobre Cooperativas de Tasba-Pri. 1983. Pamphlet.

Diócesis de San Cristóbal. 1985-86. *Caminante Informaciones*. San Cristóbal de las Casas, Chiapas, México.

Diskin, Martin and Kenneth E. Sharpe. 1986. *El Salvador:*

Confronting Revolution. Ed. by M. Blachman, W. LeoGrande., and K. Sharpe. New York: Pantheon Books.

Edwards, George C. and William J. Butler. 1987. *Guatemala: A New Beginning. Report of a Mission*. New York: American Association for the International Commission of Jurists.

Eldridge, Joseph. 1986. *With the Miskitos in Honduras*. New York: Americas Watch.

Ferris, Elizabeth. 1987. *The Central American Refugees*. New York: Praeger.

Giménez, Gilberto. 1988. Sectas religiosas en el Sureste Aspectos Sociográficos y Estadísticos. *Cuadernos de la Casa Chata* 161. Centro de Investigaciones y Estudios Superiores en Anthropología Social (CIESAS) del Sureste, México, D.F.

Guatemala. 1989. *Diagnostic, Strategies and Proposals*. Project Document presented to the International Conference on Central American Refugees (CIREFCA). Guatemala City.

Guatemala. Comisión Especial de Atención a Repatriados (CEAR). 1989. *Informe de Actividades Enero 1987-Mayo 1989*. Guatemala.

Guatemalan Church in Exile. 1987. Guatemala: Refugiados y Repatriación. *Boletín Trimestral* 2. Managua, Nicaragua.

Gutiérrez Castro, Germán. 1977-78. Informe de la Junta Directiva de la Comunidad indígena de Jinotega de inventario de bienes y distribución de tierras comunales. Mimeo.

Honduran National Commission for Refugees (CONARE). 1989. Proyecto de Asistencia al Desarrollo Social y Económico de Comunidades con presencia de refugiados y desplazados: Diagnóstico, estrategia y lineamientos para la acción. Tegucigalpa, Honduras.

Honduras. 1989. *Diagnostics, Strategies and Proposals. Project Document presented to the International Conference on Central American Refugees (CIREFCA)*. Guatemala City.

Honduras. Comisión Nacional de Refugiados. 1989. *Proyecto de Asistencia al Desarrollo Social y Económico de Comunidades con presencia de refugiados y desplazados: Diagnóstico, estrategia, y lineamentos para la acción*. Tegucigalpa, Honduras.

Inter-American Council on Refugees. 1982. *Salvadoran Refugees in Honduras, November 1981-February 1982*. Washington, D.C.

Kuntz, Diane. 1983. *Politics, Refugees, and Health: An Assessment of the Nutrition Program of the Salvadoran Refugee Camp at La Virtud, Honduras*. Unpublished MA/MPH thesis, University of California, Los Angeles.

La cuestión de las masas. *Estudios Centroamericanos* 42 (1987): 415-434. Edited by Ignacio Ellacuria, Universidad Centroamericana José Simeón Cañas, San Salvador.

Lawyers Committee for International Human Rights and Americas

Watch. 1984. *El Salvador's Other Victims: The War on the Displaced*. New York.

Lawyers Committee for International Human Rights. 1985. Honduras: A Crisis on the Border: A Report on Salvadoran Refugees in Honduras. New York.

Manz, Beatriz. 1988. *Refugees of a Hidden War: The Aftermath of Counterinsurgency in Guatemala*. Albany: SUNY Press.

_____. 1988. *Repatriation and Reintegration: An Arduous Process in Guatemala*. Washington, D.C.: HMP/CIPRA, Georgetown University.

_____. 1986. *Guatemala: Cambios en la Comunidad, Desplazamientos y Repatriación*. México: Editorial Praxis.

McClintock, Michael. 1985. *The American Connection: Vol. I,* State
    Terror and Popular Resistance in El Salvador. London: Zed
    Books.

Melville, Thomas y Marjorie Melville. 1982. *Tierra y Poder en
    Guatemala.* San José, Costa Rica: Editorial Universitaria
    Centroamericana, Segunda Edición Centroamérica.

Mexico. Comisión Mexicana de Ayuda a Refugiados. 1988. Los
    Refugiados Guatemaltecos en México. In *Memoria de COMAR
    (1982-88).* Secretaría de Gobernación, Secretaría de Relaciones
    Exteriores, Secretaría del Trabajo y Previsión Social, México,
    D.F.

Mexico. Diario Oficial de la Federación. 1990. *Decreto por el que se
    Reforma y Adiciona la Ley General Población.* Mexico, D.F.

_____. 1976. *Reglamento de la Ley General de Población. Fé de
    Erratas al Reglamento de la Ley General de Población.* México,
    D.F.

_____. 1974. *Ley General de Población.* México, D.F.

Montes, Segundo and Juan José García Vásquez. 1988. *Salvadoran
    Migration to the United States: An Exploratory Study.*
    Washington, D.C.: HMP/CIPRA, Georgetown University.

Montgomery, Tommie Sue. 1983. Liberation and Revolution:
    Christianity as a Subversive Activity in Central America. In
    Trouble in our Backyard, edited by Martin Diskin. New York:
    Pantheon Books.

Muñoz Jiménez, Krysia. 1985. *Los refugiados en Costa Rica en el
    proceso coyuntural-político: período 1978-1984.* Thesis in Political
    Science, Universidad de Costa Rica, San José.

Nicaragua. Dirección de Información y Prensa de la Presidencia de la
    República. 1987. *Autonomía: Para unir, hermanar
    definitivamente y para siempre a los Nicaragüenses.* Nicaragua.

Organization of American States. Inter-American Commission on
    Human Rights. 1984. *Report on the Situation of Human Rights of
    a Segment of the Nicaraguan Population of Miskito Origin and
    Resolution on the Friendly Settlement Regarding the Human Rights
    Situation of a Segment of the Nicaraguan Population of Miskito
    Origin.* Washington, D.C.

Ortega, Marvin. 1991. *Nicaraguan Repatriation to Mosquitia*. Washington, D.C.: HMP/CIPRA, Georgetown University.

Pacheco, Gilda. 1989. *Nicaraguan Refugees in Costa Rica: Adjustment to Camp Life*. Washington, DC: HMP/CIPRA, Georgetown University.

Pax Christi International. 1981. Salvadoran Refugees: Honduras. *Human Rights Reports*, No. 1. Belgium.

Plataforma Reivindicativa de los Refugiados de Mesa Grande Honduras, August 8, 1989.

Programa de Estudios Relaciones México-Estados Unidos de Estudios

Económicos y Sociales del Tercer Mundo, A.C., 1982. México en la Encrucijada de Guatemala. *Informe Relaciones México-Estados Unidos* 1:3. México D.F.

Ramírez, Mario A. 1989. *Refugee Policy Challenges: The Case of Nicaraguans in Costa Rica*. Washington, D.C.: HMP/CIPRA, Georgetown University.

_____. 1987. La problemática del refugiado y las perspectivas de integración socio-económica: el caso de Costa Rica. *Revista de Ciencias Sociales* 36:81.

Ramírez, Mario A. and Flor E. Solano. 1988. *La política general para los refugiados y la repatriación nicaragüenses en Costa Rica: presente y perspectivas*. San José, Costa Rica: Centro de Análisis Sociopolítico.

Rosell y Arellano, Monsignor. 1954. *About the Advances of Communism in Guatemala*. Pastoral Letter.

Salvadó, Luis Raúl. 1988. *The Other Refugees: A Study of Nonrecognized Guatemalan Refugees in Chiapas, México*. Washington, D.C.: HMP/CIPRA, Georgetown University.

Schmidt, Arthur. 1982. *Report on a Visit to Refugee Camps in Honduras*. Philadelphia: American Friends Service Committee.

Stein, Ricardo. 1989. *The Spontaneous and Planned Return of Repatriates and Displaced Persons*. In *1989 Central American Refugees: Workshop Report on Central American Refugee Research, Recommendations for Policy*, prepared by the Hemispheric Migration Project and Consejo Superior Universitario Centroamericano. Washington, D.C.: CIPRA and CSUCA.

Torres-Rivas, Edelberto. 1988. *Repression and Resistence: The Struggle for Democracy in Central America*. Boulder, Colorado: Westview Press.

_____. 1985. *Report on the Condition of Central American Refugees and Migrants*. Washington, D.C.: HMP/CIPRA, Georgetown University.

United Nations High Commissioner for Refugees. 1989. Documento de información: Situación del Programa de Refugiados en Honduras. Octubre. Tegucigalpa, Honduras.

_____. 1988. Documento de información: Situación del Programa de Refugiados en Honduras. Febrero. Tegucigalpa, Honduras.

_____. 1985. *Fact Sheet*.

_____. 1985. Notes on a Mission to Salvador and Honduras. February, 19-23.

United Nations High Commissioner for Refugees and United Nations Development Program, CIREFCA Joint Support Unit. 1991. *Status Report on Implementation of the Concerted Plan of Action of the International Conference on Central American Refugees*. Costa Rica, March.

_____. 1990. Documents presented to the First Meeting of the International Follow-up Committee, International Conference on Central American Refugees (CIREFCA). June 27-29. New York.

_____. 1989. Documents presented to the International Conference on Central American Refugees (CIREFCA). May 29-31. Guatemala City.

Washington Office on Latin America. 1989. *Uncertain Return: Refugees and Reconciliation in Guatemala*. Washington, D.C.

Wheaton, Philip. 1981. *The Iron Triangle: The Honduran Connection*. Washington, D.C.: EPICA Publications.

Wheelock R., Jaime. 1980. *Raíces indígenas de la lucha anticolonialista en Nicaragua*. Havana, Cuba: Editorial de Ciencias Sociales.

World Vision International. 1981. *A Report on the Refugee Relief Program of World Vision in Honduras. Monrovia, California.*

Zolberg, Aristide, Astri Suhrke and Sergio Aguayo. 1989. *Escape from Violence: Conflict in the Developing World*. New York: Oxford University Press.

CONTRIBUTORS

Pedro Acevedo is a research associate with the Instituto de Investigaciones Itztani, which conducts current socioeconomic research in Nicaragua. A social worker and native of Puerto Rico, Mr. Acevedo is a specialist in issues of agrarian reform and rural development.

Adolfo Aguilar Zinser is a professor of international relations at the Universidad Nacional Autónoma de Mexico (UNAM). He has been a visiting researcher at the Carnegie Endowment for International Peace and visiting professor at American University. His numerous publications focus on U.S.-Mexican relations and on Guatemalan refugees in Mexico.

Frederick C. Cuny is Chairman of INTERTECT, an international disaster assistance consulting firm based in Dallas, Texas. He is a member of the board of the non-profit Intertect Institute, which conducts research on societies in crisis and under whose auspices the case studies in this book were conducted. Mr. Cuny's publications include *Disasters and Development* and numerous training manuals on refugee operations and humanitarian assistance.

Joseph T. Eldridge is Director of the Washington office of the Laywers Committee for Human Rights. Prior to joining the Lawyers Committee, Mr. Eldridge was based in Tegucigalpa, Honduras, where he worked on human rights and economic development. Before moving to Honduras, he directed the Washington Office on Latin America, a human rights and public policy advocacy organization.

Patricia Weiss Fagen is Public Information/External Relations officer in the Washington, D.C., office of the UNHCR. Previously, Dr. Fagen was an associate at the Refugee Policy Group and a professor of history at San Jose State University in California. Among other publications, she is the author of *Exiles and Citizens, Spanish Republicans in Mexico* and an editor of *Fear at the Edge, State Terror and Resistance in Latin America* (forthcoming).

Mary Ann Larkin is Director of the Hemispheric Migration Project at CIPRA, Georgetown University. Before taking the directorship in 1990, Ms. Larkin was co-editor of the HMP monograph series. She has worked in the U.S. and Latin America on refugees, human rights, and development issues.

Marvin Ortega, an economist, is Director of the Instituto de Investigaciones Itztani, based in Managua, Nicaragua. Mr. Ortega coordinates the Institute's work on *campesinos* and rural development. His latest monograph, published by the HMP, is *Nicaraguan Repatriation to Mosquitia*.

Barry Stein is a professor of political science at Michigan State University. He has taught courses and written extensively since 1975 on refugees, displaced persons, and exiles and on issues in refugee assistance. Dr. Stein participated in the 1983 UNHCR Meeting of Experts on Refugee Aid and Development, and was co-editor of a special issue of the *International Migration Review* entitled, *Refugees Today*, among other publications.

INDEX

ABOUT THE HMP

The Hemispheric Migration Project (HMP), sponsored by Georgetown University's Center for Immigration Policy and Refugee Assistance (CIPRA), funds research on refugees and labor migrants in Latin America and the Caribbean. The project's support for Latin American and Caribbean scholars has a twofold objective: to encourage the development of research on refugees and migration in countries of origin and to bring the results of this research to the attention of policymakers in the sending, as well as receiving, countries. Since 1983, the HMP has commissioned and provided technical support for over 50 studies on the causes and consequences of population movements in the Western Hemisphere.

HEMISPHERIC MIGRATION PROJECT
Experts Review Group

Francisco Alba - El Colegio de México
Patricia Anderson, Ph.D - University of the West Indies, Jamaica
Charles Keely, Ph.D - Georgetown University
Peter Marchetti, S.J. - Universidad Centroamericana, Nicaragua
Lelio Mármora, Ph.D - Intergovernmental Committee for Migration, Argentina
Christopher Mitchell, Ph.D - New York University
Gabriel Murillo - Universidad de los Andes, Colombia
Alan Simmons, Ph.D - York University, Canada
Edelberto Torres-Rivas - Facultad Latinoamericana de las Ciencias Sociales, Costa Rica

----

HMP Staff

Francis Gillespie, Ph. D., S.J. - Director, CIPRA
Mary Ann Larkin - Director, HMP
Roxana Díaz - Administrative Assistant, HMP

HEMISPHERIC MIGRATION PROJECT
LIST OF PUBLICATIONS

Repatriation Under Conflict in Central America, Mary Ann Larkin et. al., editors, 1991. US$10.50 ($1.50 postage).

From the Shadows to Center Stage: NGOs and Central American Refugee Assistance, Sergio Aguayo, 1991. US$5.00.

Nicaraguan Repatriation to Mosquitia, Marvin Ortega, 1990. US$7.50.

Assistance and Control: Policies Toward Internally Displaced Populations in Guatemala, AVANCSO, 1990. US$7.50.

Psychological Impacts of Exile: Salvadoran and Guatemalan Families in Mexico, Cristina Bottinelli, et al., 1990. US$7.50.

Refugee Policy Challenges: The Case of Nicaraguans in Costa Rica, Mario A. Ramírez, 1989. US $7.50.

Central Americans in Mexico City: Uprooted and Silenced, Laura O'Dogherty, 1989. US $7.50.

Nicaraguan Refugees in Costa Rica: Adjustment to Camp Life, Gilda Pacheco, 1989. US $7.50.

Return in Latin America, Lelio Mármora, 1989. US $7.50.

Central American Refugees 1989. Workshop Report on Central American Refugee Research: Recommendations for Policy, April 7-8, 1989, Consejo Superior Universitario/Hemispheric Migration Project. US $5.00 *(Original version sold out, reprints available upon request)*.

On the Farm: Migration, Smallholder Agriculture, and Food Consumption in Jamaica and Saint Lucia, West Indies, Elsa M. Chaney, 1988. US $7.50.

Salvadoran Migration to the United States: An Exploratory Study, Segundo Montes Mozo, S.J. and Juan José Garcia Vasquéz, 1988. US $7.50.

The Other Refugees: A Study of Undocumented Guatemalans in Chiapas, Mexico, Luis Raúl Salvadó, 1988. US $7.50.

When Borders Don't Divide: Labor Migration and Refugee Movements in the Americas, Patricia R. Pessar, editor, 1988. [Order from Center for Migration Studies, 209 Flagg Place, Staten Island, NY 10304-1199. (718) 351-8800].

Migration, War, and Agrarian Reform: The Peasant Settlements in Nicaragua, Jon Ander Bilbao E., 1988. US $7.50.

Central Americans in Mexico and the United States, Sergio Aguayo and Patricia Weiss Fagen, 1988. *US $5.00 (Original version sold out, reprints available upon request.)*

Repatriation and Reintegration: An Arduous Process in Guatemala, Beatriz Manz, 1988. US $7.50.

Return to Rio de la Plata: Response to the Return of Exiles in Argentina and Uruguay, Lelio Mármora, 1988. US $7.50.

The New U.S. Immigration Law: Its Impact on Jamaicans at Home and Abroad, Patricia Y. Anderson, 1988. US $5.00.

The Immigration Reform and Control Act: Implications for Colombia and Colombians in the United States, Political Science Department, Universidad de los Andes, Bogotá, 1988. US $5.00.

Proceedings of the Inter-American Conference on Migration Trends and Policies, February 4-6, 1986, Mary Ann Larkin, editor, 1987 US $7.50. (Also in Spanish translation).

Western Hemisphere Migration to the U.S., Robert Bach, 1985. US $5.00.

International Migration in the Southern Cone, Jorge Balán, 1985. US $5.00.

Migration from the Caribbean Region, Elsa M. Chaney, 1985. US $5.00.

Report on the Condition of Central American Refugees and Migrants, Edelberto Torres-Rivas, 1985. US $5.00.

To order, add an additional $1.00 for postage and handling, unless otherwise specified, for each publication. Make check payable to **GEORGETOWN UNIVERSITY**, CIPRA/HMP, P.O. Box 2298-Hoya Station, Washington, D.C. 20057-1011. Phone: (202) 298-0213.

ABOUT THE INTERTECT INSTITUTE

The Intertect Institute, Inc. was established in 1987 as a non-profit scientific and educational research organization to promote in-depth study and innovative approaches to disaster-related issues. The Institute seeks to provide a continuing forum whereby the resources of the professional disaster management community, universities, government service and humanitarian assistance can be brought to bear on the critical problems of prevention, mitigation, preparedness and response in both refugee and natural disasters.

The Institute focuses its activities on cooperative research, training, demonstrative projects, and broad dissemination of data and study results worldwide. It conducts both sponsored studies and ongoing internal research programs. In addition, it organizes workshops and seminars to bring together researchers and practitioners in an environment which encourages free expression and spirited discussion of untested ideas and new directions.

Examples of research topics include:

- Exploring the economic impact of disasters on the poor, and developing appropriate economic recovery strategies.

- Studying the impact of the international debt crisis on disaster-prone countries. Analyzing the impact of disasters on the debt structure, the impact of debt on a country's ability to reconstruct, and the need and opportunities for restructuring debt after disasters.

- Integrating disaster mitigation into national development plans and internationally-financed human settlement projects.

- Studying options for the design and implementation of relief programs to promote more rapid resolution of the problems of repatriation and resettlement of refugees and displaced persons.

- Defining appropriate roles for assisting agencies in support of spontaneous voluntary refugee repatriation.

- Exploring the effectiveness of current efforts to identify early warning indicators and contingency planning data bases and how they can be supported, tested and institutionalized

The Institute seeks to maintain a broad base of support in order to enhance its position as an independent, multi-disciplinary organization. Both specific project support and general operating funds will be solicited from governmental agencies, private foundations, corporations and individuals. The Institute is now in its third year of a project to research spontaneous voluntary refugee repatriation, funded by the Ford Foundation and Georgetown University's Center for Immigration Policy and Refugee Assistance.

The Institute has been granted Federal tax exempt status under section 501(c)(3) of the U.S. Internal Revenue Code.